MESSIANIC REVOLUTION

MESSIANIC REVOLUTION

RADICAL RELIGIOUS POLITICS
TO THE END OF
THE SECOND MILLENNIUM

DAVID S. KATZ

AND RICHARD H. POPKIN

HILL AND WANG

A DIVISION OF FARRAR, STRAUS AND GIROUX | NEW YORK

Hill and Wang
A division of Farrar, Straus and Giroux
19 Union Square West, New York 10003

Copyright © 1998 by David S. Katz and Richard H. Popkin
Distributed in Canada by Douglas & McIntyre Ltd.
Printed in the United States of America
Designed by Abby Kagan
First edition, 1999

Library of Congress Cataloging-in-Publication Data
Katz, David S.
    Messianic revolution : radical religious politics to the end of
the second millennium / David S. Katz and Richard H. Pomkin.
        p.   cm.
    Includes bibliographical references and index.
    ISBN 0-8090-6885-0 (alk. paper)
    1. Messianism—History.   2. Messianism, Political—History.
3. Messianism—United States—History.   4. Messianism, Political—
United States—History.   I. Popkin, Richard Henry, 1923–   .
II. Title.
BT240.K37   1999
236'.9—dc21   98-46189

CONTENTS

A C K N O W L E D G M E N T S

We would like to thank all those who helped us along the way—especially Julie Popkin, literary agent, editorial co-worker, and helpmate, who made it possible for Dick Popkin to contribute to the volume despite the parlous state of his health during the past few years. Research assistants helped ease the burden of photocopying and library work: in Los Angeles, Robert John Arias, Kimberly Garmoe, Russell Court Ives, Anna Suranyi, and Tim Correll; in Tel Aviv, Maya Lahat-Kerman, Efrat Lev-Amitai, and Illa Ben-Porat. The authors would also like to acknowledge the help of the staff at the libraries of UCLA, the Fuller Theological Seminary in Pasadena, the Santa Monica Public Library, the Bodleian Library in Oxford (as seen from seat U151), and the library of Tel Aviv University. Much of the text was revised in friends' rooms at Siegen University and at the Centre for Early Modern Studies at Frankfurt University, and the kindnesses of these friends are gratefully acknowledged. Others who helped include Sarah Kochav, James E. Force, Authur Williamson, and Howard Brackman. We also enjoyed the help and support of Peter Robinson, literary agent at Curtis Brown, London; and the staff at Hill and Wang, especially Elisabeth Sifton and her assistant, Mia Berkman.

Throughout the writing of this book, the authors were separated by one continent, one ocean, and one sea, but remained in almost daily contact: we would therefore also like to thank the people who invented E-mail. Finally, we dedicate this book to our students, with thanks for the stimulus that teaching has given to our research, and in the hope that what we have to say might actually influence the decisions of those who need to deal with messianic revolution at the end of the second millennium.

I N T R O D U C T I O N

The idea for writing this book took shape on April 19, 1993, and was transformed into something tangible on April 19, 1995. The first date was that of the conflagration at Waco, Texas, when at least seventy-four people lost their lives because the followers of David Koresh and the federal agents outside his compound inhabited two different conceptual worlds. The second date was that of the bombing of the Federal Building in Oklahoma City, apparently by people connected with the militia movement who related their action to the anniversary of the disaster at Waco. As we watched the news reports, it was clear to us that both journalists and learned law-enforcement experts were genuinely unaware of the rich tradition of messianic revolution that stretched back unbroken at least for eight hundred years and was apparent to us in the events at Waco and in Oklahoma City. They were not police problems alone.

The FBI crisis-management negotiators who dealt with the people inside the compound at Waco had little understanding of the religious ideology behind a group like the Branch Davidians, as is clear from the transcript of their discussions with the group's leader,

David Koresh, during the FBI's fifty-one-day siege. Koresh insisted on talking about the Bible; the FBI agents were interested only in his surrender and in the safety of the people inside the compound. When Koresh interpreted his current predicament in light of biblical references, the FBI negotiator would simply wait for his own turn to speak. In the following typical exchange, Koresh is in the middle of an analysis of a passage in the Book of Nahum when an FBI negotiator named Henry interrupts him:

> HENRY [FBI]: Let's not talk in those terms, please.
>
> KORESH: No. Then you don't understand my doctrine. You don't want to hear the word of my God.
>
> HENRY: I have listened to you and listened to you, and I believe in what you say, as do a lot of other people, but the— but the bottom line is everybody now considers you David who is going to either run away from the giant or is going to come out and try to slay the giant. For God's sake, you know, give me an answer, David. I need to have an answer. Are you going to come out?
>
> KORESH: Right now listen.
>
> HENRY: Right now you're coming . . .
>
> KORESH: "He that dasheth in pieces is come up before thy face: keep the munition." What's the munition? "Watch the way."
>
> HENRY: One of the things, one of the things is I don't understand the scriptures like you, honestly, I just don't.
>
> KORESH: Okay, if you would listen, then I would show you. It says here—it says here, "The chariots shall be with flaming torches." That's what you've got out there [tanks].[1]

It took days before they realized that "Koresh" is the Hebrew name for "Cyrus," a quasi-messianic figure in the Old Testament. One FBI negotiator confessed later that some of them thought that the Seven Seals in the Book of Revelation to which Koresh constantly referred were animals.[2]

We know now that this failure to attend to the precise meaning of Koresh's references, compounded with the failure to understand the background of a group like the Branch Davidians, created very serious breaks in the chain of reasoning that might have led to an informed decision. The psychologists who advised the FBI concluded that Koresh was paranoid and that there was no point in trying to negotiate with him; the authorities eventually adopted a strategy of "stress escalation" that involved not only cutting off electricity to and training floodlights on the compound's buildings but also the use of other tactics including playing tapes of loud music, Tibetan chants, pleas from family members, and the sounds of animals being killed. Doomsday and death were part of the Branch Davidians' messianic plan, and when they died in the fire at Waco, they believed they were merely playing their parts in a divine script which they clearly understood.

Our sense was that we had seen this all before. On one level, the events at Waco reminded us of another siege by the forces of order, four and a half centuries earlier, at Münster in northern Germany. There, too, a group of religious radicals set up what they considered a divine community of Anabaptists behind a protective wall and held off the authorities for sixteen months, until June 25, 1535, when the gates of Münster mysteriously opened from within, allowing the capture of the city by Prince-Bishop Franz von Waldeck, who massacred nearly everyone inside. But even more importantly, we believe that much of modern religious radicalism can clearly be traced to earlier groups and their theologies, that it is impossible to understand sects like the Branch Davidians without this historical perspective.

Our intention in this book is not only to show the roots of messianic revolution, visible in the late Middle Ages, but also to trace the evolution of this concept. It is not enough to point out that someone like David Koresh held beliefs that were strikingly similar to those of Joachim of Fiore in twelfth-century Italy. We must demonstrate how these ideas were transmitted from a cloister in Calabria to a Texas handyman-prophet seven centuries later. One of the most intriguing aspects of our story is the way peoples and religious movements transported radical religious ideas across the Atlantic to America, where they flourished outside the control of more conventional institutions.

George Orwell once complained that "[as] with the Christian religion, the worst advertisement for Socialism is its adherents":

> In addition to this there is the horrible—the really disquieting—prevalence of cranks wherever Socialists are gathered together. One sometimes gets the impression that the mere words "Socialism" and "Communism" draw towards them with magnetic force every fruit-juice drinker, nudist, sandal-wearer, sex-maniac, Quaker, "Nature Cure" quack, pacifist and feminist in England.

The end result was that to the ordinary man, "a crank meant a Socialist and a Socialist meant a crank. Any Socialist, he probably felt, could be counted on to have *something* eccentric about him."[3]

Orwell put his finger on the tendency for radical ideas to flock together. As we shall show in this book, the most virulent manifestations of American religious extremism grew out of a rather benign interpretative school of biblical thought which located the descendants of the Lost Ten Tribes among the English-speaking peoples. Some of the key individuals who held this belief also championed more sinister concepts of racism and survivalism, and created a dangerous amalgam that overwhelmed the theoretical musings of the first biblical researchers of this theme.

The transformation of "British Israelites" into the "Aryan Nations" is only one of the bizarre developments in the history of messianic revolution, and perhaps the aspect of our story with greatest contemporary relevance. The very notion of an "Aryan race" grew out of a misunderstanding of a discovery made by an Englishman named Sir William Jones (1746–94), that many European languages share a common origin in Sanskrit. It was a short but crucial step for others to posit the existence of a superior "Aryan" race of Indo-Europeans who spoke the mother tongue of Europe, an idea with dangerous consequences. The older English theory of "British Israelism" also underwent a deadly revision, whereby later adherents in the United States began to argue that the biblical promises God made to the Israelites applied literally to their progeny alone, white Anglo-Saxon Protestants in America, and that on this basis any action might be taken to protect their "race." The militia movement in the United States draws its ideology from British Israelism, and without understanding this obscure English theory, we cannot comprehend the crimes committed by Timothy McVeigh at Oklahoma City in 1995.

This book is about ideas of messianic revolution, rather than a general history of messianism or millenarian theology, but needless to say, the concepts overlap. Our interest is particularly in those groups and individuals who both believed in the imminent Second Coming of Christ and insisted that state and society make fundamental changes in order to prepare the way for His return. This potent combination of religious radicalism and revolutionary politics is what led Oliver Cromwell to say of the messianic revolutionaries of his own seventeenth-century England that "they had tongues like Angels, but had cloven feet." We have therefore chosen to concentrate on the concept of messianic revolution in the Protestant world, or at least on those elements in the story which lead toward its most dramatic manifestations in the United States. There is much that could be said about messianic revolution in the Jewish and Islamic worlds, especially as evidenced by such groups as Habad-Lubovitch, Gush Emunim, Hisbollah, and many others. Apart from passing reference, these are subjects which we gladly leave to others.[4]

Toward the end of this book, we discuss in detail the connection between contemporary American Fundamentalism and messianic revolution. George Orwell posited 1984 as a point in the future after an all-encompassing revolution. As we shall see, date setting is a habit among messianic revolutionaries, and Orwell was prophetic in this as well, for 1984 was a year of grave danger for the Western world. That year was the exact midpoint of the presidency of Ronald Reagan, a man who not only believed in the Bible as a source for predicting future events but had grave musings about the necessity of an apocalypse preceding the Second Coming of Christ. Reagan was president of a country in which 94 percent of the people believe in God, and 71 percent are convinced that there is life after death.[5] In the United States, 65 percent of the people believe in devils, and 72 percent think that angels exist. There are more places of worship in the United States per capita than any other country in the world.[6] But merely pointing out that Reagan was firmly in the mainstream of American religious belief does not negate the fact that contemporary American Fundamentalists often interpret the Apocalypse as nuclear war, and wonder whether it is a necessary precursor of the coming of the Messiah. In a sense, Doomsday is the Fundamentalist Utopia, and the survivors of that cataclysm will reign with Christ on earth for a thousand years. Perhaps it would have been better if someone other than Ronald Reagan had his finger on the proverbial button between 1980 and 1988.

We hope that this book is not too specialized or of the shock-horror variety that plagues studies about violent modern religious cults. That too little is generally known about the messianic revolutionary tradition even in academic circles was brought home recently to one of us while attending a lecture on anarchism. The lecturer was asked whether American groups such as the Posse Comitatus or the Militia of Montana might be thought of as part of the anarchist tradition, and if not, why not. The lecturer himself was unsure, but not so a professor of Russian history, who bridled at the idea of the likes of such Americans being included in the study of the anarchist tradition, and insisted that these militias were without serious ideology, motivated by a desire to avoid paying federal taxes. A professor of French history then rallied to their defense, noting ironically that maybe the real problem was that the militiamen hadn't read the bibliography. It is our intention in this book to connect American extremist groups with the earlier history of messianism and to show that they have indeed read the bibliography. The works and ideas of everyone from Joachim of Fiore to Nesta Webster have been reprinted many times, and are available from bookshops in Cecil Court in London to Melrose Avenue in Los Angeles, sold in one form or another from the Rosicrucian Bookshop in San Jose to the mail-order catalogue of the Aryan Nation in Hayden Lake, Idaho. Call it plagiarism, call it intertextuality, but this repertoire of texts and ideas continues to be played. There has been much disconnected talk about the beliefs that motivate messianic revolutionary groups. Our book gives them a *history* as well.

Making full use of the Internet in the preparation of this book, we have found that the modern groups and key individuals mentioned in our text maintain Web sites that provide information which in the past was available only through subscriptions to unreliable periodicals or at research institutes devoted to combating racism or anti-Semitism. The groups or churches that supported these papers and institutes now devote their public-relations efforts to producing a professional-looking Web site. We have refrained from giving precise notations of these sites, as they are liable to change, especially those belonging to extremist groups, which are often evicted by their Web servers.

Despite the natural modern tendency to consider those who believe in the imminent coming of the Messiah as in some way deviant from the main line of Christian belief, in a very real sense it is precisely these people who have kept faith with the original message of the New Testament. Indeed, anyone who believes that the Bible is the literal word of God can hardly do otherwise than to accept the millenarian concept—the notion that one day soon Jesus will return and establish on this earth a regime with His saints that will endure for one thousand years. Millenarianism, or chiliasm, as it is sometimes called, from the Greek root of the word for "one thousand" instead of the Latin one, is deeply rooted in the New Testament itself. It forms the core of an entire branch of theology, eschatology, which is concerned with the *eschata*, the Greek term for the "last things."

Jesus himself spoke of his *parousia*, or arrival, and gave a good many hints about the characteristics of the Apocalypse, the revelation of Christ. The twenty-fourth chapter of the gospel of Matthew is largely devoted to this explication of the circumstances of the Messiah's return:

> And as he sat upon the mount of Olives, the disciples came unto him privately, saying, Tell us, when shall these things be? and what *shall be* the sign of thy coming, and of the end of the world?
>
> And Jesus answered and said unto them, Take heed that no man deceive you. For many shall come in my name, saying, I am Christ; and shall deceive many.
>
> And ye shall hear of wars and rumors of wars: see that ye be not troubled: for all *these things* must come to pass, but the end is not yet.
>
> For nation shall rise against nation, and kingdom against kingdom: and there shall be famines, and pestilences, and earthquakes, in divers places.
>
> All these *are* the beginning of sorrows.
>
> Then shall they deliver you up to be afflicted, and shall kill you: and ye shall be hated of all nations for my name's sake.
>
> And then shall many be offended, and shall betray one another, and shall hate one another.
>
> And many false prophets shall rise, and shall deceive many.

And because iniquity shall abound, the love of many shall wax cold.

But he that shall endure unto the end, the same shall be saved.

And this gospel of the kingdom shall be preached in all the world for a witness unto all nations; and then shall the end come.

When ye therefore shall see the abomination of desolation, spoken of by Daniel the prophet, stand in the holy place (whoso readeth, let him understand:) . . .

The time of the Second Coming will be one of "great tribulation, such as was not since the beginning of the world to this time, no, nor ever shall be."

Identifying the Messiah will be a problem, for "if any man shall say unto you, Lo, here *is* Christ, or there; believe *it* not. For there shall arise false Christs, and false prophets, and shall shew great signs and wonders." But the actual coming of the Messiah will be accompanied by unmistakable miracles:

And then shall appear the sign of the Son of man in heaven: and then shall all the tribes of the earth mourn, and they shall see the Son of man coming in the clouds of heaven with power and great glory.

And he shall send his angels with a great sound of a trumpet, and they shall gather together his elect from the four winds, from one end of heaven to the other.

These are promises for the future: the exact time of their occurrence is as yet unknown to mankind. As Jesus puts it: "But of that day and hour knoweth no *man*, no, not the angels of heaven, but my Father only . . . Watch therefore: for ye know not what hour your Lord doth come."

These are the "signs of the times" which indicate when the Messiah will come again in glory. The Book of Revelation gives us further details about what will happen afterward. Revelation 20 is the most important in this regard, in which a vision is recorded of those "which had not worshipped the beast, neither his image, neither had received *his* mark upon their foreheads, or in their hands; and they lived and reigned with Christ a thousand years." This is the basis of the idea of a thousand-year rule by Christ and the saints. The text continues to note that this glorious fate is not promised to everyone. "But the rest of the dead lived not again until the thousand years were finished. This *is* the first resurrection." The Book of Revelation continues:

> Blessed and holy *is* he that hath part in the first resurrection: on such the second death hath no power, but they shall be priests of God and of Christ, and shall reign with him a thousand years.
>
> And when the thousand years are expired, Satan shall be loosed out of his prison,
>
> And shall go out to deceive the nations which are in the four quarters of the earth, Gog and Magog, to gather them together to battle: the number of whom *is* as the sand of the sea.
>
> And they went up on the breadth of the earth, and compassed the camp of the saints about, and the beloved city: and fire came down from God out of heaven, and devoured them.

At the end of this conflagration, reports St. John the Divine in the next chapter, "I saw a new heaven and a new earth: for the first heaven and the first earth were passed away."

These are the New Testament texts which have been studied and juggled throughout the history of the concept of messianic revolution. Millenarians also take great note in the Old Testament of the seventh chapter of the Book of Daniel, with its image of "four great beasts came up from the sea, diverse one from another." They argue over the symbolism of these creatures: a lion, a bear, a leopard, and a ten-horned monster with "great iron teeth" on whose head sprouted "another little horn, before whom there were three of the first horns plucked up by the roots: and, behold, in this horn *were* eyes like the eyes of man, and a mouth speaking great things." Many people thought these four beasts represented the rise and fall of successive great world empires, perhaps Babylon, the Medes or Persians or Assyrians, Greece, and finally Rome and the Roman Catholic Church. After the fall of this last beast, a Fifth Monarchy of Saints would arise, which would rule the earth with Christ for a thousand years. By the later medieval period, these obscure phrases in the Old and New Testaments had been woven together into a coherent system. In most respects this remains the same in the theology of modern Fundamentalists.

⋖⋘⋙⋗

Even those who believe that historians always find earlier examples expressing what appear to be modern ideas before their time must surely recognize the rudiments of modern messianism in the work of the Calabrian abbot Joachim of Fiore (c. 1132–1202).[7] Any history of messianic revolution must take account of Joachim. We know little about his early life, although he seems to have served at the Sicilian court at Palermo. At some point he had a religious experience, traveled to the Holy Land, and on his return joined the Benedictine monastery at Corazzo in his mid-thirties. Joachim became abbot within a short time, and traveled to Rome in about 1183 in his project to link his monastery with the Cistercian order. He remained at the monastery of Casamari, south of Rome, for about eighteen months, writing down the visions that were now coming to him about the Apocalpyse, and trying to make sense of them.

Whether because of the nature of his own personality or the fortunate proximity to Rome, Joachim had the advantage of being a thinker with potentially explosive ideas who nevertheless remained an establishment figure. In May 1184 Pope Lucius III asked him to explain one of the Sibyl's prophecies which had intrigued him, and thereafter Joachim was encouraged to continue his research into the End of Days. At Casamari he finished two of his most famous works, the *Liber Apocalypsis* and the *Liber Concordiae*, and began the third, the *Liber Psalterii decem chordarum*. Throughout the 1180s and 1190s, Joachim was the acknowledged expert on God's divine plans and the Apocalypse, and he was consistently backed by the popes. His political views fit in very well at the time with papal policy, for he argued that since the End of Days was approaching, it was best for the Church to concentrate on religion and leave the political administration of Europe, before the accession of King Jesus, to the Holy Roman Emperor. It was not surprising that he was fêted by numerous contemporary leaders, including Emperor Henry VI, Frederick II, and even Richard the Lion-Hearted, to whom he confided the intelligence that the Antichrist had already been born at Rome.[8] When Innocent III was elected pope in 1198, it spelled the end of his direct influence at the papal court, since the new pope, as is well known, had a much more confrontational policy with the Holy Roman Emperor, perhaps not believing with Joachim that the End of the World was quite so nigh.

Joachim in any case was not completely wedded to political intrigue, and had years before, in 1190, founded a new and remote monastery of his own at Fiore in Calabria. This move was condemned by the Cistercians, who rightly perceived it as an implied criticism. Nevertheless, Joachim prevailed, and it is by the name of his new institution that he is generally known. Yet Joachim was not a rebel: in his will, written two years before his death, he ordered his followers to submit his uncensored works for papal approval, taking care, of course, to leave "the originals in safekeeping."[9]

Joachim's prophetic system, described in his three principal books, printed for the first time in Venice in 1519–27, is compelling not only by its inner logic but also because of the way in which it foreshadows later theories. Norman Cohn, in his book on medieval millenarianism, describes Joachim's system as "the most influential one known to Europe until the appearance of Marxism." The key concept in Joachim's system was that there was a secret meaning hidden in the Bible which, if properly decoded, would enable mankind both to understand the past and to predict the future. He argued that "concords" or "sequences" could be found throughout the Bible, parallels that ran throughout the scriptural texts and demonstrated its divine unity. The number twelve, for instance, was exemplified in the twelve patriarchs, the twelve tribes, the twelve apostles, and the future twelve leaders. Noah sent out a raven and a dove after the Flood, a black and a white bird, symbolizing the later religious orders of the Dominicans and Franciscans. As Cohn puts it very well:

> The idea that the Scriptures possessed a concealed meaning was far from new; traditional methods of exegesis had always given a large place to allegorical interpretations. What was new was the idea that these methods could be applied not simply for moral or dogmatic purposes but as a means of understanding and forecasting the development of history. Joachim was convinced that he had found a key which, when applied to events and personages of the Old and New Testaments and especially of the Book of Revelation, enabled him to perceive in history a pattern and a meaning to prophesy in detail its future stages.[10]

Joachim divided history into three great periods, each of which commences with a period of incubation. The first is the Age of the Father, characterized by married men, the *ordo conjugatorum*, beginning with Adam and Eve and continuing until the arrival of Jesus. The incubation period of this age extended from Creation until Abraham, when the Jews were given the Law by which the elect of mankind lived until the end of this Old Testament dispensation. The second period is the Age of the Son, symbolized by priests, the *ordo clericorum*, during which time Christians lived under grace and the New Testament dispensation. The incubation period for the Age of the Son began with Elijah, who foreshadows Christ. Since St. Matthew wrote that there were forty-two generations between Abraham and Jesus, Joachim, applying his theory of concords, wrote that there would be an equal number of generations of about thirty years each between Jesus and the onset of the third age. The old era, however, continuing for sixty-three generations, would overlap with the next one.

The third age is the most dramatic, being the Age of the Holy Spirit, the *ordo monachorum* or *ordo contemplatium*. If Joachim's calculations based on Matthew were right, it would begin about the year 1260, which meant he knew he would no longer be around to see it. The transition or incubation period would be a time of about three and one-half years (half of seven) when the Antichrist would reign, a secular king who would destroy the Christian church. Indeed, Joachim was even more specific: there would be two Antichrists, one in the incubation period and another at the end, at the time of the Second Coming. He believed that contemporary events seemed to indicate that human history was drawing to a close, and his own candidate for the first Antichrist was Saladin (1138–93), whose Islamic conquests appeared to threaten the security of Christians in Europe.[11] No wonder Joachim was on the alert for Antichrist at "all times and all places."

This last age lay wholly in the future, but Joachim thought he knew the main outlines of what would occur. Two new religious orders would arise to convert the entire world to Christianity, the *viri spirituales*, which would also include a third group of hermits. There would be twelve patriarchs whose task it would be to convince the Jews to accept the inevitable rule of Christ on earth. There would be a *novus dux*, a leader in the last days who would show mankind that it was the life of the spirit that was important, that one should free oneself from fixation on trivial mundane things. Importantly, he was not the Last Emperor, part of an entirely different mythical tradition. A holy pope, the *pastor angelicus* (apparently a different figure from the *novus dux*), would come forth to lead the Church. This would be a time of love and joy, and the understanding and knowledge of God would manifest itself in the hearts of everyone. The incubation period in this case extended from the beginning of monasticism in western Europe—that is, from the lifetime of St. Benedict (c. 480–c. 543)—to the present—that is, the thirteenth century.

History would come to an end with the Second Coming, and the final stage was not really an age, but an epilogue, the time of the *Ecclesia Spiritualis*, when the entire world would be one enormous monastery. Everyone around the globe would spend time in prayer and meditation, praising God around the clock. This was the Kingdom of the Saints, which would survive for one thousand years, until the Final Judgment and the destruction of the world.

As is readily seen, Joachim of Fiore's scheme was beautiful in its symmetry, if not altogether clear in its presentation. Apart from the three ages, there were also the two Testaments, each of which had seven parallel periods, but still, his obsession with the Trinity made the number three paramount. Just as he looked for repeating numbers in the Scriptures and in history, his notion of three ages was no accident. The Church expounded a threefold division of history: the time before the Old Testament law, the period of the Old Testament law, and the period under the grace of the New Testament and Jesus Christ. In a sense, Joachim was compelled to divide his chronology into three parts so as to remain in minimal conformity with accepted views, but his main interest was in the new order of the world to come, and in this he had many students who found his interpretation wholly convincing. Significantly, Joachim's views got a sympathetic hearing despite his direct opposition to the prevailing Augustinian view that the Kingdom of God had begun with the Church itself and that there would never be another millennium on earth apart from the one we were already enjoying under Christ.

Joachim managed to remain an accepted and revered figure within the church hierarchy, in large part because he never argued that the Church in any way impeded the progress of divine history or the implementation of God's plan. He also never set an exact time for the onset of the Second Coming: "I say openly that the time when these things will happen is near," he wrote, "but God alone knows the day and the hour. Insofar as I can estimate according to the harmony of the concordance, if peace from these evils is granted up to the year 1200, thereafter I will observe the times and the moments in every way so that these things do not happen unexpectedly."[12]

Yet his ideas were explosive, and they could hardly be controlled. Shortly after Joachim's death, a group of men arose who believed themselves to be the new spiritual order that he had promised would appear at the End of Days, in the years before 1260. These were Spiritual Franciscans, some of whom came to be called "Fraticelli" ("Little Brothers"), members of that religious order who even before the death of St. Francis of Assisi in 1226 opposed those who wanted to moderate and liberalize the original simple way of life that was their order's credo. The Spiritual Franciscans were condemned by the pope. For many of them, Joachim's views suited their self-image, and they saw Francis of Assisi as the angel of the sixth seal of the Apocalypse, who in Joachim's divine plan was to be the harbinger of the third age.

It was natural that interest in Joachim of Fiore and his system became more intense as the deadline year of 1260 approached. Gerard of Borgo San Donnino, a Spiritual Franciscan, edited excerpts from Joachim's works, including other prophecies and meditations on the New Testament, and circulated it as an Eternal Evangel, *The Everlasting Gospel*, in about 1254.[13] Gerard paid for this indiscretion by being incarcerated for life, but Joachim's prophecies now attracted more widespread attention, especially as the implication was that this new *Everlasting Gospel* was meant in the dawning of the third age to supersede both the Old and the New Testament.

The year 1260 was widely expected to be the last, and it was characterized by a penchant for penitential processions of self-flagellating sinners, a fad which began in Italy and spread north to Germany and to her eastern borders. Whether or not this movement was directly connected to Joachimism is still a subject of debate, but the timing was significant. When Jesus Christ failed to appear in that year, the date was shifted to 1290 and to other possible venues, since the calculation after all was based only on a general conception of the length of a generation. The Spiritual Franciscans were gradually eliminated, but the influence of Joachimite ideas and symbols remained widespread, and continued until modern times.[14]

Joachim's plan is still remembered and called into account. Montaigne wrote in the sixteenth century that he was very keen to see with his own eyes "the book of Joachim, the Calabrian abbot, which predicted all the future popes, their names and appearances."[15] But that Joachim never went into such detail was precisely the secret of his success. Still, it will be clear throughout this book that the basic plan behind Joachim of Fiore's program has been repeated many times over. The division of world history into three, the notion of different dispensations, the concept of an incubation period, the last of which will be characterized by worsening conditions: all this is to be found in its entirety in modern Fundamentalist theology, which has so much religious and political influence today.

MESSIANIC REVOLUTION

CHAPTER 1

RENAISSANCE MESSIANISM

We usually think of the Renaissance as a time of revival of ancient learning, an era when the humanistic values of the modern world were created and Europe became a place which a person from our own time might recognize. People like Leonardo da Vinci or even Machiavelli seem to have goals and motivations that are understandable to us. The familiar aspects of their lives and work, however, often obscure the truth that in many ways they were very different from us indeed, and they understood the world and made choices on the basis of that knowledge in ways and patterns that are wholly foreign to us. Some of the major figures of the Renaissance thought they understood the secrets of the universe, not only its construction but its very purpose in existing. Since they were Christians, they knew the universe would come to an end with the Second Coming of Christ, and their research helped them to calculate when that might take place and under what conditions.

The Renaissance men who chanced on views still held by modern scholars are often seen as scientists while those who meticulously mapped blind alleys are reduced to deluded alchemists and magicians. Nevertheless, the key methodological concept that united all these Renaissance intellectuals was eclecticism—that is, the idea that no one has a monopoly of truth but that it must be sought among all peoples and cultures. Thinkers in the Renaissance thought nothing of mixing Christian theology with Jewish philosophy and Arabic geography.

At the end of the fifteenth century, there was a keen desire to implement the new ideas coming in fast to Italy, some brought by Eastern Christian scholars who fled the fall of Constantinople in 1453, bringing with them whole treasure houses of Greek manuscripts never before seen in western Europe, others disseminated by way of the new communications revolution. This revolution was not only an effect of the invention of printing but also its cause, since increased demand for texts created the need to find a quick and efficient method of reproducing them.

| I |

The most important new idea that paved the way for a reconstructed and improved messianism was the body of knowledge that is usually called hermeticism. The hermetic tradition, in brief, was an attempt to return to a source of knowledge believed to be older than that of Rome, Greece, or even Israel—ancient Egypt. Egypt's was thought to be the most ancient philosophy, and the ancient Egyptians' intellectual and scientific achievements were held to predate those of any other civilization. The Renaissance understanding of this hermetic tradition was based on a collection of writings attributed to a certain Hermes Trismegistus, the "Thrice-Great Hermes," said to have been an Egyptian priest reporting on traditions and lore current in the Egyptian temples of his time. The *Corpus Hermeticum* had something for everyone: astrology, alchemy, texts about the secret powers of plants and stones, guides to the making of talismans, and proper philosophical treatises.[1] It is easy to imagine the excitement generated by the first reading of such secret lore.

This bulk of hermetic writings was first brought to Florence, the epicenter of the Renaissance, by a monk from Macedonia in 1453 who was one of the agents employed by Cosimo de' Medici to scour the East for manuscripts. Believing these Greek documents to be the work of an Egyptian priest who lived long before Plato, Cosimo ordered his scholars to drop everything, including their translation of Plato's *Republic*, and devote themselves to translating the *Corpus Hermeticum* into more readable Latin.

It hardly affects our argument that the hermetic texts were not nearly so old as Cosimo thought. Indeed, far from having been written before Plato, they were in fact produced in the first and second centuries of the Christian era. Needless to say, the *Corpus Hermeticum* may well contain in it older oral traditions, and the Jewish and perhaps Persian influences are readily apparent; for all we can tell, it may also contain the remains of secret Egyptian lore handed down over the generations. And there seems to be a bit about Genesis in it as well, which some people believed might predate Moses's account of creation in the Bible, and a "son of God" also appears. By the seventeenth century, when the hermetic writings were revealed as post-Christian, they were too entrenched in European culture to be discarded.

The implications of hermeticism for the messianic idea were profound, for the chief message of its writings was that humankind not only can understand the world but can actually control it, at the very least by identifying the path that nature will take. In one sense at least, hermeticism did emerge from Egyptian religion, in that its basic tenets developed in Alexandria in those first centuries of the Christian era when the direction that the organized religion would take was still unclear. Out of that cauldron also came Neoplatonism and Gnosticism, philosophies that stressed that knowledge was twofold: superstition for the masses and knowledge (*gnosis*) for the élite. Neoplatonism developed from the philosophy of Plotinus in the third century A.D., and especially emphasized the single ultimate source from which all things emanate and with which the soul seeks mystical union. The Gnostics, who considered themselves Christians, believed in a supreme God who not only was totally remote from our world but had no part in Creation, that job having been the bungled job of a lesser, perhaps evil, deity. This belief system was set out in their own texts, some of which were discovered in Egypt at Nag Hammadi in 1945, mostly written in Coptic, translated from the Greek.[2] Within our gross physical bodies, they argued, is a divine spark, the soul, trapped and searching for salvation and reunion with God. This can be achieved through *gnosis*, which enables the soul to ascend into the celestial realms controlled by the stars and planets. If we add to the Gnostics the activity of Sextus Empiricus in second-century Alexandria and the development of skepticism as a philosophical school, then certainly it can be said that hermeticism's pedigree was hardly less grand for not having come directly from ancient Egypt.[3]

In this Renaissance period of intellectual fervor, then, everything was possible, and someone interested in one aspect of the supernatural tradition was likely as not to be fascinated by another. Admittedly, not all of this was completely new: the *Asclepius*, for example, one of the most important hermetic treatises, had been known in Latin translation in the Middle Ages from the second century, and had a smaller revival during the twelfth century. But the extraordinary rehabilitation of the hermetic writings in the late fifteenth and early sixteenth centuries provided a high-quality complex text which could be studied and cited.

| II |

The most important bridge between hermeticism and the biblical scholarship from which Christian millenarianism drew its strength was the introduction to hermeticism, very early on, of the key component of Jewish mysticism, the Cabala. The Cabala entered European Christian intellectual life as part of these supernatural and esoteric interests during the Renaissance, and it never left. Its methods became an essential tool for biblical exegesis, and they have had enormous effects on messianism, because the Cabala, it was believed, could be used for calculating when the Messiah would come. Giovanni Pico della Mirandola (1463–94) was the first to use the Jewish mystical tradition as a Christian tool for biblical analysis. Pico, the youngest son of the count of Mirandola and Concordia, a small territory near Ferrara, began to study canon law at Bologna at the age of fourteen, and two years later went to Ferrara, then Padua. In Paris he encountered scholastic theologians, and back in Italy he studied Hebrew, Aramaic, and Arabic with several Jewish teachers. It was then that he developed an interest in the Cabala.[4]

Pico chose the most public way of introducing a serious consideration of the Cabala into Christian theological debate. Having settled in Rome in 1486, he proposed 900 theses and challenged any scholar to confute them, agreeing to pay his expenses. As it happened, the pope refused to allow the debate to take place, since of the 900 theses, 47 came directly from cabalistic sources, and a further 72 were Pico's own conclusions from cabalistic research. The most controversial of these theses proclaimed, "No science can better convince us of the divinity of Jesus Christ than magic and the Cabala." Indeed, the cabalistic techniques of gematria (whereby each letter stands for a significant numerical value) and notarikon (whereby words are seen as abbreviations) efficiently served Christian needs. The first three letters of the Hebrew Bible (*beth-resh-aleph*), for example, could easily be seen as an abbreviation for son-spirit-father (*ben-ruach-av*); and the placing of the Hebrew letter *shin* in the median position of the tetragrammaton produced an approximation of the name "Jesus." As this unspeakable word becomes pronounceable, so too is the ineffable made tangible, the spirit made flesh. Even the vertical arrangement of the four letters of the Hebrew name of God seemed to produce the stick figure of a man.[5]

Pico's determination to use the Cabala in Christian theological discussion promoted the first genuine scholarly interest in this important Jewish tradition, and at exactly the same time that the Jews were being expelled from Spain. Iberian Jews were instrumental in raising the study of the Cabala to new heights in Italy, for one of the intellectual effects of their expulsion from Spain was to turn the entire mystical tradition around from being focused on the origins of the world to its eventual apocalyptic destruction, a new pessimistic orientation in an era of holocaust. Pico and his spiritual descendants, then, were latching on to a Jewish philosophy in the process of rapid development. Since the Cabala was fundamentally biblical, it was spared the suspicious skepticism that might be connected with the parallel interest in the hermetic Egyptian tradition.

Through Pico's influence, Johannes Reuchlin (1455–1522) was led to cabalistic and Hebraic wisdom, which he studied in Italy under Jacob ben Jehiel Loans, the Jewish court physician of Frederick III. Reuchlin produced in 1506 the first Hebrew grammar in Latin, and wrote the first full treatises on the Cabala by a gentile.[6] Pico and Reuchlin's fascination with Hebrew and the Cabala was certainly part of Renaissance eclecticism, the notion that the truth could be found scattered in a wide variety of sources. Yet, more importantly, they reinforced the belief that the Cabala was part of the original divine message God gave Moses on Mount Sinai, and that it had remained pure, untainted by the intervention of the rabbis and their obfuscating Talmud. Many Jewish rabbis and even medical doctors now found themselves in demand among their intellectual Christian neighbors as purveyors of whatever Hebrew knowledge they might have, no matter how haphazardly acquired. Eventually, their monopoly was weakened by both the printing of cabalistic works and the rise of Lurianic Cabala, a new variety of the mystical tradition which was being developed at Safed in Palestine, but for nearly a century these Jewish teachers were very popular. Rabbi Elijah Menahem Halfan described the newfound popularity of Jewish scholars as somewhat exasperating:

In the last twenty years, knowledge has increased, and people have been seeking everywhere for instruction in Hebrew. Especially after the rise of the sect of Luther, many of the nobles and scholars of the land sought to have thorough knowledge of this glorious science [Cabala]. They have exhausted themselves in this search, because among our people there are but a small number of men learned in this wisdom, for after the great number of troubles and expulsions, but a few remain. So seven learned men grasp a Jewish man by the hem of his garment and say: "Be our master in this science!"[7]

Pico had a rabbi as well, Yohanan Isaac Allemanno, whom he met in Florence in 1488 and engaged as his teacher. But more importantly, there was Guglielmo Raimondo Moncada, a.k.a. Flavius Mithridates (c. 1450–fl. 1489), who was born in Sicily, where his father was a rabbi.[8] At some point he was baptized and took the name of the count of Aderno, becoming a priest soon afterward. He studied at the University of Naples, and picked up a few benefices, one from the pope and another from the king of Aragon; by about 1477 he was in Rome, well connected at the papal court and a professor of theology at the Sapienza. A high point of his career took place on Good Friday 1481, when he preached on the suffering of Jesus Christ before Pope Sixtus IV and the College of Cardinals in the Vatican.[9] He introduced quotations from cabalistic sources, the so-called secret Jewish doctrines, into his preaching, and even if some of them were made up, the effect was impressive. But for some reason he fell from favor in 1483, was deprived of his benefices, and was forced to flee to Germany, where he taught in Cologne and Tübingen. Two years later he was on his way back to Italy, via Basel, where he taught Rodolphus Agricola, the Dutch humanist, and Sebastian Brant, the poet.[10]

Back in Italy, and now calling himself Flavius Mithridates, he taught Pico Hebrew, Aramaic, Arabic, and the Cabala; went with him to various places in Italy; but prudently decided to stay away from Rome in 1486, when his pupil attempted to present his cabalistic theses for public debate. Instead, he went to Viterbo, meeting the young future Pope Paul III, but perhaps someone recognized him, since he was imprisoned there on the order of his former patron Pope Innocent VIII. Nothing more is heard of Flavius Mithridates after that date.

Indeed, the point has been made that the entire direction of translation was altered by the careers of these rabbis and priests. Before the Renaissance, many philosophical treatises were translated into Hebrew by Jews for the use of other Jews. But now, Jews and converts from Judaism were translating Hebrew works into Latin or Italian and writing themselves in these languages.[11]

| III |

The bigger question was whether the sort of thing Mithridates was teaching, and Pico was learning and applying, was suitable for Christian consumption. The answer was critical for the future development of both philosophy and biblical scholarship, and it would determine that, after the Reformation, the Protestants had the inside track on Jewish scholarship, which is one reason why messianism in our own day is primarily a Protestant phenomenon.

The first great battle, centered on the Talmud, featured two powerful protagonists, Johannes Reuchlin, Hebrew scholar, cabalist, eminent jurist, and member of the Supreme Court of the Swabian League, versus Johannes Pfefferkorn, a Jew who had converted to Christianity in his mid-thirties and settled in Cologne with the brief of searching out attacks on Christianity in Jewish writings. The Dominicans of Cologne helped Pfefferkorn obtain a letter of introduction to Emperor Maximilian I, written by his sister, as a result of which he was given permission to seize questionable Hebrew books for inspection. Pfefferkorn was taking no chances, and at the end of September 1509 confiscated all the Hebrew books in Frankfurt.

Even some Christians thought this was an example of overkill, and Maximilian himself issued four successive (and contradictory) mandates within a few months, in the end ordering that Pfefferkorn's allegations be investigated by the theological faculties of Cologne, Mainz, Erfurt, and Heidelberg, and by three further individuals, the Inquisition chiefs in Cologne and Carben—and Reuchlin. Heidelberg and Erfurt were evasive, while Cologne and Mainz sided with Pfefferkorn. But the only person to submit careful arguments against the suppression of Hebrew learning was Reuchlin, who produced his text in October 1510.

Reuchlin's argument was that Christians hardly knew what was written in Hebrew apart from the Bible and were therefore in no position to condemn Jewish learning wholesale. He noted that there was a good deal in Hebrew which had little to do with religion, such as Hebrew poetry, and that the Jewish commentary on the Old Testament cleared much ground for Christian commentators. Reuchlin even had some good words about the Talmud, arguing that it was not understood by those who sought to condemn it. He concluded by affirming the right of Jews not only to continue writing and publishing in Hebrew but also to practice their religion unmolested.

Most humanists were duty-bound to side with Reuchlin and to champion the ancient body of Hebrew learning and literature. But Erasmus prevaricated on the issue, his feelings of disgust about the Jews preventing him from helping Reuchlin behind the scenes. Even Maximilian I was somewhat sympathetic to Reuchlin's arguments, as was Pope Leo X. On the other hand, the king of France and the entire theological faculty of Paris, and more importantly, King Carlos el Primero of Spain (soon to become Emperor Charles V) supported Pfefferkorn. At the height of the controversy, in 1517, Pope Leo X accepted Reuchlin's dedication to him of his most recent work, *De arte cabbalistica*, the first full analysis of the Cabala by a non-Jew, written in the form of a dialogue between a Jew, a Greek, and a Muslim. Leo eventually condemned Reuchlin, in 1520, by which time he was desperate about the growing influence of Luther and Protestantism, and the dispute over the Talmud had become more of a code than a serious disagreement.

By the dawn of the Reformation, then, Jewish learning was an integral part of both the Christian mystical and the biblical tradition. As we shall see, the reign of Hebrew did not survive in the Roman Catholic world after the backlash against it during the Counter-Reformation. But the Cabala had been brought on the stage; and the notion that the Jews were privy to secrets about the building of the universe remained important in the history of messianism.

| IV |

The somewhat complacent scholarly milieu of the Renaissance was exactly what disgusted Girolamo Savonarola (1452–98), the Dominican prophet who managed single-handedly to halt the progress of the new culture in the place where it started, Florence. "How mighty must have been the soul which dwelt side by side with this narrow intellect!" enthused Jacob Burckhardt, the nineteenth-century historian of the Renaissance. "And what a flame must have glowed within him before he could constrain the Florentines, possessed as they were by the passion for knowledge and culture, to surrender themselves to a man who could thus reason!"[12]

Savonarola was born in Ferrara, a city then immersed in the spirit of the Renaissance.[13] His father, a respected court physician, gave his son a classical education with the intention of having him continue in medicine, but when he was about twenty-five, Savonarola entered the Order of Friars Preachers and became a Dominican monk. He arrived in Florence in 1482, and within two years had progressed from a sort of moralistic asceticism to outright millenarianism, which he claimed to derive from the Bible itself. Perhaps prompted by Pico della Mirandola, who was Savonarola's great admirer, Lorenzo de' Medici actually invited Savonarola to become prior of San Marco. Savonarola thereupon devoted his efforts to biting the hand that fed him, and denouncing both Renaissance culture and the rulers who had encouraged its development. Interestingly, the Medicis did not react as one might have expected— that is, by evicting the troublesome monk from their territory. They may have been keen on attracting more Dominicans to Florence, or it may simply have been that once installed, he was impossible to dislodge from Florentine life and society.

Quite apart from his effect on local politics, Savonarola was also notable because his millenarian prophecies of doom and destruction actually seemed to be coming true. The recurring appearance of the plague, crippling inflation, and the increased frequency of warfare all made life very difficult for all classes at the end of the fifteenth century. As Burckhardt taught a hundred years ago, the disorder and fragmentation of Italian city-states made for a social environment which created the free market in talent that was essential for the development of Renaissance culture. Just when Savonarola came to prominence, the machinery of devastation ground its way toward the Florentines, and everything he had been telling them seemed to be happening.

King Charles VIII of France (1483–98) regarded himself as a second Charlemagne who would restore his country to glory, and toward that end he invaded Italy at the end of 1494, on the way to Naples and, it was said, Jerusalem. Each city had to make the decision whether to surrender to the all-powerful ruler or to make a show of opposing him. Piero de' Medici, who had succeeded Lorenzo as ruler of Florence in 1492, was unwilling to risk the showcase of the Renaissance in a long and hopeless siege and willingly turned over Florence's strategic centers to France. However, he found himself deposed on his return, and Savonarola in power, for not only did Savonarola not oppose Charles VIII but he saw the French king's arrival as a sign of the imminent coming of the Messiah and the dawn of the Apocalypse. Part of his city's preparation for the Messiah's arrival would be the wholesale dismantling of Renaissance culture and its artifacts.

Savonarola did not hold specific public office but he was nevertheless Florence's dominant figure, his power wielded through his charismatic preaching, reinforced by divine communications and visions. In one of them, which he received during the Lent season of 1492, he declared:

> . . . when I was preaching in the Church of San Lorenzo in Florence on Good Friday night, I saw two crosses in the sky. The first was black and in the midst of Rome, touching heaven with its top and stretching its arms through the whole world. It was inscribed with these words: "The Cross of God's Wrath." When I saw it, immediately I beheld a tempest darkening in the air with rushing clouds, winds, lightnings, thunderbolts, hail—all mixed together with fire and sword. An innumerable multitude of men was destroyed so that those that survived on earth were few. After this I saw a peaceful and bright time come and a golden cross in the midst of Jerusalem, the same height as the other, so gleaming that it illumined the whole world and filled it with new flowers and joy. Its inscription was: "The Cross of God's Mercy." Without delay all the nations of the earth, both men and women, came together from all sides to adore it and embrace it. For this purpose I received many other, even clearer, visions, as found in the other matters I have foretold, especially about the renewal and punishment of the Church. I have been strengthened by many visions and very clear showings at different times.[14]

His "bonfire of the vanities" consumed everything from new paintings to false eyelashes. At the end of the day, he promised, Florence would become the center of millenarian activity that would intensify after the return of the savior king Charles VIII. Florence was "the chosen center of divine illumination and himself as the man sent by God, not only to warn Italy of the tribulations which had now come, but also to lead her out of the abomination of desolation."

Unfortunately, Charles VIII did not return and Savonarola's millenarian prophecy took on rather an annoying edge. The rest of Italy bitterly resented the French invader as he came swaggering down the peninsula, and in Florence here was this fanatical Dominican preacher telling them that it was for their own good and for that of King Jesus. Charles was forced to retreat to France, and he died there in 1498. Matters worsened when the corrupt Pope Alexander VI summoned Savonarola to Rome and levied on him a ban of silence. Savonarola disobeyed both orders, was excommunicated in 1497, and a papal interdict of Florence was threatened. The situation was ready-made for his rival Franciscans, who goaded him into a trial by fire, which he declined to endure. As with many popular leaders before him, his support almost instantly turned to opposition, and a crowd attacked San Marco and imprisoned Savonarola and two of his lieutenants. Interrogation and torture followed, ending with the inevitable public execution of the three friars in Florence's main square on May 23, 1498.

Marsilio Ficino, the man who had introduced hermeticism into the classical Renaissance, was at pains to explain how even he had been temporarily seduced by Savonarola. In a letter to the College of Cardinals, he gave his own theory:

I know, Venerable Prelates, that most of the Sacred College have been astonished that during the last five years one hypocrite from Ferrara has deceived so many Florentines, otherwise clever and learned men. They really ought to be astonished if they think that one man was able to outwit so many and such able men. But he is not a mortal man, but a demon of immense cleverness—not even one demon, but a crowd of them who attacked miserable mortals with hidden traps and outwitted them with marvelous artifices. No one ought to be in awe any longer. Without disagreement all will confess that our first parents, who like children of God were provided with divine wisdom and strength, established in Par-

adise, and taught by angels, were deceived by a single diabolical spirit. Why then should it seem marvelous that the
Florentines, especially at a time like this, were so unfortunate
that they were secretly possessed and seduced by a horde of
demons in the guise of an angel?[15]

As arguments go, this was one which should have convinced anyone
who had read the book of Genesis.

Significantly, Savonarola's movement did not entirely collapse,
and millenarianism continued to have a strong hold on Florence
even after his death. The Florentine republic lasted for another
fourteen years, until the Medicis were restored with the aid of Spanish troops in 1512. They were evicted yet again during the brief
flowering of the last Florentine republic between 1527 and 1530.
Savonarola's millenarian ideology, which now went under the name
of "piagnonism," was characterized by a similar burst of apocalyptic
and moralizing sermons from San Marco, and a generally puritanical
attitude toward art and culture. Though the second time it only
helped the Medicis return to power after three years of regression,
the popularity of Savonarola never died. Even Martin Luther found
much to admire in him, and a statue of Savonarola was erected in
Wittenberg, Protestantism's epicenter. Savonarola's sermons continued to be printed and to enjoy a readership in Catholic countries.
As we shall see, in a number of ways he foreshadowed many other
individuals and movements who used millenarian theology as part
of a more general political vision.

| V |

The Italian orientation of most scholars of the Renaissance has
tended to overshadow all other locations of intellectual excitement
at the end of the Middle Ages. There is also a tendency to look for
aspects of the Renaissance culture that seem modern and serve as
precursors of what was to come. One effect of this turn of mind has

been to neglect fifteenth-century Spain, which was in fact a hotbed of religious and intellectual fervor, and not all of it directed toward persecuting heretics. Spain in the last half of that century was obsessed with only one goal: the completion of the reconquest of Spain from the Muslims, who had captured much of the Iberian Peninsula centuries earlier and had been driven back gradually. The goal of Reconquista was in reach, and this gave to Spanish men and women the sense that their generation had been divinely selected to see its fulfillment with their own eyes. The generation of 1492 was composed of chosen people, for in that year, within a matter of months, three momentous events had occurred: the last remaining Muslim enclave on Spanish soil, the kingdom of Granada, was conquered; the Jews were expelled; and Columbus was sent on his voyage to the Indies. These three landmarks were connected: the Reconquest represented external cleansing, the expulsion internal cleansing, and Columbus's voyage the export of the miracle of the Reconquest to other countries. In such a highly charged religious and emotional atmosphere, it is hardly surprising that millenarianism should flourish.[16]

In a sense, it is odd that modern historiography has underestimated the millenarian dimension of Columbus's voyages, as the Admiral himself openly expressed his apocalyptic motivation. After returning from his third journey, when he was ignominiously brought back from the New World in chains, he wrote to a member of the royal court that "God made me the messenger of the new heaven and the new earth of which he spoke in the Apocalypse of St. John after having spoken of it through the mouth of Isaiah; and he showed me the spot where to find it."[17] He tried to rehabilitate his image as a great discoverer, and published a book of prophecies with an open letter to Ferdinand and Isabella as the preface. "Not unworthily nor without reason, Most Splendid Rulers," he wrote, "do I assert that even greater things are reserved for you, when we read that Joachim the Calabrian Abbot predicted that the future ruler who would recover Mount Sion would come from Spain."[18]

Columbus's plan in his fourth voyage was no less than to liberate the Holy Sepulcher from the clutches of Islam.

These views come out even more clearly in his account of his fourth and final voyage (1502–4), a document known as the *Lettera Rarissima*. Columbus begins his argument by noting that the chief reason for trade is to obtain gold and that merchants take their commodities "to the ends of the earth to exchange them for gold." This precious metal had more than monetary value, since "he who possesses it has all he needs in this world, as also the means for rescuing souls from purgatory, and restoring them to the enjoyment of paradise," presumably a reference not only to indulgences but also to masses said for the dead. Citing both biblical and classical evidence, Columbus suggested that the gold which Solomon brought back to the Holy Land came from "the Aurea"—that is, the Malay Peninsula. If this is true, Columbus noted,

> I contend that these mines of the Aurea are identical with those of Veragua, which, as I have said before, extends westward twenty days' journey, at an equal distance from the Pole and the Line. Solomon bought all of it—gold, precious stones, and silver—but your Majesties need only send to seek them to have them at your pleasure. David, in his will, left three thousand quintals of Indian gold to Solomon, to assist in building the Temple; and, according to Josephus, it came from these lands.

Gold was available for the taking, and Columbus could prove it from the Bible, and from Josephus, whose writings had already acquired a quasi-scriptural status as the text which linked the New Testament with the Old. Columbus offered himself as the man for the job, citing the fact that "Jerusalem and Mount Sion are to be rebuilt by the hands of the Christians, as God has declared by the mouth of his prophet in the fourteenth Psalm. The Abbot Joachim said that he who should do this was to come from Spain."[19]

Admittedly, much of what Columbus thought and did in the apocalyptic sphere is appropriately obscure. Even his signature is a mystery. After discovering America, he usually signed his name with this curious collection of letters:

	.S.	
.S.	A	.S.
X	M	Y
Xpo	F E R E N S	

Apart from the bottom line, which is certainly "Christoferens"—that is, "Christ-bearer"—it is not clear what Columbus was trying to express.

Even the book of prophecies which Columbus worked on remains mysterious, despite his own wish that this text would explain his view of the historical role which he thought he had played and would continue to play in his projected fourth voyage. All that survive at the Biblioteca Colombina in Seville are fragments, compiled by Columbus and a friend, a Carthusian monk named Gaspar Gorricio. What we find are passages from the Scriptures, selections from secular authors both ancient and medieval, and some Spanish verses, apart from Columbus's letter, which is itself not complete. The psalms which he selected reflected on the End of Days and the restoration of Jerusalem and Mount Zion. There are different handwritings: that of Columbus and Gorricio, but also passages written out by Columbus's son Ferdinand and his brother Bartolomeo. Nevertheless, it is clear from this text that the Admiral's motivations by this stage, if not before, were clearly millenarian as much as they were commercial or in the mode of the conventional explorer.

Christopher Columbus was in large measure a self-educated thinker, so it is not surprising that he should have relied on the reading of others. One source which he used with great frequency was the *Imago mundi* of Pierre d'Ailly, an early-fifteenth-century compendium of knowledge.[20] Columbus had a printed copy, already a nicely symbolic indication of the way in which ideas would be distributed in the postmedieval world. This book, which survives in Seville, is heavily annotated, especially the eighth chapter, relating to geography; from it more than from any other text Columbus was misled as to the width of the Atlantic. At least in this sense, the great Admiral was rather conventional in his geography.

D'Ailly was also the author of a number of short *opuscula*, published by John of Westphalia in 1480–83. These include summaries of metaphysical matters, with a good deal about the End of Days. Much of d'Ailly in turn came from Roger Bacon, of which he sometimes incorporated large sections verbatim. Bacon, in turn, derived his chronology from the ninth-century Arabian astronomer Albumasar, whose works were translated into Latin three centuries later, and whose notion that empires and religions no less than the lives of individuals were controlled by the stars made sensational reading to alchemists everywhere. So d'Ailly's work was part of a chain of tradition that became available to Columbus. One lesson he learned from it was that the Antichrist would follow Islam.[21] He was especially intrigued by material that d'Ailly got from a writer named Pseudo-Methodius, which indicated that the "king of the Romans" would defeat Islam and follow up this victory by living in Jerusalem for ten and a half years, after which time the Antichrist would appear.[22]

Columbus's millenarian motivation for his voyages is therefore hardly in doubt, and we will need to reevaluate the importance of the apocalyptic motif in this greatest of enterprises. But on what sort of soil did Columbus's seeds fall? One advantage of the unchallenged supremacy of the Catholic Church in Spain was that it allowed for a certain amount of religious speculation within the boundaries of orthodoxy. Fields of study that would become immediately suspect in Germany, for example, such as Hebrew scholarship and textual criticism, were able to flourish relatively unchallenged in the closed community south of the Pyrenees. Nowhere is this flirting with the apocalyptic within the academy more apparent than in the work that went into the Complutensian Polyglot Bible.

This great *Biblia Sacra Polyglotta*, a Spanish initiative, was undertaken in the generation that saw the conquest of Granada, the discovery of the New World, and the expulsion of the Jews and Muslims from Iberia.[23] The driving figure behind the work was the famous Cardinal Francisco Ximénez de Cisneros (1437–1517), confessor to Queen Isabella, provincial of the Franciscan order in Castile, primate of Spain, and Inquisitor General of Castile and León.[24] Ximénez had studied at Salamanca and Rome until 1465, and established the University of Alcalá (*Complutum* in Latin) in 1500 as a trilingual college.[25] In short, he was of impeccable orthodox credentials (despite having been imprisoned for six months by a previous archbishop of Toledo in his youth). He was a great crusader against Marranos, burning hundreds of backsliding Jews, in no way deterred by his love of the Hebrew language from persecuting its purveyors.

According to the story, Ximénez began to learn Hebrew when he was over sixty in order to work on his new Bible. The point of his new edition was to lay the various versions of Scripture side by side, and thus enable the scholar to arrive at the divine truth which had been clouded by centuries of miscopying and obscurantism, and which now could be revealed by the new textual tools that had been developed in the past fifty years. He paid for the work itself, which cost more than 50,000 ducats, including 4,000 ducats alone for the purchase of seven manuscripts of the Hebrew Bible.[26]

The Complutensian Polyglot was begun in about 1502 and finished just as the Protestant threat to the Church began. The Medici pope Leo X (1513–21), Lorenzo the Magnificent's second son, was always a soft touch for the humanists, and he issued a bull in 1520 giving permission for its printing, but the Bible was not circulated in its six volumes until 1522, after the pope's death.[27] Six hundred copies of the Complutensian Polyglot were printed, including about three on vellum. The price, 6.5 ducats, was set by the pope himself:

too dear for casual use. It may be that Leo X had cold feet once the work was actually done: he it was who had made the shady deal with Albrecht of Mainz (1490–1548) over the sale of indulgences for the rebuilding of St. Peter's, the deal which sparked Luther's crusade, and it was Leo who had to excommunicate Luther in January 1521.[28] Ximénez himself lived at least to see the volumes printed and was very gratified, as told in a contemporary anecdote:

> I have often heard John Brocarius, son of Arnoldus Brocarius, who printed the Polyglot, relate to his friends, that, when his father had put the finishing stroke to the last volume, he deputed him to carry it to the Cardinal. John Brocarius was then a lad; and having dressed himself in a very elegant suit of clothes, he approached Ximenes, and delivered the volume into his hands. "I render thanks to thee, O God!" exclaimed Ximenes, "that thou hast protracted my life to the completion of these biblical labours!" And afterwards conversing with his friends, the Cardinal would often observe, that the surmounting of the various difficulties of his political situation, afforded him not half the solace of that which arose from the finishing of his Polyglot. Ximenes died the same year (1517), not many weeks afterwards.[29]

The structure of the Polyglot showed what could be done by applying the spirit of the Renaissance to biblical scholarship. The first Old Testament volumes showed the Latin Vulgate in the center of each page, the Greek Septuagint with interlinear Latin translation on the inside column, and the Hebrew text on the outside column. Below the text of the first five books of the Bible (the Pentateuch) is the Aramaic Targum of Onkelos with Arabic vowels, and a Latin translation. The margin notes Hebrew and Aramaic roots. The apocryphal books which the Church accepted as Scripture appear in the

Septuagint Greek version, with the Vulgate printed interlinearly, although III Maccabees appears in Greek only.[30]

The contribution of Ximénez and his Polyglot to Old Testament scholarship can hardly be overestimated. His edition was the first to divide the Hebrew text into chapters, and it was the first time that the Septuagint was printed, the text being based on manuscripts from the Vatican library, the library of St. Mark at Venice, and from Ximénez's own private collection. In the dedication to the pope, the editors boasted that they had used "the oldest examples out of the apostolic library," although they missed Vatican B, one of the most ancient manuscripts. Sometimes they cheated a bit, in accordance with time-honored practice: when passages were present in the Vulgate but absent in the Septuagint, they filled in the gaps by translating back into Greek from the Latin text.

According to the colophon dated January 10, 1514, the New Testament (in Greek) was actually printed first, and it forms the fifth volume of the Polyglot. Thus it predates Erasmus's more famous edition by two years. A sort of primitive concordance appears in the margin, noting similar passages in other parts of the Bible.

In many ways, the sixth volume of the Polyglot was the most revolutionary, consisting as it did of innovative study aids. One highlight was the Hebrew and Aramaic dictionary, far superior to Reuchlin's and far more user-friendly. The lexicon included Latin catchwords and Hebrew roots in the margins, and passages from the Latin Old Testament to provide examples of the use of Hebrew words. Ximénez also added a short Hebrew grammar for general use. The primacy of the Hebrew and even Aramaic elements in scriptural study was thus implied unequivocally, and made explicit in the dedication:

Certainly since there can be no word, no combination of letters, from which there does not arise, and as it were spring forth, the most concealed senses of the heavenly wisdom; and since the most learned interpreter cannot explain more than one of these, it is unavoidable that after translation the Scripture yet remains pregnant and filled with both various and sublime insights which cannot become known from any other sources than from the very fountain of the original language.[31]

This proclamation of reliance on the primary text of Scripture, and the need to look at the Bible as one would with any other ancient document, is probably more representative of the preface than this oft-quoted sentence: "We have placed the Latin translation of the blessed Jerome as though between the Synagogue and the Eastern Church, placing them like the two thieves one on each side, and Jesus, that is the Roman or Latin Church, between them."[32]

Such a prodigious effort as the Complutensian Polyglot quite obviously could only be accomplished with a good deal of effort from many sources. Certainly at this time, at the end of the fifteenth century, the Jews held a near-monopoly in Hebrew scholarship. Ximénez's chief Jewish adviser was the convert Alfonso de Zamora (c. 1474–1544), who may have left Spain at the expulsion, but who certainly was baptized at least by 1506. Zamora became professor of Hebrew at Salamanca, and even published a letter to the Jews of Rome calling on them to follow his lead and convert to Christianity. Zamora was aided in his Hebraic work by two other converts from Judaism, Pablo Coronel and Alfonso de Alcalá. A Christian named Nebrija worked with them as well. Benjamin Kennicott, the great eighteenth-century English biblical critic, would claim that one of the problems with the Complutensian Polyglot was that the Hebraists were former Jews and therefore used Jewish Masoretic manuscripts in which the variations between the texts had already been smoothed over. More recent criticism, however, suggests that Zamora and his colleagues seem to have been using a manuscript that dated no further back than the ninth century, before the codification of the Masoretes, which can be determined by certain idiosyncrasies in the text. As this so-called Babylonian Codex no longer survives among Ximénez's manuscripts in Madrid, we will never have any final proof, but the work of the Jewish converts seems to have been more flexible than Kennicott understood.[33]

Why were so many resources expended to produce this text? And why were Jews involved in the project? Ximénez himself did not mind becoming involved with people who could never pass any racial test of *limpieza de sangre*. Apart from the Jews, he was close to Archbishop Hernando de Talavera of Granada, whom the Inquisition arrested in 1506 and accused of Judaizing, telling people that Elijah and Moses had already arrived. Ximénez reacted by appointing himself Grand Inquisitor and arresting the Inquisitor who had arrested Talavera.[34] But more intriguing, perhaps, is the attitude of Zamora toward all this activity. Despite his conversion to Christianity, he seems to have written very little about his new faith. He wrote a letter to the Jews of Rome which appeared in the second edition of his Hebrew grammar in Latin, published in 1520, also a Hebrew work that was never published, *Sefer Hochmat Elohim*, which, he claimed, would bring about the conversion of the Jews.[35] Neither document was polemical: they were both simply compilations of texts, and, significantly, both were produced after Ximénez had died and could no longer protect him from charges of heterodoxy.

Zamora discussed his situation more directly in a somewhat obscure postscript to a letter supposedly sent by a Professor Zornosa of the University of Alcalá to Pope Paul III and Cardinal de Santa Balvina in 1544. The letter, written in Hebrew, appears to be a request by this professor for protection against a certain D. Juan Tavera, who is persecuting the university. Presumably Zamora translated the letter into Hebrew if he did not write it himself. What is curious, however, is his own personal postscript:

> This letter was written and completed for the service of God on Monday, the thirty-first day of the month of March in the year one thousand, five hundred, forty-four of our salvation in

the university ["yeshiva"] of Alcalá de Henares by me, Alfonso de Zamora, a teacher of the Jewish language in this university ["yeshiva"] to all who want to learn it. And behold I am about seventy years old and I have not yet managed to see a single good day. And I wrote this letter with vocalization so that any middling man can understand it even if he be not learned, since learned men have no need of vocalization but supply by themselves the parts that I omit. Because I alone am left of all the learned men of Spain since the expulsion of the Kingdom of Castile that was in the year five thousand two hundred and two and fifty since the creation of the world according to the way all Jews today calculate wherever they are in exile throughout the world in their seasons.

Sof Shevach l'Al

finis laus deo and in all the letters I have used I have made this sign √ so that the reader will recognize it and not be confused with others that they see.

What is Zamora trying to say in this strange letter, Zamora, the engine behind Christian Spanish millenarianism after 1492? What was the fate of the letter, and why was it sent? Curiously, we have no record that it was ever received in Rome. The text comes from a collection at the University of Leiden based on materials assembled by a Dutch official at Constantinople in the seventeenth century. The official also obtained an introduction written in Aramaic to a work on Isaiah which Zamora began at Salamanca in 1532, in which he notes that he did it to be deposited in the library there for the use of scholars. So it would seem that Zamora sent the letter with his earlier translation to a Jewish community in the Ottoman Empire, in an attempt to explain that despite his conversion to Christianity, he was still Jewish.

There is an exciting possibility that the reason these Jews worked on the Polyglot Bible was their desire to keep alive the flame of Jewish learning in Spain. Zamora represents the end of one line of

Spanish millenarianism, one which could hardly be sustained without the input of resident Jews. The millenarian impulse was later taken over by very different sorts of mystics, people like the New Christians Isabel de la Cruz and Ruiz de Alcazar, who avoided making any commitment to the divinity of Christ or to the institutional church and awaited the imminent divine fulfillment of history. This line was to flourish in the seventeenth century, with such luminaries as Teresa of Avila and Juan de la Cruz; an earlier representative was Gregorio López (1542–96), known as the perfect man, who on his deathbed had nothing to confess.[36] Their millenarianism was mystical, their religion based on the direct apprehension of God within them. This sort of approach to God was readily understandable throughout the Christian world, especially after the Counter-Reformation, right through the Romantics to our own day. Zamora's brand of Hebraic scholarship in the service of Christian messianism looked very old-fashioned even in his own time, and it came to a swift end by the mid-sixteenth century, when the Counter-Reformation Church ruled that Hebrew matters were not a fit subject for study by Christians. Columbus's messianism was therefore not a demonstration of intellectual deviation by a partially educated self-taught sailor but part of a much larger world of Spanish millenarianism, which continued at least until the middle of the next century, when it was consumed by the newer-model mystical variety of apocalyptic thought.

One Jewish thinker, not yet mentioned, was probably part of the same movement in ways too subterranean to trace. Isaac Abrabanel (1437–1508), born in Lisbon, began a career there which combined scholarship with politics and high finance. Abrabanel's father Judah (d. 1471) was also in government service in Portugal, becoming the treasurer of King Alfonso V, a post in which Isaac succeeded him. Judah Abrabanel had also served the Braganza family, and when King Alfonso died in 1481 and the Braganza brother-in-law of the new king, João II, rebelled, it was only natural that Isaac would be implicated. He escaped to Spain in 1483 and thereby avoided the sentence of death decreed two years later. Although he initially devoted himself solely to scholarship, he soon became involved in government finance for Ferdinand and Isabella, and, with Abraham Señor, was one of the main Jewish notables who pleaded with the Catholic kings in vain in an attempt to reverse the edict of expulsion in 1492.

We know that Isaac Abrabanel was at Alcalá de Henares in 1488, and in any case as a leading Jewish scholar and public figure he must have met and discussed matters of mutual interest with Cardinal Ximénez. He may even have turned to Ximénez for help during the last desperate months before the expulsion. In any case, his views after 1492 are clearer to us, since from his exile in Naples, Corfu, and ultimately Venice he worked on biblical commentaries that sought to explain the misfortunes which had befallen the Jews as the tribulations of the Messiah. He also wrote three books designed to demonstrate the imminent coming of the Messiah, generally known under the collective title of *Migdal Yeshu'ot (Tower of Salvation)*. Abrabanel was convinced, from his reading of the Book of Daniel, that the Messiah would arrive in 1503, the dead would be resurrected and judged, and the Jews would return in glory to the Holy Land, to be ruled over by King Messiah, their enemies cast into eternal damnation. The mundane world would vanish, and disembodied souls would eternally bask in the divine presence. Abrabanel died in Venice, confident that he had discovered the plan behind the terrible events of the past two decades.

The influence of Abrabanel on the Jewish conception of the millennium was prodigious. His work remained a touchstone of millenarian thinking for both Jews and Christians, and given his extraordinary importance in pre-expulsion Spain, it is reasonable to surmise that Cardinal Ximénez and possibly Columbus knew something of his views. Zamora certainly did, and the transmutation of active Spanish messianic fervor into contemplative mysticism occurred under his very eyes, as we have seen, and fueled his feeling of despair.

| VI |

It is clear that many of the ideas which seem so modern to us have their origins, or at least their flowering, in the period of intellectual ferment which we call the Renaissance. To a modern nonbeliever, many of these ideas seem patently false. Millenarianism, messianism, prophecy are notions that sometimes seem to fit awkwardly with twentieth-century conceptions of how the universe is organized. There is a natural tendency to look in the past for those people and movements that represent concepts we find correct or familiar.

Nowhere is this turn of mind more apparent than in the theories of Paracelsus.[37] Philippus Aureolos Theophrastus Bombastus von Hohenheim (1493–1541) was a German alchemist, physician, and mystical philosopher who took the name of Paracelsus since he claimed to be greater than the classical Greek physician Celsus. He was born near Zurich, but he traveled so widely throughout Europe that it would be hard to imagine him in any particular place. He made his name at Basel by curing of a grave illness the great printer Johann Froben (who had published Erasmus), and he became city physician and professor of medicine at the university there. Paracelsus was a complete rebel against the medicine of his time. He objected to the contemporary system which placed the physician on a pedestal as a scholar who never dirtied his hands, and had the actual work done by surgeons and apothecaries, working according to the physician's orders. He also lectured in the local Swiss German dialect instead of in Latin, and threw open the secrets of the profession to outsiders. In about 1527, after Froben's death, Paracelsus fled Basel, having lost his protector and patron, and spent the remaining fourteen years of his life on the road, writing manuscripts and leaving them for safekeeping with students and followers.

His message was important, even if obscured by a style so boastful and incomprehensible that he might as well have written in Latin. His basic thesis was no less than that he had discovered the building blocks of the universe; the key was chemistry. His alchemical training led him to believe that if one took the hermetic idea developed by Ficino and others that the universe was built of overlapping microcosm and macrocosm, which differed in size rather than in inherent nature, then anything that held true in his little laboratory must also be true in the universe at large. There were correspondences, sympathies, between the body and soul of a person, and the world-body and world-soul of the universe. In other words, the universe, the macrocosm, was one enormous chemical laboratory, and, more important, Creation itself was a chemical operation by means of which God had distilled the pure from the impure in chaos.

For the physician, this meant that the human body, the microcosm, was essentially a chemical system that could be cured of disease by chemical treatment, by adjustment of the basic components. In this, Paracelsus opposed the prevailing concept of medicine based on Galen's theories, which posited four humors whose imbalance caused disease. Paracelsus argued that diseases were caused not by humoral imbalance but by living parasites in the body, and that one could use homeopathic remedies and detoxified poisons to make medicines that killed these parasites. All of this was well within the alchemical tradition of the Middle Ages. Paracelsus just happened to be right, and his patients tended to survive, at least as much because his chemical cures killed less frequently than the harsher Galenic remedies. He also invented "laudanum," which became a famous painkiller, and Paracelsus discovered how to make and use ether. These made the patient more comfortable even if he was dying and, for the ones with hope, gave them rest, which was often just what they needed.

His chemical explanation of messianic prophecy was at least as important. If the beginning of the world was a chemical operation, he reasoned, then the end would be as well. Joachim of Fiore had cited Malachi 4:5: "Behold, I will send you Elijah the prophet before the coming of the great and dreadful day of the Lord." Paracelsus claimed that fifty-eight years after his own death (which, as it turned out, meant 1599) Elijah would return as "Elias Artista," Elijah the alchemist. Elias would show us how to turn iron into gold, and would bring forward the end of the world. Contrary to popular opinion, Paracelsus posited, there would be no battle at Armageddon, and no Second Coming. The end of the world would be Creation in reverse: a chemical act of separation. The millennium would be a chemical millennium, a sort of alchemist's utopia.

From our point of view, what is significant is that Paracelsus—in his voyages from Italy to Scandinavia, from Alsace to Bohemia—proclaimed that our millennium lay with science, that if only we understood the actual structure of the universe, we could reproduce the process of Creation and prophesy the End of Days. He was convinced that these last days would be brought forward by a great scientist who would know how to unleash the power that would bring us full circle. In this chapter, it may seem that sometimes we have strayed from our brief of examining the origins and development of messianic revolution. But much of the groundwork was laid in the Renaissance, and when we look at the modern period, we have a general sense of déjà vu, for many groups have kidnapped ideas that flowered hundreds of years ago and survived in various written and oral forms until they were adapted to an overtly millenarian purpose in later centuries.

CHAPTER 2

THE MESSIANIC IDEA
DURING THE REFORMATION

During the period of the Reformation, in the first half of the sixteenth century, what had begun as a theoretical formulation of the nature of the universe took on practical use, as religious radicals began to see the messianic idea as a brief for fundamental change in society. Certainly, there was a good deal to change. Recent historiography of the Reformation tends to emphasize what is sometimes called its "magisterial" elements and to present the rise of Protestantism as the result of the power of individual personalities, such as Luther, and their use of coercive measures to force compliance with their views. The Reformation, then, becomes the victory of a minority determined to impose its doctrinal views on an indifferent majority by the use of force. But even revisionist historians would not deny that a "radical Reformation" lurked beneath their magisterial one.

If social oppression is a prerequisite of demands for change, there is no doubt that the period immediately preceding the Reformation fulfills this criterion. It was an era of violent economic and social dislocation, to put it mildly. Historians tend to put the primary blame on the rapid growth in Europe's population, itself the result of a number of other factors. In any case, the vastly increased numbers of mouths to feed led inevitably to rising food prices, higher rents, lower wages, unemployment, and a migration to towns and cities. The gulf between the rich and poor widened, with peasants and artisans especially affected not only by the low wages and high prices but by rising taxation, as landlords tried simultaneously to maintain their grand lifestyles in a period of inflation and also to supply the demands of the state against them. Landlords lost the paternalistic element in their self-definition of honor and proper standards, and gradually became transformed into rural capitalists exploiting cheap and plentiful labor.

Some historians have posited this poverty, social disorientation, and anger as sufficient explanation for the Reformation itself. While there was certainly a good deal of discontent, and many people longed for the stability that the disciplined and rational messages of Luther and Calvin offered, the appeal of Protestantism was equally strong among ruling élites, among princes, nobles, and city corporations eager to gain control over their own political communities. Still, it was in the lower reaches of society that the social changes of the past decades were translated into radical religion, especially messianism.

| I |

In a very real sense, the radical Reformation was quite different from the grand "magisterial Reformation" of Martin Luther. His Reformation was implemented with the agreement of secular authority: Luther would first convince the prince of a particular German state, say, and this prince would convince his people, usually by making them an offer they could not refuse. More importantly, his Reformation developed within the established political structure of the German Empire, composed as it was of hundreds of petty principalities. A prince who became "convinced" of the Protestant message suddenly found himself rich and powerful, for he confiscated lands and property belonging to the Roman Catholic Church, about one-third of his territory on average, and at a stroke eliminated the only rival to authority which he had at his doorstep.

Yet Luther was a also a sorcerer's apprentice, for his doctrines of *sola fide* ("by faith alone") and *sola scriptura* ("by scripture alone") meant that everyone could decide for himself in matters of religion, so long as he could show that a particular view could be found in Scripture. The Bible, as is readily seen, is a very long book. Luther eventually came to think of himself as the man who changed the face of Christianity forever, but in showing people that they could think for themselves, he found that many of them thought different thoughts than he did. Many new nominally Protestant leaders and nominally Protestant sects flowered almost immediately, arguing that Luther had traveled down the right road but had quit before reaching his destination. These radical groups, whose members viewed Luther as a halfway prophet, were not within his control, and he came to regret having opened this particular Pandora's box.

Whereas Luther was mainly interested in the German-speaking countries, the radical Protestants were more truly international. These political and social revolutionaries were at best indifferent and at worst opposed to the authority of the state, especially if it was "ungodly." They were also more willing to jettison the practices, institutions, and discipline of the medieval Church, and especially its concept of a clergy. They also had a much stronger concept of the millennium than Luther did, and looked forward to the day when Christ Jesus would return to earth to rule as king.

Some of these radical millenarians were spiritualists, mystics who argued against Luther that there was more to revelation than *sola scriptura*, than the Bible alone. They emphasized a concept of continuous revelation, insisting that God was still with us, communicating information that was not current at the time of the codification of the Scriptures. True understanding came not from God, but from the inner experience of Christ, the interior word. These spiritualists were therefore indifferent to all outward forms of religion, especially ceremonies and ecclesiastical organization. The true church, they believed, was the invisible communion of the faithful.

The two most characteristic representatives of this spiritualist orientation, which would be so important in the following centuries, were Sebastian Franck (c. 1499–c. 1542) and Kaspar Schwenckfeld (1490–1561). Franck, a champion of complete freedom of thought, argued for a minimalist, undogmatic form of Christianity. He spent his later years at Basel, where he was hounded by both Protestants and Roman Catholics, who rightly saw him a threat to the entire notion of an organized church. Schwenckfeld was even more of a mystic: when he came to see Luther at Wittenberg in 1522, hoping to find a fellow traveler, the two men disagreed on the interpretation of *sola fide* and on the significance of the Eucharist, which for Luther still held some vestige of supernatural power. For a man who was not in favor of outward forms of religion, Schwenckfeld did rather well: his followers continued in Germany until 1826, and, transplanted to Philadelphia in 1734, his sect still survives.

In a sense, though, mysticism of the soul is a luxury that can hardly be enjoyed by those who have great difficulty in keeping it chained within the body. Within quite a short time, Luther's exhortation to read the Bible and to try to understand it oneself had unleashed a fury of rebellion claiming to be based on his new religious ideology. At the top of the scale were the so-called Imperial Knights, who in 1522–23 made a bid for political power within the Holy Roman Empire using Protestantism as a crusading ideology. Their leader, Franz von Sickingen, had the aid of a humanist spokesman, Ulrich von Hutten, who found Luther's ideas a more convincing excuse for aggression than any other. In September 1522 they attacked the city of Trier, which was governed by an archbishop, claiming that they were not merely pillaging and stealing but cleansing the Church. By May 1523, Sickingen was dead and Hutten driven into exile, as the Imperial Knights were defeated and their castles destroyed. All they had achieved was to give Roman Catholic princes a cause around which to rally.

More interesting is the radical religious use made of early Protestantism by the rebellious peasants in southwestern Germany. The Bundschuh movement, which took its name from the tied cloth shoes they wore, had been going on for twenty-five years before Luther came on the scene, with peasants protesting against the oppression of their landlords, especially the larger ones, including the Church, which held property on a provincial, not merely local, scale. The movement spread along the rivers, down the Danube to Austria (skipping Bavaria) and down the Rhine to central and northern Germany. Castles were destroyed, monasteries were sacked, and landlords were attacked. When Luther appeared, the peasant leaders grafted on an ideological element grander than economic deprivation.

The involvement of Thomas Müntzer (c. 1490–1525) added a certain danger to this Peasants' Revolt. Müntzer had studied at Leipzig and probably met Luther there in 1519, at the famous debate when Luther was forced to admit certain sympathies with heretical Hussite doctrines of the century before. Müntzer became involved with the prophets of Zwickau the following year, extreme mystics who claimed to hear the word of God as He updated the biblical text, but they didn't want Müntzer and he was forced to move on. He disputed with Luther at Wittenberg, and then went to Alstedt, where he preached adult baptism and revolt. Müntzer was driven out of one town and another until he found his niche in the Peasants' Revolt.

Müntzer's message was by this time explicitly apocalyptic. In a sermon preached before two Saxon princes in 1524, for example, he chose as his text the second chapter of Daniel, with the description of the dream of the great statue:

It is true, and I know it to be so, that the Spirit of God has in our day revealed to many pious and chosen people how very necessary an excellent, invincible future reformation now is, and that it must be brought about, no matter how men may resist it. The prophecy of Daniel remains unaffected even though no one will believe in it. The text is as clear as the sun, and the work of ending the fifth monarchy of the world is even now in full swing. The first of them, represented by the golden head, was the empire of Babylon. The second—the silver breast and arms—was that of the Medes and Persians. The third was the empire of the Greeks, resounding with intelligence, as is indicated by the sounding brass. The fourth was the empire of Rome, won by the sword, a government of force. But the fifth is that which we have before our eyes. It too is of iron and would like to use force, but it is stuck together with muddy clay, as we see before our sensible eyes—vain pretences of that hypocrisy which writhes and wriggles all over the earth.[1]

Thus did the image of the Fifth Monarchy enter the Reformation at its earliest days; it provided a powerful means to conceptualize the changes that were about to occur.

Like other religious revolutionaries, Müntzer was unwilling to wait until King Jesus chose to terminate the last monarchy before His Second Coming. He was very involved in the drafting of the "Twelve Articles of the Peasantry," a manifesto detailing the grievances of the rebels. Reading it now, the seams of the document show clearly, between Müntzer's more ideological statements and the peasants' more commonplace, fairly moderate demands concerning rents, fishing rights, and land enclosure. Müntzer confronts his critics directly, acknowledging that they may ask, "Is this the fruit of the new teaching, that no one should obey but all should everywhere rise in revolt and rush together to reform or perhaps destroy altogether the authorities, both ecclesiastic and lay?" One of his goals in this document, he says, is "to give a Christian excuse for the disobedience or even the revolt of the entire peasantry."[2]

Within a few short years of Luther's initial protest, then, Protestantism was being used as the justification for political and social revolution.

This was too much for the moderate Reformed princes in Germany to bear. Led by Philip, landgrave of Hesse (reg. 1509–67), the Swabian League of Protestant princes broke the rebel force at Frankenhausen (May 15, 1525), in Saxony, where the Peasants' Revolt had been most concentrated. Müntzer himself was executed two days later, although his partner Andreas Carlstadt escaped and found refuge in Luther's own house. The net effect of Müntzer's millenarian revolution had been to strengthen the position of the princes and their state churches at the expense of the peasantry and lower classes, albeit lessening the power of their overlords and the emperor in the bargain.

Luther himself had little idea of how to react to his name being taken in vain. At first he published a moderate response, an "Admonition for Peace on the Twelve Articles." When he saw that not only did his plea have no effect whatsoever but the rebellion was increasing in intensity and violence, he changed tack and wrote "Against the Robbing and Murdering Hordes of Peasants" in May 1525, immediately after the revolt was suppressed. "Therefore," he instructed, "let everyone who can, smite, slay and stab, secretly or openly, remembering that nothing can be more poisonous, hurtful or devilish than a rebel. It is just as when one must kill a mad dog; if you do not strike him, he will strike you, and a whole land with you." Luther said that "one who is killed fighting on the ruler's side may be a true martyr in the eyes of God." The belief that the fallen in religious warfare rise straight to heaven was not an invention of Islamic Fundamentalists. As for Müntzer's millenarian claims, Luther explained:

And even though it happens that the peasants gain the upper hand (which God forbid!)—for to God all things are possible, and we do not know whether it may be his will, through the devil, to destroy all order and rule and cast the world upon a desolate heap, as a prelude to the Last Day, which cannot be far off—nevertheless, they may die without worry and go to the scaffold with a good conscience, who are found exercising their office of the sword.[3]

By statements such as these, Luther tied himself irrevocably to the existing political powers, and his entire movement toward supporting the status quo. Luther's first patron, Frederick the Wise of Saxony, died that same year, but his successors all supported him, not only because he proclaimed his intention to support the political structure of the German empire as it was but also because the rebellious friar had put their ministate on the map.

The idea of political and social revolution based on a religious gospel was too useful to be abandoned, however, with the execution of Thomas Müntzer. Many others fervently believed that Luther had halted his revolution only halfway by compromising with existing governments and churches. The most radical of these people were the Anabaptists. The prefix "ana" is Greek for "up," or "again," and the Anabaptists favored adult baptism, or baptism "again," since all Christians had been baptized in infancy. This in itself was a revolutionary idea, for an important social function of infant baptism was to induct the unprotesting infants into the fold. Since baptism conferred a permanent mark on the soul, it was impossible to leave the Church without taking the impossible step of renouncing it altogether.

More worrying, however, were the additional doctrinal points that Anabaptists held. Like others before them, they denied that God had said His last word in the biblical text as we have it, but that instead He remained in direct communication with us by means of revelations and visions. The Anabaptists were also called *Schwärmer*, or "enthusiasts," and their particular brand of belief in divine inspiration came to be known as "enthusiasm." Religious authority was thus much more fragmented than Luther would have had it, for some of these divine communications, the Anabaptists claimed, recommended radical social and political changes. They argued that the elect should separate from existing churches and political institutions, share their goods in common, establish independent communities, and work to destroy the existing order so as to bring forward the Kingdom of Christ on earth. At a later stage they championed polygamy. The Anabaptists were often drawn from the skilled and semiskilled classes of underprivileged craftsmen and peasants, so they brought with them a host of social and economic demands.

Eager to put their ideas into practice, a group of Anabaptists seized the town hall at Münster in Westphalia on February 9, 1534, and established a Kingdom of the Saints. Their leader seems to have been the so-called Jan of Leiden, a.k.a. Jan Bokelson or Beukels (1510–36), a former tailor or innkeeper. Others included Melchior Hoffmann (d. 1543) and Jan Matthys (d. 1534), a baker from Haarlem, and Bernhard Knipperdolling, a local cloth merchant. By the beginning of March they had ruled that all who refused to be baptized once again would be banished from the Kingdom of Zion. The Anabaptist utopia survived for sixteen months, until June 25, 1535, when the gates of Münster were mysteriously opened from within, allowing the capture of the city by Prince-Bishop Franz von Waldeck, who did not spare the sword.

The results of the Anabaptist experiment were essentially threefold. First, it led to even greater conservatism among Protestant leaders. Those who had not been fearful about the continuation of the Peasants' Revolt under the Protestant banner were shocked by this new genre of Reformed revolt. Heinrich Bullinger, for example, Zwingli's successor at Zurich, proclaimed that "God opened the eyes of governments by the revolution at Münster," and no one thereafter should trust Anabaptists, however innocent they claimed to be. In 1536, the city council at Zurich ordered Anabaptists to be drowned. Indeed, any deviation from its official Protestant line was liable to be branded as "Anabaptism," and the stigmata of rebellion, disorder, and polygamy haunted religious radicals for centuries.

A second consequence of the defeat of the Anabaptists at Münster was the establishment of a number of alternative religious communities which still survive today. One of these is the Hutterites, followers of Jacob Hutter (d. 1536), Anabaptists who found asylum in Moravia after the catastrophe. They established settlements centered on a *Bruderhof* ("brother house") based on common ownership of property. They migrated to the United States in 1874, and thrive in North America. Another group was the Mennonites, followers of Menno Simons (d. 1561), who reorganized survivors of Münster in Holland. They became pacifists, and today they are an important community of liberal views, numbering several hundred thousand. They, too, found a home in the United States, where their even more extreme offshoot, the Amish, are perhaps the most widely known.

The last result of the debacle at Münster was its effect on Martin Luther himself. It confirmed decisions he had made after the Peasants' Revolt and wed him irrevocably to the existing political authorities in the current structure of the Holy Roman Empire. He developed a more organized political theory, and began to conceive of a final situation in which each area within the empire would have a single religion, in order to reduce conflict. This, in turn, would give a far greater role to the prince than to the religious authority. This political conception of the German Empire was eventually adopted by Luther's venerable adversary, Emperor Charles V, and made the basis for the stabilizing Peace of Augsburg in 1555. Luther's ideas became fully developed in his doctrine of the two kingdoms, by which he argued that man is a citizen in both a temporal kingdom, where he is subject to the sword and to secular law, and a spiritual kingdom, where he is guided by God as recorded in the Bible. In the first, temporal kingdom, man is in bondage, rightly placed in a system based on coercion and fear, for God wants order imposed on chaos, which was His first act of creation. Luther firmly grounded the ruler's political authority on Providence and Scripture.

On the one hand, Luther achieved some final consolidation of the vague ideas that he had promulgated when he began the Reformation at Wittenberg in 1517. On the other hand, his political theory was a charter for injustice, for it urged the church to tolerate, or at least not to oppose, almost any kind of social and economic injustice if it tended to threaten the established political structure. This domination of the church by the state became the most obvious feature of Lutheranism, as German princes took over religious authority in their own kingdoms, the *Landeskirche*. Many centuries later, the Swiss theologian Karl Barth (1886–1968) wrote a famous letter in 1939, citing Luther for having instilled in the Germans their stereotypical tendency to follow orders and not to question political power no matter how unjust, as if it were divinely ordained.

| II |

In most conventional histories of the Reformation, John Calvin (1509–64) is classified along with Luther as one of the makers of the "magisterial Reformation." In our view, this misrepresents the revolutionary implications of Calvin's theology and its crucial importance in the development of messianic and other radical groups, up to and including those formed in our own time, since nearly all revolutionary religious sects are Calvinist in some way. Calvinism was a response to the success of Lutheranism, which spread throughout central Europe in the 1530s, particularly in northern Germany, an area characterized by large territorial states. Luther stayed close to his method of convincing the princes to accept Protestantism, leaving it to them to enforce the change in their own little countries. Tolerating more than one version of Christianity in a single principality was never contemplated.

Politically, Protestantism created a second camp, an alternative to Roman Catholicism and a permanent force of opposition to it. But the economic changes were in some ways even greater. In territories that became Protestant, church land was confiscated by the newly Protestant ruler, who frequently sold or gave away much of it to nobles and merchants, who then became transformed into what amounted to a middle class. In the intellectual sphere, the effects of Protestantism were to suggest that there was now more than one answer on offer to the problems of the universe.

But what was one to do if the prince refused to accept the temptations of Lutheranism? In areas in which the ruler already had de facto control over church appointments, revenues, and so on, which was the case in France and Spain, Luther made little headway. Was Protestantism simply to give up? The answer of John Calvin was an emphatic "no": Calvinism evolved to answer the need for a more aggressive crusading version of the Protestant faith which would bring the Reformation to France, England, and other countries where the prince could not or would not go over to the new religion. This Calvin did by creating an extremist religious and ideological élite which from its center in Geneva sent missionaries, secret agents, to other countries to subvert the established powers from within. Calvinism is clearly part of the radical Reformation and, like Lutheranism, is a theological idea with enormous practical consequences. Its great success was due in large part to the religious survival of the fittest.

Calvin's greatest contribution to the development of radical religion in general, and messianism in particular, was his understanding of the key concept of predestination. This is the doctrine that God not only knows the future but has already decided what form it will take. From the personal point of view, this means that God judges people before they are born, and that one's eternity in heaven or hell is a foregone conclusion no matter what one does in life.

Predestination was not Calvin's invention: he understood it to be set forth in the Old Testament, with its references to the Book of Life, and in the New Testament Jesus warned, "Ye shall drink indeed of my cup, and be baptized with the baptism that I am baptized with: but to sit on my right hand, and on my left, is not mine to give, but *it shall be given to them* for whom it is prepared of my Father." St. Paul characteristically made the same point even clearer, in Romans 8:28–30:

> And we know that all things work together for good to them that love God, to them who are the called according to *his* purpose. For whom he did foreknow, he also did predestinate *to be* conformed to the image of his Son, that he might be the firstborn among many brethren. Moreover whom he did predestinate, them he also called: and whom he called, them he also justified: and whom he justified, them he also glorified.

Among the Church Fathers who debated it in the centuries when Christian doctrine was becoming clarified, St. Augustine (354–430 A.D.) was the most prominent of those who argued that it is not human merit that is the criterion for salvation, but the will of God. Holiness is therefore the *result* of election, and not its cause. Augustine's view became official church teaching by the early fifth century, despite the efforts of Pelagius (360–420 A.D.) to ascribe greater prominence to free will and individual efforts. By the end of the Middle Ages, however, Augustine's view had become somewhat eroded, not only by the great theologian Thomas Aquinas but by Renaissance thinkers such as Erasmus, who affirmed the power of free will, which was a key concept of the period.

Luther, reviving the Augustinian doctrine, spoke of *sola gratia*, the idea that it is only through the grace of God, and not because of our puny efforts, that one is chosen for eternal life. Luther saw this grace as an undeserved gift: all men since Adam deserve hellfire, but God in His inscrutable mercy has rescued some of those who believe in Him for heaven. It is for this reason that we really have no cause for complaint if we are condemned to eternal damnation: it is the penalty incurred by all mankind since the disobedience in Eden. The whole point of God's grace, he emphasized, is that He "justifies" sinners, people who are undeserving, because His concepts of justice are not ours. This was Luther's "Theology of the Cross," explaining that even the way God chose to redeem the world, through the suffering of Jesus, challenges the way we look at justice, in that being crucified would normally be considered a sign of being shamed and defeated.

Calvin, a lawyer by training, was unable to tolerate Luther's idea of a God who sends people to hell only indirectly, as it were, by deciding not to save them. Calvin's uncompromising doctrine of "double predestination" had it that some people are eternally destined for glory, while God chose others, specifically and actually, to be sent to eternal torment. For Calvin, God was completely sovereign and active, and would not act merely by default. We may not understand the operation of His divine grace and justice, but we can witness its effects.

If we look for a moment at the Calvinist lexicon, we can already have a sense of how this doctrine developed, and how important it became in the evolution of radical religion in the next four centuries. The first word is "election," the decision to save unworthy souls. It is interesting that in both Hebrew and Greek the word also has the meaning of "choice." The point was that just as God had once chosen the Children of Israel, so now has he chosen the Calvinists as His people, the New Israel, and transferred His promises to them. This choice was an act of divine grace, not made because of any particular merits in the case, but because it fulfilled a divine purpose: the elected become God's servants within His general plan for salvation. Once "saved," then one begins to do righteous deeds and good works. These have no causative effect on one's final destination, which has been set by God at the beginning of the world.

The second key is "covenant," the agreement between God and

His people. The "covenant of grace" was two-sided: it laid down God's obligations to His people and their religious and social duty to God. The parallel with the Children of Israel, the previous beneficiaries of the covenant, was to become even more explicit in the New World, where Calvinists conceived in biblical terms their crossing of the Atlantic and their colonization of new lands. "Church" was another important word, the structure by which God brings us into His fellowship. For Calvinists, there was an "invisible church" within the visible one, whose members, known only to God, included all the elect from the beginning of the world. Calvin was very keen on organization, however, and did not neglect the "visible church" of Calvinists who hoped that they were members of the secret congregation as well.

The last central Calvinist word is "calling," or "vocation," two versions of the same word. This expressed the notion that man is required to serve God by helping in the community, which we do through our "callings." This was more than a job or even profession, but a way of working and living that defines us in the most essential way. Everyone has more than one calling: we might be simultaneously teachers, mothers, husbands, daughters, and citizens. But in each of these callings we become God's instruments on earth, just as our work here helps to curb selfishness and point us to divine service. The catch, as it were, was that success in one's calling was likely to be a sign that one was destined for heaven and glory, though—contrary to what many people now think about Calvinism—not necessarily economic success, although this variety was most easily measured. A man might be a failure at farming but an excellent son to his mother. The point was that through application to one's calling, through self-discipline, one could demonstrate godliness and confirm one's eternal destination before traveling, for one's own benefit, and to advertise it to the neighbors.

Interestingly, Calvin conceived of politics as the highest calling, since the vocation of a statesman involves to some extent taking God's place on earth. A ruler is God's instrument and thus is permitted to use force and violence, but should he forget for a moment that he is merely a sinner wielding divine power, should he overstep his bounds and begin to act unjustly, the judgment of God against him will be harsh and unremitting. He will certainly be doubly punished in the next world but also quite likely in this one: either through the judgment of history or by being overthrown. Calvin suggested that a ruler's downfall might occur through the agency of a kind of divine hero, such as Alexander the Great or King David, but failing that, it could be brought about by subordinate magistrates. This would especially be the case in a kingdom with an anti-Calvinist ruler.

The effects of Calvin's doctrine of predestination can hardly be overemphasized. People looked for the signs of predestination for heaven, and their searching came to acquire a classic pattern of recovery from a period of degradation. The Puritan leader Oliver Cromwell, for example, came to Christ after having lost everything, including his land, being forced to rent a farm from someone else. After humbling himself in this way, and cleaving to the Almighty, he was left a large legacy which restored him to greater glory. Others had different experiences. The Puritan preacher Richard Baxter was always troubled by the fact that he had never personally suffered. At last he came to understand that God breaks hearts in different ways. Even more interesting was the Quaker George Fox, who was convinced that he was always destined to be saved and did not need any heavenly pyrotechnics to show him that. The point is that these people had supreme self-confidence, and it was simply impossible to argue with a man who believed that he had been destined from Creation to sit at the right hand of God. Many Calvinists spent their lives in paroxysms of doubt, but the religion tended to appeal to those who imagined they were probably on the sunny side of the street. Calvinists kept diaries in which they reviewed the day's events, searching for signs. They worried themselves sick, but they knew that election, once manifested convincingly, guaranteed them divine approval for their foreordained actions.

Such people were also extremely dangerous. Calvin, as we have seen, had argued that the highest calling was politics and that unjust rulers might be deposed. There was no doubt in his mind, for example, that the king of France was an unjust ruler, since he stubbornly refused to abandon his Roman Catholic faith and persecuted Protestants whenever they turned up. Calvin's teachings created a new spiritual élite of saints—saints, but an elite nonetheless, with all the dangers that an élite brings with it. French Calvinists, called Huguenots, thought nothing of plotting to murder their king, since as an anti-Calvinist Roman Catholic he was obviously not to be numbered among the elect. As we shall see in the next chapter, the same phenomenon manifested itself in England, where Calvinists, called Puritans, actually succeeded in putting their king on trial for his life, and finding him guilty, executed him off the window of his palace.

Apart from the political dangers inherent in a group of self-confident saints destined for heaven no matter what they did, there was also the theoretical problem of what would happen to everyone else, including all those who were not so sure of their destiny. Both Roman Catholicism and Lutheranism were essentially geographically based: people went along to their local church, and expected to be welcomed there as part of the service that the religious establishment provided. Calvinism, on the other hand, was an élitist religion. Not everyone could be allowed to attend the local church, since once it had been taken over by the Calvinists, a religious test of righteousness first needed to be passed. As obvious reprobates and sinners were clearly not to be found among the elect, such people were excluded. In practice, this meant that many people found themselves completely outside of any sort of religious relief. Entire areas, such as much of the north of England, were thought to contain few people who demonstrated signs of election, and they were excluded, until the Methodists in the eighteenth century tried to instill religious values into a people abandoned. "Humble toward God, Haughty toward Man, This is the Race that Jesus ran," complained the poet William Blake about the Puritans, and his comments might equally have applied to Calvin.

John Calvin was not particularly a millenarian, although his theology might be described as messianic in that it was oriented toward that great day in the future when the Messiah would return and raise His elect to glory. But Calvinist notions of election, covenant, New Israel, and so on, as we will see, suited well the groups and sects that preached a much more militant theology.

| III |

In January 1517, the Roman Catholic Church had a monopoly on Christianity in the West. By the end of the year its troubles had begun, and within forty years it was clear that its primacy, now shattered, would never be put back together again. It was a time for self-examination, or at least for closing the barn door. This process is generally known as the Counter-Reformation, over the protests of Catholics since the nineteenth century who have tried to popularize the term "Catholic Reformation" as if the popes and cardinals would have made any necessary reforms even if Luther had never appeared on the scene. We should always remember that there was also a financial motivation for reform as well. Luther's victories in Europe deprived the papacy of substantial revenues, since Protestant countries immediately ceased sending taxes to Rome.

It was Pope Paul III (1534–49), a worldly pope from the powerful Farnese family, who was finally pressured into convoking a church council to deal with the problems that had accumulated over the past decades. Emperor Charles V, who had been dealing with Luther and Protestantism firsthand from the inception of the revolt, was determined that only a general council would suffice. The pope, on the other hand, was afraid that such a conclave would reduce his own power, reconcile Charles V and the Protestants, and give the emperor power in Italy. When Paul finally called the council, he made sure that it would be in Trent, which although nominally part of the Holy Roman Empire, being in Tyrol, was in spirit Italian, and two-thirds of the delegates were in any case Italian. The chairmen consistently adopted procedural rules which also allowed the pope to have the upper hand, especially the measure of voting individually rather than by nation, and since two-thirds of the delegates were Italian, the decisions were likely to go his way.

The Council of Trent (1545–63) was a great success for the Roman Catholic Church. It produced more legislation than all of the previous eighteen ecumenical and general councils put together, and was the last of its type until Vatican I (1869–70). The Roman Catholic Church emerged from Trent rigid over doctrine, and absolutist in its power structure, paralleling in this trends which were becoming apparent in governments throughout Europe. Most importantly, it was ready to wage war on heresy, having defined what heresy was, and determined to impose a uniform religious life on all Catholic parishes.

The decisions taken at Trent had numerous implications for both radical religion and the messianic idea. First of all was the stand which the Church took against anything Jewish. In this, it went entirely against the Renaissance trend of looking for truth wherever it might be found, even among the writings of those who rejected Christ. Among the casualties was the Jewish mystical tradition, the Cabala, which would be an important messianic tool in its Protestant sanctuary.

The turnabout of the Church against Jewish learning was somewhat unexpected. Until the Counter-Reformation, the papacy might have been numbered among the chief protectors of the Jews in Europe. It tried to reduce popular violence against Jews, showed doubts concerning forced baptism, such as had occurred in Portugal, and allowed Jews exiled from Iberia to settle in the Papal States. Pope Paul III in 1541 had invited the Jews whom Charles V had expelled from Naples to settle in his port city of Ancona, and later included in this invitation Jews who had actually renounced their so-called permanent baptism and reverted to the faith of their fathers. Within a few years there were more than one hundred baptized Portuguese Jewish families in Ancona, not including Jews who had come from Turkey or from within Italy itself.

Paul's successor, Pope Julius III (1550–55), was hostile to Jews, however, despite his devotion to Renaissance values, and was under the influence of his Grand Inquisitor, Giovanni Pietro Caraffa. In August 1553 he issued an infamous decree whereby the Jews were ordered to turn over all copies of the Talmud to be destroyed. Many other Hebrew books were also consigned to the flames. This change in papal attitude was not personal—Julius was not above having a Jewish physician, the famous Amatus Lusitanus—but he recognized that Renaissance eclecticism had created genuine intellectual and social contacts between gentiles and Jews, and that while many Christians had begun to study Jewish sources in order to understand their own religion more fully, others found Jewish traditions a treasure of genuinely interesting material and had lost sight of their original purpose in opening the books in the first place. Jewish scholars such as Isaac Abrabanel's son Judah (c. 1460–c. 1535, also known as Leone Ebreo), and Azariah de Rossi (c. 1511–c. 1578) participated fully in Renaissance culture, even doctoring Jewish traditions somewhat in order to make them more palatable and understandable to a gentile audience. All of this was shattered in the Counter-Reformation, beginning in 1553. Julius's successor, Marcellus II, might have reversed the trend, for he was a Hebraist who wanted to reconsider the wholesale prohibition of Hebrew works, but he survived less than a month in office in the spring of 1555.

His successor was the Jews' worst nightmare: the very same Caraffa who had masterminded the attack on their culture. He took office as Pope Paul IV (1555–59). He was not only anti-Jewish but also violently anti-Protestant, and the Council of Trent did not continue its meetings during his tenure, since he saw no need whatsoever for change in the eternal Church. He was also militarily ambitious: allied with France, papal forces attacked a Spanish possession, his native Naples, and lost to the infamous duke of Alva. Caraffa believed that the rapprochement between Christianity and Judaism had gone too far and that Hebrew influences should be kept out of the Church. Furthermore, he believed that increasing the heat on Jews might persuade them to convert. In his bull *Cum nimis absurdum* (July 14, 1555) he segregated the Jews into ghettos in Rome and in all the Papal States and forced them to wear distinguishing badges. It was forbidden for a single town to have more than one synagogue. Paul decreed that even forced baptisms were eternally valid, which threw the Portuguese refugees into the greatest alarm. Paul sent representatives to Ancona particularly to uncover baptized Jews who had now reverted to Judaism. Many escaped, but fifty-one were caught, examined, and tortured; some were sent to the galleys, and twenty-five were burned alive. World Jewry attempted to retaliate. The House of Mendes in the person of Doña Gracia and Don Joseph Nasi, important former Marranos in the sultan's court, arranged for a commercial boycott of Ancona, and rerouted the profitable Jewish trade through the port of Pesaro in the neighboring duchy of Urbino, to which many Jews from Ancona had fled. Sultan Suleiman the Magnificent even sent a letter of protest to Pope Paul IV, but the pontiff refused outright to give in. It was a shrewd commercial move, because the unbaptized Jews who remained in Ancona were unhappy about the boycott, and knew that they were better placed to service the trade. In the end, the Marranos were expelled from Urbino in 1558: the pope had won.

Pope Paul IV died in 1559, and although his successor, Pius IV (1559–65), was not nearly so anti-Jewish, the tone of the Counter-Reformation had been set. When the Council of Trent finished its deliberations by instituting an Index of Prohibited Books (1564), they quite naturally included the Talmud. But there was nothing wrong with printing the Talmud as long as its name was left off and certain anti-Christian passages deleted. It could be called *The Six Orders*, and even editions printed abroad for Italian use followed this practice. But the papacy also managed to stop the printing of

Jewish books in vernacular languages, which restricted the access that gentiles might otherwise have had to Hebrew learning of all sorts.

The end of this particular story came with the accession of Pope Pius V (1565–72), who was rewarded with sainthood for his efforts on the papal throne. Pius was a harsh moralist with firm views. He excommunicated Queen Elizabeth I of England in 1570 and financed the great naval victory against the Turks at Lepanto the following year. But he hated Jews even more than Paul IV did, and in his bull *Hebraeorum gens* (February 26, 1569) actually expelled the Jews from all church-governed lands in Italy and France, apart from Ancona and Rome, where they were allowed to stay. (The decree regarding the French lands, especially Avignon, was suspended.) Many Jewish communities were destroyed, including some which had survived since ancient times. Bologna was the hardest hit, but synagogues everywhere were closed and Jewish refugees took to the roads. Though papal authorities in later years turned a blind eye to the expulsion decree, it was emblematic of how the Counter-Reformation viewed the Jewish contribution to Christian religion and culture.

Another element of the Counter-Reformation was its attitude toward the place of reason in religion. The Tridentine Confession of Faith (1564), agreed on in Trent and required of every Catholic until modern times, made it quite clear that the Counter-Reformation Church was not going to change its position on transubstantiation, on the "real presence" of Christ in the Eucharist, on purgatory, or on other theological doctrines that seemed unreasonable to Luther and other Protestants. Little attempt was made to explain how these concepts could be reconciled with Protestant objections.

After the Counter-Reformation, there was a general shift in Roman Catholicism away from rationality to emotionalism. This is readily seen in contemporary religious painting and sculpture, such as Bernini's "Ecstasy of St. Teresa," which shows her in an attitude not normally associated with conventional religion: eyes closed, mouth open, distorted features, face turned upward, an asymptotic point of ideal behavior when praying. The agonies of Jesus on the cross were now presented in graphic, almost pornographic detail, as were the sufferings of martyrs and saints, with a special emphasis on blood. Death enjoyed somewhat of a rebirth, and putting representations of skulls on tombstones became standard practice.

This overheated emotionalism, so characteristic of the Church after Trent, found practical religious expression in the flowering of mysticism. The notion that some part of the mind or the soul can have a direct apprehension of God, the aspiration that man with divine grace can perfect himself gradually and come to see God face to face, is an old one. We have already seen that elements of this appear in Gnosticism thirteen or fourteen centuries before the Counter-Reformation, and even in the views of some radical Protestants. In late-sixteenth-century Counter-Reformation thought, the Church co-opted the entire concept instead of treating it as a dangerous heresy.

It is easy to see how the two might go together. The Counter-Reformation Church, opposing Luther's notion of *sola gratia*, emphasized man's freedom of will and his ability to cooperate in his own salvation through good works and sacraments. So too does mysticism stress self-help, the application of a disciplined program of spiritual exercises and a training of the will. The two systems fit very well together, and mysticism even improved the Counter-Reformation Church, which became more administrative and impersonal with its obsession with the difference between holy and unholy, and the necessity for parochial uniformity. Mysticism gave believers a warm feeling of piety, a quality that to some extent had been lost in Trent, with its insistence on getting the theology right, even at the expense of love, family participation, and community sentiments. To Trent's religious precision, mysticism offered brief moments of ecstasy in the divine presence.

Two chief Spanish mystics who contributed to this new turn of mind were Teresa of Avila (1515–82) and her colleague John of the Cross (1542–91). Both were canonized: Teresa only forty years after her death, and John in 1726, which gives some indication of their standing in the Church. Even more dramatically, in 1970 Teresa was declared a Doctor of the Church, one of several dozen extraordinarily saintly theologians (*Doctores Ecclesiae*), the first woman to reach this pinnacle of holiness. John, a century behind her in sainthood, had attained this academic honor in 1926. Teresa wrote several mystical works—*The Way of Perfection* (1565), *The Interior Castle* (1577), as well as her powerful *Autobiography* (1561–62)—and John was a great poet, among whose best works are "The Ascent of Mount Carmel" and "The Dark Night of the Soul." They were not only mystics but effective administrators. Teresa and John established seventeen convents and founded the first house of the reformed Discalced (i.e., barefoot) Carmelites. While they did have their difficulties with the Church, which like all religious authorities was wary of loose "canons," the Counter-Reformation was in general receptive to leaders who emphasized the spirit rather than the study of the text. Instead of persecuting them, which the Church might have done even a few years before, they co-opted the two Spaniards and proclaimed them as living (and then dead) examples of what might be achieved by devotion to the Godhead.

This was the direction that the Church took in the centuries after the Counter-Reformation: emphasizing a warm, emotional piety that encouraged exactly those elements which so disgusted Protestants. Catholics also looked for the coming of the Messiah, but they were not so bold as to believe that they could easily understand the workings of God's plan merely by studying the Bible. Nevertheless, their messianism was no less fervent than that of the Protestants, though historians sometimes unjustly underplay the messianic elements in Counter-Reformation mysticism, simply because the style of discourse is so hard to pin down. Catholics, like Protestants, believed that what they did in this world had an effect in bringing forward the date of Christ's arrival: Catholics, however, used completely different methods toward that meritorious goal.

One path to perfection was devotion to the cult of the Virgin Mary, which grew to a popularity that it had not enjoyed since the High Middle Ages. Belief in the doctrine of the Immaculate Conception of Mary became obligatory. (Pope Pius IX would define this as dogma in 1854 in his bull *Ineffabilis Deus*, a sign that the road taken from Trent was repaved but not diverted.) The cults of various other figures also prospered, especially the Baby Jesus, St. Joseph (who had been a comical figure in the Middle Ages), and the entire Holy Family. The worship of saints thrived, especially St. Peter, leader of the Apostles. Great emphasis was placed on the supernatural elements of Christianity, especially the doctrine of the Real Presence in the Eucharist. Also, great efforts were taken to make the church buildings themselves especially glorious, to inspire emotive religion, so different from the plain whitewashed walls of a Protestant church.

The shock troops that put the Counter-Reformation into action were the Jesuits, who not only infused a new and vigorous Catholic spirit into Europe but also won back areas that had been lost to Protestantism, such as parts of Poland, Austria, and Bavaria, and brought the faith to more distant places in America, Africa, and Asia. The order itself was founded by Ignatius Loyola (1491–1556) and his companions at Montmartre, Paris, in 1534, and received papal recognition six years later. Loyola was born into a wealthy Basque family and became a page at the imperial court. He was wounded in the legs by a cannonball at Pamplona while fighting for Navarre against France, and read the lives of the saints while recovering, which led to a spiritual transformation accompanied by a vision of the Madonna and child. Loyola tried various religious paths, including life as a beggar in a cave near Barcelona, a pilgrimage to the Holy Land, and university studies in Spain and France, until he had the idea of organizing a religious order along military lines. Jesuits gave their absolute loyalty to their General, who was elected for life. Loyola reluctantly became the first General of the Jesuits in 1541, the same year in which he completed his *Spiritual Exercises*, a kind of manual for self-hypnosis which enabled believers to imagine themselves into a state of heightened religious awareness. One of his "rules for thinking with the Church" in that book enjoined the reader that "if she shall have defined anything to be black which to our eyes appears to be white, we ought in like manner to pronounce it to be black." This complete devotion to the authority of the Catholic Church enabled Loyola to distance himself from the *alumbrados*, the Spanish mystics whose religiosity made them suspicious to the Inquisition, but in truth he too is connected to the messianic fervor of his day. At the same time, despite the fact that Jesuit schools shaped the outlook of the ruling classes of Catholic countries forever after, they were always under attack by religious rivals such as the Dominicans and the Jansenists while secularists saw their confessors and advisers as being too close to the ears of kings and princes. Jesuit missionaries such as Francis Xavier (1506–52) exported their particular brand of Catholicism to India, Japan, China, and the New World. Eventually, the Jesuits would be expelled, for being too powerful, from Portugal (1759), France (1764), and even Spain (1767), until Pope Clement XIV suppressed the entire order in 1773. The godless French Revolution and Napoleon's treatment of the papacy made many Catholics think that it was impossible to do without the Jesuits, so they were restored in 1814 and continue to thrive.

Even by the end of the sixteenth century, then, the psychological gap between Roman Catholicism and Protestantism was unbridgeable. Yet both Catholics and Protestants directed their efforts toward the End of Days, the difference being that Catholics believed that sacraments, good works, and mystical union helped to bring that joyful day forward, while Protestants placed greater emphasis on learning God's plan in a spirit of resignation.

CHAPTER 3

THE MESSIAH DURING
THE THIRTY YEARS' WAR

If the theory that crisis brings with it an upsurge of millenarianism is correct, then we would expect to find the millenarian epicenter in the seventeenth century, when the Old Regime began to collapse. For reasons which have long been the subject of dispute among historians, the seventeenth century was a period of almost constant warfare and struggle, some of which changed the face of Europe forever. The most dramatic part of this disruption was the English Civil War; on the Continent, the emerging nation-states were ripped apart by the first large-scale European conflict, the Thirty Years' War.

To true believers, there was no doubt that the End of the World was close. There were signs everywhere, like the new star which appeared in the heavens in 1572, a nova which blazed for seventeen months and then disappeared. This was the first new star since the one which guided the wise men to Bethlehem, and according to contemporary astronomical theory should not have existed at all. There was also the comet of 1577, especially important because comets were abnormal and sporadic occurrences whose appearance was believed to be a well-known method of divine communication with mankind. The conjunction of Saturn and Jupiter in Aries took place in 1603, a phenomenon which occurs only once in eight hundred years. Contemporaries were entranced by the eclipse of August 12, 1654; indeed, no fewer than thirty-eight authors in Europe tried to explain its significance. There was sometimes a nice symmetry to these observations. Halley's Comet of 1682 was the same one that Paracelsus wrote about in 1531! These divine signs and others made it quite clear to most believers that God was trying to tell them something. Generally speaking, on the analogy of the story of Creation, the world was unlikely to exist more than six thousand years, followed by the thousand-year Sabbath of Creation, the eschatological reign of Christ on earth.[1]

Parallel to these dramatic astronomical events we find a new codification of the messianic idea, and at a greater level of intensity. Certainly it is true that many of these new groups were peddling recycled concepts. Many of the themes which we have found in the Renaissance and the Reformation were repeated, but the messianists of the seventeenth century considered themselves inheritors of a tradition who were advancing the cause of mankind through their knowledge and actions.

Sometimes they envisioned an actual reign on earth of King Jesus: this was the vision of the Fifth Monarchy men, who thrived in Cromwell's England. Sometimes they saw this Utopia as the result of a scientific revolution that would uncover the secrets of the universe, Paracelsus style, and bring forth a chemical Apocalypse, a techno-millennium. This was the hope of the Rosicrucian movement. But in both cases, what underlies them is the desire to control Nature, to transform life on earth into something completely different.

| I |

The history of the Rosicrucians is so shrouded in mystery, and so much the subject of debate among historians, that to summarize the state of research and to describe what we know about them is to invite controversy.[2] The origins seem to be connected to the royal wedding in February 1613 of the daughter of King James I of England, Princess Elizabeth Stuart, and Frederick V, Elector Palatine of the Rhine, whose capital was Heidelberg. Frederick cherished the idea of becoming the leader of the Protestant princes in Europe, and marriage to the daughter of King James was an excellent idea, since the English monarch was perceived (wrongly, as it turned out) as one of the brave champions of Protestantism, now under political threat.

Frederick's ambitions were soon to outstretch his support. In 1612, Emperor Rudolph II died. Although a Habsburg, he had stayed away from traditional Roman Catholic extremist politics, shunned King Philip II of Spain, and became involved in occult studies of various kinds. He moved his imperial court from Vienna to Prague, which soon became a magnet for anyone with supernatural ideas from Paracelsianism to millenarianism. Drawn to the emperor were such adepts as John Dee, Edward Kelley, Giordano Bruno, and Johannes Kepler. Prague was the center of an occult renaissance, and after Rudolph moved on to a better world, everyone wondered what would happen next.

At first, nothing happened. As there were no children to inherit, Rudolph's brother Matthias was elected to the throne of the Holy Roman Empire, but he was old and ineffectual, and his seven-year reign little more than a breathing space. Indeed, it seemed as if the occult world would continue to thrive, for in the midst of the continuing excitement three extremely bizarre documents appeared. These Rosicrucian pamphlets—the *Fama Fraternitatis* (in German) (Cassel, 1614), the *Confessio Rosae Crucis* (in Latin) (Cassel, 1615), and the *Chymische Hochzeit [Chemical Wedding] Christiani Rosenkreutz* (in German) (Strasbourg, 1616)—tell a wonderful story. The first two pamphlets spin a tale of a certain Christian Rosenkreutz, who was said to have been born in 1378 and to have died in 1484, aged 106. In 1604, they said, on the 120th anniversary of his decease, his followers, according to instructions, opened his tomb and found his undecayed body and various texts that summarized his teachings, the fruits of the wisdom he had acquired while traveling in the East, especially in Egypt and the Holy Land. The influence of Renaissance doctrines of alchemy, hermeticism, Gnosticism, Cabala, and Paracelsianism was clear. Rosenkreutz, according to the tale, founded during his lifetime with three companions a Society of the Rose Cross, which (like Paracelsus) was devoted to caring for the ill without charge. Members of the Society were charged with gathering information and knowledge from around the world in their travels, and to report annually in person or by post to the Rose Cross center, the Home of the Holy Spirit. Like the Jesuits, they would often wear no distinguishing clothing, but they were to use the rose cross as a seal or symbol. The members of the Rose Cross would look for those to succeed them before they joined their founder in eternity.

The last text, much longer and more complicated, described an alchemical initiation in the guise of a wedding, the actual marriage ceremony of Frederick and Elizabeth. The little book recounted Rosenkreutz's participation in the wedding, to which he was called on Easter Eve. He traveled to a magical castle full of wonders, joined the wedding party, and as the week progressed he took part in many marvels and was initiated as a Red Cross knight, based on the ceremony of the Order of the Garter, whose symbol, incidentally, is the Red Cross of St. George. Christian Rosenkreutz is transformed almost alchemically, as are the Rosicrucian elect. Alchemical symbols abound. The union of the bride and groom represents the marriage of the soul, the fusion of the elements in alchemy. Death and resurrection are connected to alchemic transmutation. Even the name Rosicrucian may be more complicated: some believe that the word is "*ros*," dew, the solvent of gold, with "*crux*," cross, representing light.[3]

Who was behind the Rosicrucian excitement, and what did it mean? Most historians give the credit to Johann Valentin Andreae

(1586–1654), a Lutheran theologian and mystic, who was thought even in the seventeenth century to have written the text. He was from Württemberg, and his grandfather had been a key Reformation figure in his area. Andreae was certainly the author of the *Chemical Wedding*, but it remains unclear if the first two pamphlets should be ascribed to him. Frances Yates, whose work on the Rosicrucians is both brilliant and controversial, thought so. More recent historians, however, have pointed out that Andreae described his book as only a *ludibrium*, a fantasy, a word which he always uses in a negative connotation, and that he soon regretted that his tale had become another of the very texts he was satirizing. Other candidates have been put forward, such as Raphael Eglinus of Marburg, who also wrote on alchemy, revelation, and chronology. Some historians ascribe key significance to Guillaume Postel, the French Hebraist; to Helias Roselin, a Paracelsian astronomer; and to Simon Studion, whose enormously long apocalyptic and prophetic work *Naometria* (1604) uses numerology and is based on the prophecies concerning Solomon's Temple. Studion posited the year 1620 as the end of the reign of Antichrist with the downfall of both the pope and Islam, to be followed about three years later by the millennium. They all talked about the coming of "Elias Artista" as proclaimed by Paracelsus, and were entranced by the new star that appeared in the skies in 1604, which seemed to be repeating the New Testament's announcement of a new Messiah.[4] Some even argued that the Rosicrucians were in their totality a sort of corporate Elias, all according to the divine plan.[5]

Whoever wrote the first two Rosicrucian works, it is clear that the entire *ludibrium* was related to traditional millenarian concerns about the Second Coming, adding to this religious background the Paracelsian dream of using knowledge and science to advance the day. This is why the Oxford historian Hugh Trevor-Roper, in a penetrating phrase, noted that indeed "without Paracelsus the whole Rosicrucian idea—the form of its message and the extraordinary echo of that little voice—is unintelligible."[6]

It is interesting to note how many of the key millenarian and occult figures were involved in the Rosicrucian movement. Those who took it seriously searched out these secret adepts, to no avail. Among those were John Dee and Edward Kelley, who were in Prague in 1583 trying to influence Rudolph II. Frances Yates even argues that since Dee returned to England passing through Germany in 1589, we should see the entire Rosicrucian movement as "a delayed result of Dee's mission."[7] Dee invented a peculiar symbol called the "Hieroglyphic Monad," consisting of seven elements: this symbol is in the margin of a poem Christian Rosenkreutz reads, and the same symbol appears on the title page of the book. Another occult figure involved early on in the movement was Robert Fludd (1574–1637), whose *History of the Macrocosm and Microcosm* (Oppenheim, 1617–19) showed what an English Paracelsian physician practicing in London might do with the entire range of concepts. Like his Renaissance forbears, he tried to explain philosophy with reference to correspondences in the universe and the parallel harmonies in man, using much hermetic material and other parts of the occult tradition. Fludd came up with a wonderful cosmic scheme that has Jehovah in the middle, ruling over concentric circles consisting of angels, stars, elements, and so on, with man at the center united with the other parts by various ethereal connections. His work also made great play of numerology, showing how all arts and sciences could be explained that way. Fludd's work is a sort of encyclopedia of Renaissance magic and Cabala, topped up by Paracelsus and Dee. In brief, he would have been an ideal member of the Rosicrucian Society, if only it had existed. This is what made Fludd an easy target for Marin Mersenne, a French monk who was the philosopher Descartes's friend. Mersenne attacked the entire range of Renaissance magic, Cabala, Ficino, Pico, Agrippa, but especially Fludd. But despite his rejection of the occult tradition, he believed that the Rosicrucians were real—and that Fludd was one of them.

In any case, much of this discussion would prove to be irrelevant.

Two years before his death, Emperor Matthias had secured the election of the Habsburg archduke Ferdinand of Styria to the throne of Bohemia, the traditional royal waiting room to the imperial crown. Ferdinand was a pupil of the Jesuits and a fanatic Roman Catholic, and immediately he began implementing measures to destroy the Bohemian Church. The Bohemians therefore took the rebellious step of offering their crown to Frederick of the Palatinate instead. To his misfortune, he accepted, and therefore found himself in open rebellion against Ferdinand, who was duly elected Holy Roman Emperor in August 1619.

The winter of 1619–20 is legendary in Rosicrucian history as a kind of idyllic calm before the storm. We do not know exactly how the "Winter King and Queen," as they came to be called, reacted to Rudolph's collection of occult curiosities, but one hopes that they were sympathetic, since they had shown such inclinations for dramatic effects in Heidelberg. But the inevitable was not long in coming: the duke of Bavaria, commanding the Roman Catholic forces loyal to the emperor, defeated the Bohemian rebels at the Battle of the White Mountain (November 8, 1620) outside Prague. Oddly enough, one of those present on the winning side that day was Descartes, who entered Prague with the victors and saw their defeat. The hope that Frederick had had of an English cavalry force coming over the hill never materialized. In his haste, he and his wife fled Prague, leaving behind the insignia of the English Order of the Garter. Caricaturists seized on this image and usually portrayed him with one stocking coming down, an ironic illusion as well to his misplaced hopes for aid. Spanish troops under the emperor's aegis meanwhile invaded the Palatinate, and Frederick was completely bereft. The sometime royal family were reunited at The Hague, where they kept a rather pathetic and indigent court.

In 1618 Descartes had left France for Holland and there enlisted in the army of Prince Maurice of Nassau. The following year he was in Germany, where he joined the duke of Bavaria. On November 10, 1619, a year before White Mountain, Descartes had some famous dreams which led him to realize that mathematics was the only key to understanding the nature of the universe. He became interested in the Rosicrucians, and when he returned to France, he was accused of being one, a smear which was hard to live down. In the 1640s, he lived near Leiden, in the Netherlands, to be near his patroness, Princess Elizabeth of the Palatinate, eldest daughter of the defeated Frederick and Elizabeth, and dedicated his *Principia* (1644) to her as the daughter of the king of Bohemia. When her brother was restored to the Palatinate, she suggested that Descartes come to live with them, but he preferred the more lucrative offer of tutoring Queen Christina of Sweden, herself entranced by the occult tradition. Descartes died in Sweden, having failed to survive the queen's icy early morning tutorials. What this all means is still a mystery, but it is clear that any thinking person in those years found both the Rosicrucians and Prague fascinating subjects.[8]

The imperial attack on Bohemia and on the Palatinate set in motion a long period of warfare which goes by the name of the Thirty Years' War (1618–48). Initially, it seemed to be a struggle between Catholics and Protestants, but French fears of German hegemony moved the goalposts, and it became more of a general European war first and a confessional conflict second. From the point of view of those with a millenarian and supernatural bent, this period of destruction seemed to be connected to the false dawn of the hermetic enlightenment. Rosicrucian and millenarian works which continued to be published on the Continent and in England throughout the century had the effect of giving continuous popular life to many of the philosophical ideas that had first become prominent during the Renaissance and Reformation.

| II |

The Rosicrucians attained a high level of intellectual distinction, but it was in more proletarian England that some of these ideas were actually put into practice. The Fifth Monarchy Men have become rather well-known in recent years, in part because scholars have shown us how important and influential radical groups were in shaping the English Revolution. These religious extremists were convinced, more than the philosophically minded Rosicrucians, that the Kingdom of God would be established imminently on earth, not through science or understanding but through devotion to God's eternal plan as revealed in the Holy Scriptures. They saw themselves as the natural ministers in a theocratic regime in which the Saints would rule England and prepare the people for the Second Coming. What made them more dangerous than the other groups that we have discussed was the fact that they were willing to resort to force and violence to arrange worldly matters to the satisfaction of King Jesus. As we shall see, the Fifth Monarchy Men had detailed plans on what the new millennium would look like, including provisions far removed from any connection with religion. This is why Oliver Cromwell said that "they had tongues like Angels, but had cloven feet."

Like other readers of the Book of Daniel before them, the Fifth Monarchy Men were entranced by the image given in it of four beasts, thought to represent the rise and fall of four successive world empires, each of which would degenerate into nonexistence. The last and fifth empire, they believed, would go on forever, under the reign of King Jesus. Scholars at least since Joachim have debated the precise identity of these empires: the first was usually said to be Babylon; the second that of the Persians and Medes, or possibly Assyria; the third Greece; and the fourth Rome, including the Roman Catholic Church. The fourth beast, according to Daniel, had ten horns, said to be kings, and a little horn which destroyed some of the ten. After this great event, the kingdom was given to the Saints forever: that was to be the Fifth Monarchy.

In much of their theology and theorizing, the Fifth Monarchy Men were no different than Rosicrucians and some of the Renaissance thinkers whom we have already studied. What made them innovative was their belief that the Kingdom of Heaven could be advanced by their actions in this world, that once the divine plan was grasped, the essential part of its truth became known. In this, they eliminated part of the great gap of Gnostic systems of thought, which posited a different layer of knowledge for the adepts as opposed to the ordinary spiritual followers.

For Englishmen in the early seventeenth century, there were three high priests of millenarian thought. The first was Thomas Brightman (1562–1607), a Cambridge-educated minister of Presbyterian convictions. Brightman's argument was that we are even now deep in the millennium, and that Jesus would reappear at the *end* of this current period of gradual improvement, postmillennium. Understandably, this very optimistic point of view was difficult to sustain in periods of adversity, although postmillennialism continued as a minority school of thought until the First World War, when it became virtually extinct, only to be successfully revived in our own time under the names of Christian Reconstructionism and Dominion Theology.

The second millenarian theorist was Johannes Alsted (1588–1638), professor of philosophy at Herborn in Germany. Unlike Brightman, he was a "premillennialist"—that is, he believed the millennium to lie wholly in the future. Jesus Christ would appear, and only after this revelation would follow a thousand-year rule of the Messiah and His Saints, at the end of which period a Final Judgment would take place and the world would be destroyed. Alsted studied the last verses of the Book of Daniel, which make reference to two periods of 1,290 and 1,335 days, beginning "from the time that the daily sacrifice shall be taken away, and the abomination that maketh desolate set up." Considering a day to be symbolic for a year (a concept derived from Ezekiel 4:6), Alsted argued that the first period began in 69 A.D. with the destruction of the Second Temple, and ended with the appearance of John Wyclif in England, the "morning star of the Reformation," in about 1359. The second period would end 1,335 years later in 2694 A.D. This would be the date of the Last Judgment, at the end of the thousand-year millennium, when Christ would rule on earth with His Saints. In other words, the Second Coming would take place during the year 1694, and the dead would be resurrected.[9]

Alsted's chief English interpreter was Joseph Mede (1586–1668), fellow of Christ's College, Cambridge, who, despite his firm views about millenarianism, stayed within the Anglican Church. His major contribution was a sophisticated textual analysis of Scripture based on the idea of synchronism, whereby the Book of Revelation was seen to be describing events taking place at the same time, in exactly equal time frames.

As we have seen, the millenarian idea was far from new, but it became far more explosive during the period of the English Civil War, since for the first time press censorship broke down. Some historians have maintained that these ideas were held throughout the early modern period, and it is merely the breakdown of censorship that gives us a window through which to see what had always been present. This is probably true, but we can never know for sure.

One thing we do know is that the messianic idea was adopted by the Puritan preachers. In the absence of any mass media, the monopoly of attention enjoyed by the clergy in the pulpit gave them many opportunities to convince others. It is impossible to estimate how many Puritan preachers accepted the general millenarian schema, but Bernard Capp, who has examined the works of 112 ministers who wrote three or more books published between 1640 and 1653, has found that 78—that is, 70 percent of them—expressed millenarian views.[10]

But according to Capp, by the time of the Fifth Monarchy Men, millenarianism was already losing appeal as an acceptable solution to England's woes. What had begun as a religious and even philosophical approach to the conundrum of the Second Coming had begun to take on a radical tinge that was unacceptable to many people. The forcible eviction of conservative members from Parliament in December 1648 (Pride's Purge), and the increasing radicalization of the army before and after the Levellers, led many to realize how little they relished the egalitarian principles of the most radical revolutionaries. With the execution of Charles I in January 1649—a momentous event in European political consciousness, the first time in which a legitimate anointed king was judicially executed after a public trial by his people—the image of Münster and Jan of Leiden was uppermost, and people feared England's moving along the same path toward rebellion and ultimate destruction. The Fifth Monarchy movement began to organize more efficiently after 1651, centering on such leaders as Christopher Feake and John Simpson, later meeting at Blackfriars in London, the city's traditional center of religious radicalism. There was some evidence that seemed to point to the year 1656 as the messianic year, and excitement grew as it approached.[11]

Their first aim during the initial years of the English Republic after the execution of the king was the end of the traditional form of parliamentary government, organized as it was around geographical districts whose votes sent representatives to the legislature. The radicals did not see why people who were obviously predestined for hell should have any input in deciding on states' affairs, and they promoted the idea of a parliament composed of representatives from the various godly churches in the land.

Among the most interesting ideas which emerged was a plan to model the new parliament on the Jewish Sanhedrin of seventy members. The main obstacle seems to have been that an assembly of seventy members alone would be much too small to represent adequately all the English counties, Scotland, Ireland, and Wales. Cromwell later claimed that he had therefore doubled it to 140 members on this Judaical basis, and indeed until the last stage he intended to summon only 130 men to the nominated parliament. A very strong biblical element appears at the very outset of the Puritans' search for a parliamentary solution, which illustrates the penetration of the Old Testament ideas and values into the realm of political action.

"Barebone's Parliament," or the "Parliament of the Saints," began to sit in July 1653, entertained at its first meeting in an airless and stiflingly hot room by an invigorating millenarian exposition by Oliver Cromwell himself which went on for hours. As it was conceived, the Parliament (named after one of its more absurd members, "Praise-God" Barbon), was meant to conduct the business of God on earth. This biblical orientation is also apparent in debates over legal reform, which threatened to divide it. The ultimate hope was that "the great volumes of law would come to be reduced into the bigness of a pocket book, as it is proportionable in New-England and elsewhere." The reference was to the radical code of laws enacted in Massachusetts in 1643 and revised the following year as "The Laws and Liberties."[12] One of the comprehensive plans which was not finally accepted in Massachusetts was John Cotton's "Moses his Judicials," so called because it aimed at being a synthesis between the biblical commandments and common-law practice. Although other plans were thought to be more workable, Cotton's code was printed in England as well and appealed to radical instincts everywhere.[13] As it was, the final code had numerous biblical overtones: the list of capital offenses included idolatry, blasphemy, witchcraft, adultery, rape, sodomy, kidnapping, and cursing or smiting a parent. In the event, like parliamentarians everywhere, they fell to arguing about numerous issues, especially the status of the tithe in the run-up to the millennium, and Cromwell was forced to send them away in December, which was for him a great personal defeat.[14]

There were a significant number of rather distinguished Fifth Monarchy Men in Barebone's Parliament, possibly an even dozen: five former members of the Council of State, six justices of the peace, two former sheriffs, and nine with army or at least militia connections. Even though they made up only a twelfth of the body, they voted as a group and discussed strategy beforehand. Indeed, one can make a case that the Fifth Monarchy Men were the first political party in parliamentary history.

In any case, after the dissolution of Parliament, they went into permanent opposition to the government of Oliver Cromwell and the army. Their view is best summarized by the public question of the millenarian preacher Vavasor Powell just at that time: "Lord, wilt Thou have Oliver Cromwell or Jesus Christ to reign over us?" Powell was arrested and held for a few days, but he continued attacking the government, and eventually thought it better to hole up in Wales until the Second Coming or the defeat of Cromwell, whichever came first.

As the first organized millenarian political movement, the Fifth Monarchy Men demand our attention not only on the level of strictly narrative history, but also from a sociological perspective. They were largely urban, coming either from London or from the large towns. The old theory that English dissent grows out of the independent conditions of the wood-pasture areas, while satisfyingly wholesome, does not seem to be true in this case. Interestingly, the towns that nurtured Fifth Monarchist views share few characteristics, apart from the fact that towns tended to have higher literacy, choice of clergy, fewer social controls, and a mixture of people from different backgrounds, including immigrants and merchants. The army was another breeding ground for Fifth Monarchism, but that may be because the army was a sort of mobile town.

We can estimate the number of people involved as well. Christopher Feake, one of the movement's leaders, thought that there were probably 40,000 Fifth Monarchy Men in 1655; Royalist estimates in 1659 postulated maybe 20,000–30,000 armed men. Despite these high numbers, it seems likely that the politically committed among them never numbered more than about 10,000.

Among 233 Fifth Monarchy Men for whom we have such data, there were two distinct groups: army officers and clergy, and the others. Landowning gentry comprised about 8–9 percent, and beneficed ministers a little over 20.6 percent. Of the remaining men, cloth and leather trades made up about 33 percent, and other occupations disproportionately represented include agriculture, woodwork and metal, and food. The impression is of a working-class movement, but not necessarily victims of early industrial society, for many of these people came from independent trades which gave some measure of security even during times of economic crisis. The key determinant of participation was religious rather than anything else.

Since a good part of the millenarians' support came from the army, they were rightly perceived as a security problem. Their most well-known supporters in the army were Major General Thomas Harrison (1606–60), eventually executed as a regicide by King Charles II after the Restoration, and Major General Robert Overton (c. 1609–c. 1668). Eventually, Cromwell removed them, and the Fifth Monarchists did exactly what the government feared most: they sought alliances with other disaffected groups and tried to subvert the army. By the beginning of 1657, they began to transform their vague millenarian longings into a concrete military plan.

The center of plotting was a congregation under the leadership of Thomas Venner (fl. 1638–d. 1661), a master cooper who had gone to Massachusetts in 1638 and returned to England in 1651 after the execution of the king. Venner became the spiritual leader of a radical church in London in 1656, and plotted his revolution from there. He had a secret organization with five groups of twenty-five members each, only one member in each cell knowing the details of the others.

The Venner plotters hoped to attack a troop of government horse, and then proceed through Epping Forest to East Anglia, fighting the republican army as their chief enemy. About eighty Fifth Monarchy Men were supposed to meet on the outskirts of London on the evening of April 9, 1657, but the government troops got there first and arrested about twenty of them. Thomas Venner himself was sent to prison for two years.

What exactly did they want? How did they envision the transformation of the millenarian idea into concrete political action? These questions are crucial for understanding how the concept of messianic revolution developed in this first example of the violent transformation of this ideological conception into such a dangerous movement. As it happens, we know the answer precisely, since the government troops not only arrested the rebels but also seized five hundred copies of their manifesto, already printed and ready for distribution. This curious document bears careful examination: what is most striking is the almost comical combination of high-sounding religious and messianic desires with much more mundane and prosaic demands.

The first article began by demanding "That all earthly governments, and worldly constitutions may be broken and removed by the first administration of the Kingdom of Christ, appointed unto him by the decree of the Father, and is the inheritance of the Saints, as joint heirs with him," a clear indication of their own self-perception as co-rulers on earth with Jesus, and stated long before the definition of the all-inclusive authority of Jesus in the sixth article. Like so many millenarian groups, they found their textual guide in Scripture. According to the seventh article, "the scriptures, given by inspiration of God with his holy spirit, are the revealed will and rule of this legislator, to be constantly owned and submitted unto in times of war and peace, as a constant standing rule, for the inward and outward man." As for the particular form of government preferred by the Messiah, the Fifth Monarchy Men posited "a Sanhedrin, or Supreme Council (this interest now up once removed)," of course, for the present Parliament would have to be overthrown. The Sanhedrin would "be duly chosen and constituted upon and according to the principles of right and freedom." Indeed, "such a Council, so constituted, shall be the Representative, for our Lord and King, of the whole body of the Saints, whose day this is, and people in the nations."

The Fifth Monarchists described the powers of the Sanhedrin in a lofty sort of way that almost puts one in mind of the later Constitution of the United States:

That the said Representative, as princes under Christ, from whom, with his people, their power is derived, shall rule in judgement or have the exercise of the chief-magistracy and the power of administering the laws residing in them: shall consult and provide for the safety and welfare of the state and people; shall determine and give judgement in all supreme matters of civil counsel, (not to prescribe forms of worship for their brethren, nor to take the power upon them given to the church) according to their present light; and shall rule and govern the people with just judgement; and that freely without respect of persons, or taking of gifts or bribes, and the poor with righteousness and equity; and shall save the children of the needy, with him that hath no helper. So that all just and honourable ends, for which they are entrusted, may be answered.

Lest anyone take the analogy with a modern liberal constitution too literally, we should look at the eleventh article, the next one, which states "That the power of ordering and disposing the militia, and forces of Zion at sea and land . . . be in this Representative." The "forces of Zion": this was no ordinary assembly: it was a Sanhedrin.

At the same time as entrusting their lives to Christ in a general sense, in a more immediate and mundane perspective, the Fifth Monarchists set about drawing up basic principles by which the new state could be governed. They limited the term of membership of the new Sanhedrin to a year, and made it clear that the power of the Sanhedrin to "take away, give up or enervate any of the foundations of common right and freedom" should be severely limited. Still, everyone would be subject to its laws, no matter "what rank, degree, or quality soever." The twenty-first article was even more specific, and rather different in tone: it covered such legal issues as habeas corpus, military impressment, excise, customs, taxation without representation, land tenure, and tithes. It would be difficult to find a better example of the principle of trusting in God and keeping your powder dry.[15]

Obviously, it would take more than a prison sentence to daunt the exuberance of the Fifth Monarchy Men, and their fervent desire to create Christ's Kingdom on Earth before the coming of the Messiah. Cromwell's death in 1658 was a great boost to them, and after the failure of his son to carry the torch, and with the revival of the original revolutionary Parliament, some people regarded them as the ones who had remained faithful to the original revolutionary message before Cromwell's military dictatorship had seized control. But they were unwilling to compromise on any major issue, and actually may have helped create the polarized atmosphere in 1659 and 1660 that led to a general feeling that only the son of the executed king could restore peace.

The Restoration of King Charles II was a moment of intense defeat for radicals everywhere, but nowhere was it more intensely felt than among the Fifth Monarchists. Readers of Milton's *Paradise Lost* already know that the Restoration reminded them of how mankind had been sent out of the Garden of Eden into the cruel and harsh world outside. Not all the Fifth Monarchists were convinced that this was God's will. On January 6, 1661, about fifty of Venner's faithful followers marched to St. Paul's Cathedral armed with rather vague plans. Nevertheless, they did manage to defeat an armed party sent against them, and to retire to the woods near Highgate, in the north of London. Three days later, a number of them reappeared in the City of London itself and fought it out with the Life Guards and a whole regiment of better-armed and -trained men. About twenty-six rebels were killed and twenty captured, while about twenty government soldiers lost their lives. Contemporaries swore that the Fifth Monarchists numbered maybe three or four hundred, but no more than fifty were ever seen together. Of the twenty brought to trial, a dozen were executed, as well as the infamous Thomas Venner, who was finally put to death as well. But the millenarian ideal itself, of course, did not die, even in England,

and the Fifth Monarchy Men remained both a model for the messianic revolution and a warning for the advocates of stable government.

| III |

We have seen how the consideration of the Bible's millenarian message led groups such as the Fifth Monarchy Men to think that they had understood God's divine plan and were empowered to put it into action. Yet even less committed Englishmen might agree with the basic points of their understanding of the biblical text, and in some ways, aspects of their thought became a permanent part of the Anglo-American heritage. For study of the Bible often led the English to consider the separate functions of divine providence and chance, being the first and most common manifestation of scriptural politics: the Bible as a providential prism, a method for interpreting mundane events.

During the mid-seventeenth century, it was taken for granted, and not only in Puritan circles, that the divine plan was extremely detailed, if not complete, and that God was continuously intervening in worldly affairs, sowing small clues that directed mankind's attention to His pleasure. Apart from conspicuous and meaningful signs and "providences," the largest single collection of clues was to be found in God's written word, His legacy to mankind—the Bible. The so-called godly were convinced that the Bible provided an infallible guide in a wide variety of human experience, and were prepared to seek guidance in Holy Writ. The end result was to create a new climate of Bible worship.

The underlying assumption of Puritan veneration for the Bible and its message, then, is that God has a divine plan and that mankind can go a good deal along the way toward discovering it. The usual explanation was that God demonstrates His concern for His human creations by means of His "general" and "particular" providence. His "general" providence consisted in His having created the world in the first place, in having ordained the courses of the planets and the laws of physics. His "particular" providence was His suspension of the laws He had ordained in order to achieve a specific goal. The extreme cases of particular providence are what we would call "miracles" and fulfilled prophecies. The Bible recounts many instances of God's particular providence and demonstrates His extraordinary intervention on behalf of mankind in crucial historical moments, so there was no reason to rule out the possibility that He was still active in human affairs.

The biblical axiom of divine intervention as a regulatory mechanism worked in a wide variety of applications in seventeenth-century England. Thieves might see capture and punishment as their just reward. A righteous man unjustly suffering could compare himself with Job, enduring trial after trial in his quest for eternal compensation. When punishments fit the crime, such as the contraction of syphilis after a lifetime of philandering, God's will seemed a full and justified explanation.

The necessity of distinguishing between an act of providence and pure chance hardly concerned those who were already convinced they had succeeded in deciphering the meaning of a particular temporal event. Thomas Gataker studied the problem from the Puritan point of view in the early years of Charles I's reign and concluded that the essential ingredient for distinguishing between providence and the mere course of events was a clear connection between the sign and the resulting outcome.[16] A storm before a dangerous journey was likely to be a message from above. It was a good bet at all times that lightning had a hidden meaning, especially when it struck down someone who deserved it. Even those who did not think that the notion of chance was in some way an insult to God's Dominion were impressed by the context of a divine message.

In the very long Calvinist run, it seemed likely that there was a connection between success in this world and one's final and eternal destination. As Tyndale nicely put it in his translation of Genesis 39:2: "And the Lorde was with Joseph, and he was a luckie felowe."[17] Max Weber's later insight about the relationship between Calvinism and the rise of capitalism touched on only one part of a complex equation. It was equally apparent that temporal failure might be a divine portent. It now seems clear that one of the reasons for the development of laissez-faire economics even in the nineteenth century was the desire to allow God to manifest his providences unimpeded by human safeguards or cushions. If a man was doomed to become bankrupt, he should be allowed to free-fall to the very bottom.[18]

Certainly Christians everywhere agreed that the Bible was a useful guide with regard to general moral conduct. The text of the Ten Commandments was enjoying a general European revival during the early modern period, and even in Roman Catholic countries it was coming to replace the Seven Deadly Sins as the yardstick for human behavior.[19] When it came to specific advice on which course to follow out of several possible alternatives, one could always open the Bible at random and pull out a verse. Theologians might argue that this procedure implied that God could be compelled to intervene, and itself infringed on the notion of God's absolute sovereignty, but biblical fishing remained popular. Creative exegesis of the Bible, combined with a careful study of providences and portents, might thus illuminate the path for mankind.

Undoubtedly, one pioneer in the prophetic field during the period of the English Civil War and after was the Baptist clergyman Henry Jessey (1602–63), and it is worth looking at him for a moment to see how from biblical soil might spring up an entire science of prophecy and prediction. Apart from his courageous stand for the theological position that would become known as semiseparatism, Jessey was also prominent for his philo-Semitism and his active support for Rabbi Menasseh ben Israel and the readmission of the Jews to England. He was also a great believer in God's constant intervention in human affairs, and published a "Scripture-Kalender" between 1645 and his death in 1663.[20] In August 1660, Jessey published another work of this nature, "a True *Relation* of some Late, Various, and Wonderful *Judgments*, or Handy-works of God, by Earthquake, Lightening, Whirlewind, great multitudes of Toads and Flyes; and also the striking with Sudden Deaths, of divers persons in several places." Although no direct reference was made to the Restoration, the implication was that the political changes of the past year would have some awe-inspiring divine effect.[21] This work seems to have been a trial run for his three-volume edition of "prodigies," which appeared in 1661 and 1662.[22] Jessey's work was an account of "many remarkable *Accidents*, and signal *Judgments* which have befel divers Persons who have Apostatized from the Truth, and have been Persecutors of the Lord's faithful Servants." More exactly, it was a list of strange occurrences between the summer of 1660 and the autumn of 1662; 146 prodigies seen in the skies, 75 observed on the earth, 26 in the rivers and seas, and 91 examples of divine judgment.[23] Jessey explained: "Let every one rather from these things be convinced, that upon us the ends of the world are come, and that God is now making hast to consummate his whole work in the earth, and to prepare the way for his Son to take unto himself his great power and reign."[24] These were "certain Harbengers and immediate fore-runners."[25] Henry Jessey may have sincerely believed that the biblical-style signs and portents he had collected pointed the way to certain divine action. During the Interregnum, when he was widely respected, he found signs of God's pleasure all around him. But from the point of view of the newly restored Royalist government, however, his latest researches seemed to imply divine dissatisfaction with the recent changes. Certainly Jessey included numerous examples of Nonconformists who went over to the Established Church and subsequently met bad and often violent ends. The publication of such a work on such a grand scale was an incitement to disorder that the government could not ignore. Jessey spent the next two years in and out of prison, until he was finally released in February 1663, with only a few months to live.[26] He was buried after a funeral attended by upwards of five thousand people, which was itself seen as a danger to public order. He always believed that the Bible gave the key for interpreting seemingly innocuous occurrences around us, and seeing them as partially disguised divine messages. God's method of communication had not changed very much between the time of Moses and the era of Cromwell.

| IV |

One lasting contribution to the notion of messianic revolution was undoubtedly the fascination during this period with the whereabouts of the Lost Ten Tribes of Israel, a subject that became the ideological underpinning of twentieth-century racist groups such as the Aryan Nation and the Christian Identity movement. The discovery of the New World seemed to point to a solution to this old chestnut. Ever since Columbus, the presence of Native Americans in a part of the world apparently so distant from the scene of biblical events had been a problem for Christian and Jewish theologians. Columbus himself had no difficulty with their discovery: he died in the belief that he had landed on the east coast of Asia: the native peoples were Asiatics whose presence was interesting but unremarkable. Columbus reported in his journal that when he sent a reconnaissance party into the interior, he included one Luis de Torres, a converted Marrano who "understood Hebrew and Chaldee and even some Arabic." Torres was meant to act as the interpreter of the expedition, in case they encountered any Hebrew-speaking Indians.[27] It was entirely possible, he reasoned, that these strange people might be the barbarized descendants of the Ten Tribes of Israel whose fate was described in II Kings 17: 6, 23:

> In the ninth year of Hoshea the king of Assyria took Samaria, and carried Israel away into Assyria, and placed them in Halah and in Habor *by* the river of Gozan, and in the cities

of the Medes . . . So was Israel carried away out of their own land to Assyria unto this day.[28]

The Apocrypha continued the story and revealed further that after the conquest the Ten Tribes

> took this counsel among themselves, that they would leave the multitude of the heathen, and go forth into a further country, where never mankind dwelt, That they might there keep their statutes, which they never kept in their own land . . . Then dwelt they there until the latter time; and now when they shall begin to come, The Highest shall stay the springs of the stream again, that they may go through.[29]

Although some proto-anthropologists suggested that the native peoples of the Americas might be entirely outside the Scripture story (such as Isaac La Peyrère), virtually everyone who wrote about their origin agreed that they must in some way be descended from Adam and Eve, if not from Noah as well: the chief difficulty was to describe the route of migration and to fit the chronology with the timetable in Genesis.[30] Their identification with the Lost Ten Tribes was a convenient and popular solution that found supporters not only in the Spanish-speaking world but also in England and France.[31]

These speculations took on renewed urgency in 1644, when a Marrano named Antonio de Montezinos, recently returned from Quito province in Ecuador, testified under oath before the Amsterdam rabbi Menasseh ben Israel (1604–57) that he had met Israelites of the tribe of Reuben, living secretly deep in the interior of the territory. Montezinos had made a good choice in selecting Menasseh as his witness, for in many respects he had become the Jewish ambassador to the gentile intellectual world. Menasseh ben Israel was to be the man who convinced Oliver Cromwell to hold a public conference in London in 1655 to discuss the possibility of granting

Jews a formal readmission to England, nearly four centuries after their expulsion by Edward I. Although this Whitehall Conference never came to any formal decision, the very fact that the issue was debated publicly with aggressive support from Cromwell was to encourage Jews to come out of the Marrano closet when war with Spain in 1656 presented them with the option of being either enemy aliens or quasi-legal Jewish residents of England.

During the five years before his arrival in England in 1655, Menasseh's chief goal had been to obtain a position at the court of Queen Christina of Sweden as her Jewish librarian, bibliographer, and tutor. In the early 1650s, Menasseh's situation had verged on the desperate. Despite his fame among prominent gentiles, in fact he had never succeeded in establishing himself as a respected and financially secure scholar in the Jewish community of Amsterdam, and was forced to turn to publishing in order to supplement his meager income, which he received as a teacher in the primary school of the newly united synagogues of Amsterdam after 1639. At one stage, Menasseh even considered emigration to the New World, and it was only his appointment as director of the community school and lecturer at the yeshiva that changed his mind. This was followed in 1644 by his appointment as principal of a newly established Talmudic academy founded by Abraham and Isaac Pereira. In spite of these rather minor and poorly paid posts, however, the Jews of Amsterdam never considered Menasseh a great mind, which only encouraged him to seek his honors elsewhere.[32] When he published his book *The Hope of Israel* in 1650, dedicated to the English Parliament, he had reached rock bottom, both financially and in terms of any hopes he might have still entertained for a formal position in Amsterdam. Queen Christina's abdication in 1654 spelled the end of his dream of making a career for himself on the circuit of international intellectuals.[33]

But the seeds he had planted in that important book came to fruition, and he now had the leisure and the will to turn to England, where his works were widely known and respected in the circle of

John Dury, one of Cromwell's closest spiritual companions and his unofficial emissary to the Protestant churches of Europe. For the theme of *The Hope of Israel* concerned a central question that had preoccupied English and Continental theologians since the Reformation—that is, the mystery of the Lost Ten Tribes, who would have to receive the Protestant message in order to complete the circle.

His chief piece of evidence was the testimony of Antonio de Montezinos from 1644, which was both fantastic and exciting. Montezinos recounted his arrival at a secret kingdom where the inhabitants repeated the Jewish credo, the *Shema*, along with nine vague remarks and prophecies, but refused to allow him to cross the river Sambatyon, which bordered their country. Montezinos estimated that he spoke with nearly three hundred Israelite Indians during his three days there, but they would see him only in small groups, and declined to elaborate on their nine cryptic statements. Montezinos's Indian guide explained afterwards that these were Israelites who had come to the New World and defeated the local populace in the area. Since then, no outsider had been allowed to cross the river and enter the kingdom itself. These Israelites of the Lost Ten Tribes believed that the arrival of the Spanish in the New World, the coming of ships to the South Seas, and the visit of Montezinos fulfilled certain prophecies. Montezinos testified that following his visit he returned to the coast and met other native peoples who had visited the Lost Ten Tribes as well.[34]

This startling firsthand account of the current whereabouts and activities of the Lost Ten Tribes was first revealed to the gentile world in 1649 by the American missionary Edward Winslow, who wrote excitedly to Parliament and the Council of State begging to

> acquaint your Honors, that a godly Minister of this City writing to Rabbi-ben-Israel, a great Dr. of the Jewes, now living at Amsterdam, to know whether after all their labor, travells, and most diligent enquiry, they did yet know what was become of

the ten Tribes of Israel? His answer was to this effect, if not in these words, That they were certainly transported into America, and that they had infallible tokens of their being there.[35]

It was no secret that this "godly Minister" of London was John Dury, international crusader for Christian unity. Menasseh had sent Dury a French translation of the testimony, and Dury had it rendered into English and published in Thomas Thorowgood's book *Ievves in America*, which appeared in 1650, to which Dury contributed an "Epistolicall Discourse." Although "at first blush," he confessed, "the thing which you offer to be believed, will seeme to most men incredible, and extravigent; yet when all things are laid rationally and without prejudice together, there will be nothing of improbability found therein."[36]

Menasseh himself published a full account in *The Hope of Israel*, which in 1650 appeared at Amsterdam in Latin and Spanish, and in London in an English edition, translated by Milton's friend Moses Wall; a second English edition is dated 1652.[37] Menasseh's little book gave the debate over the Lost Ten Tribes a text on which it could center. The author himself was instantly famous, not only in the circle of philo-Semitic intellectuals such as Dury and his colleague Samuel Hartlib, but among a much wider group of enthralled readers.

Menasseh and Dury worked in concert, although their aims were quite different. Dury and his group believed that the conversion of the Lost Ten Tribes was a harbinger of the conversion of the European Jews, which in turn was a prelude to the Second Coming and the millennium, when Christ would rule on earth for a thousand years with His Saints. Menasseh, on the other hand, who had no intention of converting to Christianity, cited Isaiah, who had prophesied that the Lord would "assemble the outcasts of Israel, and gather together the dispersed of Judah from the four corners of the earth" before the coming of the Messiah. Russia and Palestine might be two corners; South America a newly discovered third. England was probably the fourth, in part because its designation in medieval Hebrew literature was often "the end of the earth," an overly literal and etymologically false translation of "Angleterre."[38]

The issue of the Lost Ten Tribes, then, connected an unemployed and underpaid Dutch rabbi with circles in London who hoped simultaneously to bring the Jews to England, to convert them to true and pure English Protestant Christianity, and thereby bring closer the Second Coming. There was an identity of purpose between Christian and Jew in seventeenth-century England, which was already sensitized to philo-Semitism on the basis of the values of the Renaissance and the Reformation common to northern European culture.

Most importantly, the chimera of the Lost Ten Tribes stayed fresh, and survives as a powerful force, especially among groups that stressed the inerrancy of the Bible and refuse to accept the new biblical criticism, even more so among denominations which give the Jews, with or without the Lost Ten Tribes (and sometimes the Israelite Indians), a critical role to play at the End of Days. The first of these religious groups was the Mormons, whose truths were revealed to Joseph Smith on September 21, 1823, by the angel Moroni, son of Mormon. These were written on gold plates in the Reformed Egyptian language which could be deciphered with the aid of an accompanying pair of eyeglasses made from two transparent stones, the Urim and Thummim described in the Old Testament. Only four years later was Smith allowed to take possession of the plates, and to begin the process of translation. The result was *The Book of Mormon*, a 275,000-word chronicle about the inhabitants of pre-Columbian America.

The story begins in 600 B.C. in Palestine, when a group of Israelites is inspired to leave Jerusalem immediately before the Babylonian invasion. They flee by caravan to the Indian Ocean, and then by boat to the Promised Land on the west coast of North America. There they divide into two disagreeing groups, the Nephites and the Lamanites, and spend centuries building a civilization and fighting with one another. Following His crucifixion and resurrection, Christ appears to them in America, announcing that He will also visit other remnants of the Lost Ten Tribes of Israel. "I go unto the Father," He told them as He prepared to leave, "and also to show myself unto the lost tribes of Israel, for they are not lost unto the Father, for he knoweth whither he hath taken them." The Nephites and the Lamanites live in harmony after the divine visitation for about two centuries, then begin warring again, and finally, in about 421 A.D., the Nephites are totally vanquished and destroyed. The victorious Lamanites, however, gradually sink into barbarism, lose their fair skins, and become the ancestors of the Native Americans. Moroni, the last prophet of the exterminated Nephites, buries the history of the American Israelites in the hill Cumorah, where they remain until revealed to Joseph Smith in 1823. As is fitting for the first genuine indigenous American variety of Christianity, America is given a starring role: it had been the scene of Christ's work on earth as much as Palestine, and would be once again, as the true American church would arise against the apostate churches of ungodly Europe.[39]

The Articles of Faith of the Church of Jesus Christ of Latter-day Saints made quite clear the role the Jews and the Lost Ten Tribes were expected to play. The tenth of thirteen articles affirms: "We believe in the literal gathering of Israel and in the restoration of the Ten Tribes; that Zion will be built upon this [the American] continent; that Christ will reign personally upon the earth; and, that the earth will be renewed and receive its paradisiacal glory."[40] This Zion was revealed to be Jackson County, Missouri, confirmed by revelations received by Joseph Smith. This had been promised by Jesus Christ himself during His manifestation before the American Israelites after His resurrection, fortelling the redemption of

> as many of the house of Israel as shall come, that they may build a city, which shall be called the New Jerusalem. And

then shall they assist my people that they may be gathered in, who are scattered upon all the face of the land, in unto the New Jerusalem. And then shall the power of heaven come down among them; and I also will be in the midst . . . at that day shall the work of the Father commence among all the dispersed of my people, yea, even the tribes which have been lost, which the Father hath led away out of Jerusalem.[41]

The Jews themselves, however, as opposed to the Lost Tribes, would be redeemed in a different location, as prophesied in the Book of Isaiah:

I would gather them together in mine own due time, that I would give unto them again the land of their fathers for their inheritance, which is the land of Jerusalem, which is the promised land unto them forever, saith the Father. And it shall come to pass that the time cometh, when the fulness of my gospel shall be preached unto them; And they shall believe in me, that I am Jesus Christ, the Son of God, and shall pray unto the Father in my name. Then shall their watchmen lift up their voice, and with the voice together shall they sing; for they shall see eye to eye. Then will the Father gather them together again, and give unto them Jerusalem for the land of their inheritance.[42]

The conversion of the Jews to Christianity, then, would precede the Second Coming, the return of the Jews to the Holy Land of Palestine, and the establishment of a New Jerusalem in Missouri populated by Mormons and found Israelites.

The Mormon attitude toward the Bible was somewhat less straightforward. As Joseph Smith explained it in 1842: "We believe the Bible to be the word of God as far as it is translated correctly."[43] Believing the Bible to have been incorrectly translated, Smith began the work afresh as early as 1830, though he had no knowledge of either Hebrew or Greek, producing a text that amended the Authorized Version, with corrections and expansions. He credited inspiration as his guide, a problematic claim to which one might only reply, "Judge not, that ye be not judged," or as Smith elegantly put it: "Judge not unrighteously, that ye be not judged; but judge righteous judgment."[44]

The Mormons remain steadfastly philo-Semitic and supportive of Jewish temporal interests, especially the welfare of the modern state of Israel, which most Protestant groups have come to see as part of the divine plan rather than as a human attempt to jump the gun. A vast and beautiful Mormon college sits on Mount Scopus in Jerusalem, built only recently and with full support from one of Israel's right-wing nationalist governments.

CHAPTER 4

MEASURING THE APOCALYPSE: ISAAC NEWTON AND THE MESSIAH

The nature and significance of the theology of Isaac Newton (1642–1727) have become extremely controversial in recent years.[1] On the one hand, much of what Newton wrote was striking and original, demonstrating a clear grasp of the major scriptural issues of his day, combined with a special insight about their application to history and the natural world. At the same time, a good deal of the primary material consists of Newton's notes derived from his reading, and the orderly presentation of the great man's ideas necessarily involves a good deal of interpretation. Others have argued that Newton's theology is useful for understanding his science, but is insufficiently original to warrant independent study, or for supporting the argument that it would be worth studying Newton's religion if he had not become the leading scientist of the early modern period.

Nevertheless, it is undeniable that Newton represents for us the earliest attempt to apply modern scientific concepts to an understanding of the apocalyptic implications of the coming of the Messiah. His interest in the millennium was known since at least 1733, when his *Observations upon the Prophecies* was published.[2] Newton was convinced that he had discovered the key to God's divine plan, which in the hands of mankind could only lead to a better life on earth. His science was, for him, a vehicle for demonstrating the truth of religion, and his biblical criticism was a means of deciphering the mysteries of his faith. Like many of his contemporaries, Newton believed that it was no accident that the prophetic books were being unsealed at the same time that there was a revelation of scientific knowledge.

| I |

An examination of Newton's millenarianism should probably begin with a consideration of his revision of conventional chronology, which first came to light through a combination of gossip and royal pressure. Newton had discussed his work with the Abbé Conti, a Venetian nobleman and hanger-on who in turn communicated this bit of news to Caroline of Anspach, princess of Wales and wife of the future George II, and Newton's greatest admirer. Newton was summoned to court and was requested to provide a copy, or at least a summary, of his work in this fascinating field. Newton worked up an "Abstract," what would become his "Short Chronology," and gave it to the princess, although he refused to pass it on to Conti as well. Not to be denied a look at this compelling document, Conti simply asked Caroline to order Newton to hand it over, and he could do nothing but comply.

As Newton suspected and feared, Conti immediately showed the manuscript around. His twenty-page chronology of ancient history was a minor bombshell, since apart from anything else, Newton had cut off about four centuries from Greek history, basing his calculations on astronomy and the points of the equinox, and refused to accept any written Greek authority before Herodotus. The summary was published without Newton's permission as the appendix to a French translation of Humphrey Prideaux's history of the Jews. Newton denounced the pirated edition, but refused to recant on his ideas. Conti, for his part, was soon arguing that he had discovered the Italian counterpart to Newton's chronological research: *The New Science* of Giambattista Vico (1668–1744). Vico sent a copy of the first edition of his book to Newton via a rabbi of Livorno, but the book seems not to have been delivered.

The importance of Newton's work can hardly be overestimated. For the first time, a scholar conversant in both the written sources and what was called the "Book of Nature" had managed to combine the two approaches to understanding the divine message. Once the biblical and gentile written record was linked to the unimpeachable astronomical evidence, it should have been easy to verify or correct the accepted chronological schema. Although Newton refused to allow anything further to be published under his name, after his death in 1727 it was inevitable that every word written by the great man would appear in print. We know that Newton was working on the manuscript only a few days before his death. The following year, *The Chronology of Ancient Kingdoms Amended* was published, including the troubled "Abstract," produced by John Conduitt, who had married Newton's niece.[3]

His most important biographer, Richard S. Westfall, described Newton's chronology as a "work of colossal tedium, it excited for a brief time the interest and opposition of the handful able to get excited over the date of the Argonauts before it sank into oblivion. It is read today only by the tiniest remnant who for their sins must pass through its purgatory."[4] In many ways, this is an unfair assessment of a book whose importance outweighs its uselessness as a scientific decipherment of a significant problem. The study of biblical chronology has always required a good deal of ingenuity and a substantial amount of patience and mathematical skill. Different methods need to be applied in order to find the exact date of a biblical event. The first is based on simple addition and subtraction.

Others had dealt with the issue of chronology before Newton, the true study of which began with the Irish archbishop James Ussher of Armagh (1581–1656). Ussher's greatest achievement was to have improved the system of chronology devised by J. J. Scaliger (1540–1609), the inventor of the "Julian Period," a cycle of 7,980 years within which no day was in exactly the same position according to three parallel systems of measurement: the solar cycle of nineteen years, the lunar cycle of twenty-eight years, and the Roman civil cycle (Indiction) of fifteen years. Scaliger had managed to bridge the gap between recorded history and the Old Testament, and thereby to calculate the day of Creation as Sunday, October 25, 3950 B.C. Ussher, however, pointed out that Scaliger had missed the crucial fact that Terah was twice married and that Abraham's mother was his *second* wife. Furthermore, even assuming that the sun readjusted itself after standing still for Joshua and moving backward for Hezekiah, recalculating the entire calendar pushed the date of Creation back to 4004 B.C.: Sunday, October 23, to be precise. Scaliger, Ussher complained to his friend John Selden, "intending higher matters, did not heed so much his ordinary arithmetic."[5]

The systems of Ussher and Scaliger were marvels of exactitude which enabled the Christian world to assimilate the histories of the gentile nations to the biblical plan, and to provide a comforting framework within which to accommodate all known historical facts. Ussher pinpointed not only the Creation, but all other key dates, such as the Flood (2349 B.C.) and the Exodus (1492 B.C.). Edward Gibbon, the great eighteenth-century historian of Rome, described the effect that the study of chronology had on his schoolboy mind:

> from Strauchius I imbibed the elements of chronology: the tables of Helvicus and Anderson, the annals of Ussher and Prideaux distinguished the connection of events, and I engraved the multitude of names and dates in a clear and indelible series. But in the discussion of the first ages I overleaped the bounds of modesty and use. In my childish balance I presumed to weigh the systems of Scaliger and

Petavius, of Marsham and Newton, which I could seldom study in the originals; the dynasties of Assyria and Egypt were my top and cricket-ball; and my sleep has been disturbed by the difficulty of reconciling the Septuagint with the Hebrew computation.[6]

Even more recently, the historian Hugh Trevor-Roper described the pleasure he had as a boy derived from the labors of Archbishop Ussher:

When I was a child I was taken regularly, on Sundays, to our local parish church, from whose formal proceedings I fear my attention was inclined to wander. Happily, it found a rival attraction still within the holy circle of orthodoxy. The prayer books supplied in the pews contained a series of tables which, I now realize, came ultimately from the Archbishop: tables of fascinating complexity which enabled the reader to work out, via the Epact and the Golden Year, the date of Easter in any year, past or future. I never discovered what the Epact and the Golden Year were, but many a mechanical litany, many a dull sermon, formed a comfortable continuo while I conjured with these fascinating tables, checking that they worked and applying them to random years in the past and the future.[7]

Both Gibbon in the eighteenth century and Lord Dacre two hundred years later give us a sense of the comforting quality of chronology, whose claims brought strength to the faith of the devout Christian and fascinated even the doubting one. The problem with an exact science, however, is that one needs to be exact: even the differences between Scaliger and Ussher, so much in agreement about the generalities, would in the long run undermine the whole. As the intellectual historian Paul Hazard pointed out fifty years ago, when the chronologists finished their task and concluded their hairsplitting arguments, "they will have sown more seeds of unrest in quiet minds, and done more to undermine faith in history, than all your open scoffers and anti-religious fanatics ever succeeded in doing."[8] Paradoxically, the reason for this was the very fact that they were believers rather than skeptics.

Newton agreed with his predecessors that the main challenge of chronology was to find a way of organizing world history using biblical history as the base. Yet to this difficult task he added the ambitious project of incorporating as well the events recorded by Egyptians, Assyrians, Babylonians, Persians, Greeks, and Romans, and possibly the Chinese, whose detailed chronology posed an especially difficult quandary. The problem, he lamented, was that "All Nations, before they began to keep exact accounts of Time, have been prone to raise their Antiquities; and this humour has been promoted, by the Contentions between Nations about their Originals."[9] His innovation was to use astronomical proofs in order to set a number of dates as axes around which the entire chronology could be set. The variation of the equinox was the key. As long as he could find the date in a reliable ancient record, such as his favorite, Pliny, of the position of the sun at the time of the equinox relative to the fixed stars, Newton knew that he could extrapolate backward from the stars' present astronomical position to arrive at the desired date of the event, since the "Equinox goes back fifty seconds in one year, and one degree in seventy and two years." Others had tried to find the position of heavenly bodies at certain key points in history. The Polish astronomer Hevelius claimed to have been able to set the exact location of the sun over Eden at the moment of Creation, and Newton's sometime protégé William Whiston did his best to date the comet that in his view had caused the Flood. Following this astronomical method, Newton was able to calculate the date of the Argonautic expedition as 43 or 44 years after the death of Solomon—that is, at about 936 B.C. As for the period when the Greek historian Hesiod lived, Newton noted, "*Hesiod* tells us that sixty days after the winter Solstice the Star *Arcturus* rose just at Sunset: and thence it follows that *Hesiod* flourished about an hundred years after the death of *Solomon*, or in the Generation or Age next after the *Trojan* war, as *Hesiod* himself declares."[10]

Another of Newton's innovations was to calculate the average length of a king's reign in ancient times. "The *Egyptians* reckoned the Reigns of Kings equipollent to Generations of men," Newton noted, "and three Generations to an hundred years." As a result, "so did the *Greeks* and *Latines*: and accordingly they have made their Kings Reign one with another thirty and three years a-piece." Newton studied the records of the Jews, the Persians, the Hellenistic kings, as well as those of England and France, and came up with a more representative figure of eighteen to twenty years per monarch. Indeed, Newton concluded, in "the later Ages, since Chronology hath been exact, there is scarce an instance to be found of ten Kings Reigning any where in continual Succession above 260 years." In brief: "Let the reckoning be reduced to the course of nature, by putting the Reigns of Kings one with another, at about eighteen or twenty years a-piece." The net result was that the existing chronologies needed to be shortened by almost half. Using this method, and considering mythological gods as real historical rulers who had later been accorded divine status, Newton arrived at the same date for the Argonauts that he had calculated astronomically. What further proof could be desired? Biblical history could now be comfortably assimilated into the shortened ancient record.[11]

Newton's belief that the mythical Greek gods were kings who had become divine in popular history was based on a method called "euhemerism," which had acquired a kind of acceptance. The philosopher Euhemerus, who lived in the fourth century B.C., was the first to have the idea of explaining myth on a historical basis and, by extension, to explain religious beliefs or phenomena in nonsupernatural terms. Since classical and biblical archaeology as we know it was not yet born, there was little evidence for Newton to work with apart from literary sources. Virtually every symbolic element in ancient culture could be explained in this euhemerist fashion. Newton even argued that hieroglyphs were originally an ordinary alphabet. Whereas others looked for complicated spiritual meaning in the cultural artifacts of ancient cultures, Newton tried to reduce everything into political history, with the aim of comparing these civilizations with that of the Israelites as recorded in the Bible.

The point of all this frenetic chronological activity was to prove the supreme antiquity of the Hebrews and their civilization. In this, of course, Newton had numerous allies. Most prominent among them was Theophilus Gale, whose massive multivolume work on *The Court of the Gentiles* argued that all of philosophy began with the Jews, whose religion Gale thought was the only authentic one in the ancient world. One problem was that even the Bible seems to suggest that Egyptian and Assyrian royal houses had predated the establishment of an Israelite kingship. Newton's response was to argue that there was a significant difference in kind: the Israelites had the first properly developed monarchy, while their neighbors ruled over petty little tribal groups that did not deserve to be called kingdoms. In any case, for Newton, the battle between Israelites and Egyptians for antiquity was merely a preliminary skirmish before the great fight between Jews and Greeks, between Moses and Homer. Though it had come to be accepted since the Renaissance that Western civilization owed its origins to the Greeks, Newton took pains to restore the Jewish element to the fore.

We can get a clearer idea of Newton's views on this subject by looking for a moment at his manuscript entitled "Theologiae gentilis origines philosophicae" ("The Philosophical Origins of Gentile Theology").[12] Apart from Newton's supreme confidence in pronouncing on prehistoric events for which there is hardly any record, this document expresses his views on the earliest history and influence of the biblical text.

Newton argued that the ancient peoples worshipped the same twelve gods under different names, the gods being originally Noah and his sons and grandchildren. Why twelve gods exactly? Because the number twelve expressed a total of the seven planets, the four elements, and the single quintessence—that is, the most prominent objects that nature presents to the primitive mind. In earliest times, people identified their most famous ancestors with these supremely important factors. As this religion of Noah was transmitted to other nations farther away from the original time and place of the Flood, its mode of metaphysics was adapted to local conditions: each nation would identify its own kings and heroes according to the same pattern. This is why one finds similar structures among the mythologies of different peoples. Noah evolved into Saturn or Janus, for example, but all these characters were united in having three sons. Ham represented the original model of the supreme God, the divine who is depicted as a mature man in all civilizations—Zeus or Jupiter or Hammon, the connection is the same. Interestingly, Ham, who was so reviled by both Jewish and Christian theology, thus becomes a central figure in Newton's scheme. All peoples have a goddess, too, who is a beautiful woman, Newton notes. This was originally Ham's daughter, and later became Aphrodite, Venus or Astarte, or others. When one nation colonized another, as when Egypt or Phoenicia colonized Greece, then the theology of the mother state was exported and adapted to local conditions.

Newton's general point was that while at first glance the myths and religions of the world present a chaos of conflicting views, in fact they have an underlying unity, based on true biblical history as recounted in Genesis. Furthermore, as the beginnings of mythology were found to be a primitive interpretation of the physical world, it might be said that gentile theology began with the study of natural philosophy, or science.

In his *Irenicum*, Newton proclaimed, "All nations were originally of one religion & this religion consisted in the Precepts of the sons of Noah": love of God and love of neighbor, "the Moral law of all nations." Noah was the key figure of Jewish history no less than of the world: Abraham was the man who simply revitalized an old principle, further strengthened by Isaac and Jacob. Moses taught these principles to the Israelites after they had forgotten Noah's precepts.

Basing his account on Genesis and other ancient sources, Newton described how Noah's religion spread. The Egyptians were descendants of Ham. Noah's son Cush received the East, and two centuries after the Flood went beyond Arabia and conquered the family of Shem, establishing an empire in Babylon. It was Cush's son Nimrod who led an expedition from Babylon, establishing Nineveh and Assyria. No wonder, then, that the same themes should appear both in local religion and in mythology.

Despite these promising beginnings, Newton explains, Noah's religion was not destined to prevail outside the Jewish world. The Egyptians began the decline by creating false gods from their ancestors, and by developing a religion based on the stars, "sidereal" theology. This was gentile theology to which Newton referred in his unpublished manuscript, the corruption of true religion. A staunch anti-Trinitarian, Newton in this way explained the growth of what he considered the aberration of worshipping Jesus Christ as a god: it was no different from the Egyptians' worship of dead men as divinities. Jesus had been merely the latest prophet, who, like Abraham and Moses, had sought to recall the Jews to the original religion of Noah. He had not intended to form a totally new faith, and Newton blamed Athanasius (an Egyptian) for corrupting Christianity by introducing the concept of Jesus's divinity. The coming of Jesus was therefore no longer the central fulcrum of Christian history but merely the latest manifestation of a pattern in Jewish history which had begun with Abraham. Christianity, therefore, was hardly different than Judaism, in that it was simply the religion of Noah, which gave praise to God and His creation. The main distinction between Judaism and Christianity was that to the first two precepts of Noah, Christianity adds a third one: that we should believe that Jesus is the Christ foretold in prophecy. Nothing is to be found here about the redemption of mankind by a man who was also a god. That was too similar to corrupt gentile and Egyptian theology to be true.

Ever on the lookout for divine teaching, Newton also developed a keen interest in the exact form of the Temple of Solomon. "The Temple of *Solomon* being destroyed by the *Babylonians*, it may not be amiss here to give a description of that edifice," he explained in his *Chronology*.[13] He was taken with the idea that the Temple was a building that had God as its architect, with divine secrets no doubt contained in its very proportions and structure, and he spent a good deal of time trying to determine the exact length of a cubit.[14]

Newton argued that Moses had restored the original religion of Noah, and had also given the Israelites the basic form of the tabernacle, which Solomon would later re-create. Moses installed a perpetual flame in the tabernacle, which thus served as a model of nature, the fire representing the sun in a heliocentric universe: "Now the rationale of this institution was that the God of Nature should be worshiped in a temple which imitates nature, in a temple which is, as it were, a reflection of God. Everyone agrees that a Sanctum with a fire in the middle was an emblem of the system of the world."[15] When Solomon built his temple, according to the instructions given by God and recorded in the Book of Ezekiel, he also placed a fire in the center, surrounded by seven lamps representing the seven planets. We were to understand by this that the heavens themselves are God's temple, no less than the building erected by Solomon. When false religion came to dominate the Egyptians, it was similarly reflected in their misunderstanding of nature: the fire in the center was misconceived, not as the sun, but as some fire in the center of the earth, and the earth was placed in the center of the planets. Not by accident was Ptolemy an Egyptian.

| II |

Given these theories, it is not surprising that Newton should have strong views about the text of the Bible itself. Ironically, his very critical attitude toward the biblical text as we have it had the effect of strengthening the authority of prophecy, with implications for messianic theory. These views were most strikingly expressed in two letters he wrote to the great philosopher John Locke. In a cover letter to both, dated November 14, 1690, Newton instructed Locke that "if at present you get only what concerns ye first done into French, that of ye other may stay till we see what successe the first will have." Locke had a copy made of both letters, and sent it to Jean Le Clerc, a reformed theologian who was later a professor of philosophy at the Arminian Remonstrants Seminary at Amsterdam. Le Clerc read it and agreed to translate it into either Latin or French, but he thought that Newton should "read with care" the work of the controversial French theologian Richard Simon first. Newton, who had not known that Locke had sent his work to Le Clerc, did not seem to mind, and followed the theologian's advice to read Simon's *Histoire critique du Texte du Nouveau Testament*, which had been published at Rotterdam the year before. Newton did make some changes as a consequence, which Locke passed on to Le Clerc, who intended to incorporate them in the Latin translation.[16]

Newton got cold feet, however, and declined on this occasion, as he had on many others, to expose himself to public display of his heterodoxical views. Le Clerc promised not to broadcast the work, and deposited the manuscript in the Remonstrants' library, where it lay undisturbed until long after Newton's death. It was not published until 1754 in London, under the misleading title *Two Letters of Sir Isaac Newton to Mr. Le Clerc*.[17] A better copy was published from the original manuscript in 1785.[18]

Newton begins his discussion with the controversial proof text of I John 5:7, which had long been believed to establish the concept of the Trinity, by noting:

But whilst we exclaim against the pious frauds of ye Roman Church, & make it a part of our religion to detect & renounce all things of that kind: we must acknowledge it a greater crime in us to favour such practises, than in the Papists we so much blame on that account. For they act according to their religion but we contrary to our's. In the eastern nations, & for a long time in the western the faith subsisted without this text & it is rather a danger to religion than an advantage to make it now lean upon a bruised reed. There cannot be better service done to the truth than to purge it of things spurious: & therefore knowing your prudence & calmnesse of temper, I am confident I shal not offend you by telling you my mind plainly: especially since 'tis no article of faith, no point of discipline, nothing but a criticism concerning a text of scripture wch I am going to write about.

Newton then enters into a long discussion of the history of the text itself through the centuries, the upshot being that "the testimony of the three in heaven, wch in the times of those controversies would have been in every bodies mouth had it been in their books, was wholy unknown to the Churches of those ages." He is particularly scathing about the claim that the Trinitarian text had been censored during the Arian controversy. He found it outrageous that the Church Fathers "without proof accuse hereticks of corrupting books, & upon that pretense correct them at their pleasure without the authority of ancient manuscripts."

Yes truly those Arians were crafty Knaves that could conspire so cunningly & slyly all the world over at once (as at the word of Mithridates) in the latter end of the reign of the Emperor Constantius to get all men's books into their hands & correct them without being perceived: Ay & Conjurers too, to do it without leaving any blot or chasm in the books, whereby the knavery might be suspected & discovered; & to wipe even the memory of it out of all men's brains, so that neither Athanasius nor any body else could afterwards remember that they had even seen it in their books before, & out of their own too so yt when they turned to the consubstantial faith, as they generally did in the West soon after the death of Constantius, they could remember no more of it than any body else.

Newton goes on to analyze the contribution of Erasmus to the misunderstanding of this central text, and of Cardinal Ximenes's Polyglot Bible, which ratified the mistake. Erasmus "omitted it in his two first editions & inserted it unwillingly against the authority of his manuscripts in his three last," having promised to include the text if it could be found in a single manuscript.[19]

Newton's letter exhibits an extraordinary amount of thought and research given to a central problem of biblical theology, and considerable historical and religious understanding. The forthright nature of his views is remarkable, and in striking contrast to his political caution. Newton himself was aware of the paradox:

> You see what freedome I have used in this discourse & I hope you will interpret it candidly. For if ye ancient Churches in debating & deciding the great mysteries of religion, knew nothing of these two texts: I understand not why we should be so fond of them now the debates are over. And whilst it's ye character of an honest man to be pleased, & of a man of interest to be troubled at the detection of frauds, & both to run into those passions when the detection is made plainest: I hope this letter will to one of your integrity prove so much the more acceptable, as it makes a further discovery than you have hitherto met with in Commentators.

In short, Newton established to his satisfaction that the text of the New Testament was defective, not only because of the passage of time, but because various groups over the centuries had deliberately falsified it and deliberately distorted its original meaning. Nevertheless, he had no doubt that the prophetic portions of the Bible accurately expressed God's will. Generally speaking, his attitude toward the prophecies was exactly opposite of the esoteric approach that had been so popular during the Renaissance and that would remain an essential tool in biblical interpretation. Whereas the esoteric tradition saw mystical truths in even the most commonplace statements in the Bible, Newton had realistic interpretations of every supernatural passage. He accepted that the Bible was written in a secret language; the text could be seen to be composed of "hieroglyphs." But these "hieroglyphs" could be understood, the code could be cracked, by anyone who took the trouble to learn the key.

> He that would understand a book written in a strange language must first learn ye language & if he would understand it well must learn the language perfectly. Such a language was that wherein the Prophets wrote, & the want of sufficient skill in that language is the main reason why they are so little understood . . . they all wrote in one & the same mystical language, as well known without doubt to ye sons of ye Prophets as ye Hieroglypic language of ye Egyptians to their Priests, and this language, as far as I can find, was as certain & definite in its signification as is the vulgar language of any nation whatsoever.[20]

Newton spelled out the rules for the interpretation of prophecy. He wanted to "prepare the Reader also for understanding the Prophetique language," to make certain that "the Language of the Prophets will become certain and the liberty of wresting it to private imaginations be cut of." His final goal was to compare the different parts of the Apocalypse and reduce its message to "Propositions."

The first almost axiomatic principle was that the reader must "assigne but one meaning to one place of scripture, unles it be by way of conjecture." In other words, the images of the Bible are so consistent that it is impossible for them to have more than one meaning. In this they are even less flexible than words in a language. For example:

> if any man interpret a Beast to signify some great vice, this is to be rejected as his private imagination becaus acording to the stile and tenour of the Apocalyps and of all other Prophetique scriptures a Beast signifies a body politique and sometimes a single person which heads that body, and there is no ground in scripture for any other interpretation.

The important thing is to "keep as close as may be to the same sense of words, especially in the same vision." That being said, one should "chose those interpretations which are most according to the litterall meaning of the scriptures unles where the tenour and circumstances of the place plainly require an Allegory." There is no necessity to see figurative language in each and every place in the Bible. Another example:

> if they describe the overthrow of nations by a tempest of Hail, thunder, lightning and shaking of the world, the usuall signification of this figure is to be esteemed the proper and direct sense of the place as much as if it had been the litteral meaning, this being a language as common amongst them as any national language is amongst the people of that nation.

When Newton reached his more specific "Rules for methodising the Apocalyps," he insisted that one ought to "prefer those interpretations which, caeteris paribus, are of the most considerable things. For it was Gods designe in these prophesies to typefy and describe not trifles but the most considerable things in the world during the time of the Prophesies." Thus, when we see references to the whore of Babylon or the woman clothed with the Sun, we should prefer an interpretation which relates these figures not to individuals but to "Kingdoms Churches and other great bodies of men." One should also take into account that the Apocalypse was meant to be a continuous narrative "without any breach or interfering." For the interpretation of the Apocalypse should not become overly clever: "Truth is ever to be found in simplicity, and not in the multiplicity and confusion of things."

This, of course, was Newton's principle in his search for general laws of physics:

> It is the perfection of God's works that they are all done with the greatest simplicity. He is the God of order and not of confusion. And therefore as they that would understand the frame of the world must indeavour to reduce their knowledg to all possible simplicity, so it must be in seeking to understand these visions. And they that shall do otherwise do not onely make sure never to understand them, but derogate from the perfection of the prophecy; and make it suspicious also that their designe is not to understand it but to shuffle it of and confound the understandings of men by making it intricate and confused.

The interpretation of the Apocalypse was in a sense similar to the construction of a mechanical device. One should "chose those constructions which without straining reduce contemporary visions to the greatest harmony of their parts." The key is to avoid "straining":

> For as of an Engin made by an excellent Artificer a man readily beleives that the parts are right set together when he sees them joyn truly with one another notwithstanding that they may be strained into another posture; and as a man acquiesces in the meaning of an Author how intricate so ever when he sees the words construed or set in order according to the laws of Grammar, notwithstanding that there may be a possibility

of forcing the words to some other harsher construction: so a man ought with equal reason to acquiesce in that construction of these Prophecies when he sees their parts set in order according to their suitableness and the characters imprinted in them for that purpose.

But the analogy with machinery should not be carried too far:

Tis true that an Artificer may make an Engin capable of being with equal congruity set together more ways than one, and that a sentence may be ambiguous: but this Objection can have no place in the Apocalyps, becaus God who knew how to frame it without ambiguity intended it for a rule of faith.

The important point was that the divine plan could be understood, if only we had the key, and Newton believed he could provide it.

Thus did Isaac Newton apply the full force of his scientific genius to the nature of biblical prophecy and the chronology of Apocalypse. His work was of enormous importance in framing the messianic canon of authoritative interpreters of the divine message. Although his modern biographers usually prefer not to dwell on his theological views, for groups like the Seventh-day Adventists, he remains an important link in the chain of messianic theorists, and is so depicted passing the torch down the line to John Wesley in a wall mural at their headquarters in Takoma Park, Maryland.[21] His research into messianic interpretation helped to bridge the gap between Renaissance mysticism and modern science, and ensured that apocalypticism would never be dismissed as the delusions of a superstitious age.

CHAPTER 5

THE RADICAL ENLIGHTENMENT

If we were to look for a general characterization of the age of the Enlightenment," wrote Ernst Cassirer in his classic study of that period, "the traditional answer would be that its fundamental feature is obviously a critical and skeptical attitude toward religion."[1] Voltaire (1694–1778) claimed that religion began when the first rogue met the first fool, and in a famous letter to Frederick William of Prussia, coined his maxim "*Si Dieu n'existait pas, il faudrait l'inventer.*" The Encyclopedist Denis Diderot (1713–84) dreamed of the day when religion and tyranny would perish together as "the last king is strangled with the entrails of the last priest." This intellectual movement symbolized by Voltaire and Diderot is described in every European language through the use of a metaphor of light: *siècle des lumières, Aufklärung, illuminismo, ilustración,* Enlightenment. Only in the beginning of the eighteenth century, they believed, were the centuries of darkness finally dispelled and the blinding power of priestcraft broken, an achievement made secure by the achievements of the French Revolution.

Certainly this view of the Enlightenment period has a strong basis in fact, and like most stereotypes, it contains a hard kernel of truth. The key concept of the period was reason, by which was meant many different things. Some used the term to signify the demonstration of God's existence and attributes by the use of mathematically inclined proofs. Others used reason to study the miracles of the New Testament. Reason might also imply the formulation of Christian doctrine on the basis of eternal moral principles. But whichever understanding of reason was emphasized, its Christian protagonists were united in the belief that the human intellect was charged with studying and examining the rational elements of Christian belief in an effort to determine which parts of that faith could be shown to be true.

| **I** |

The French Revolution was a historical event of such importance that it could be described only in cosmic terms. Protestants throughout Europe saw the papacy as a particularly sinister combination of ecclesiastical and civil oppression. France withdrew its support for the pope and for Roman Catholicism in general during the Revolution, and thereby took the first and necessary step toward the millennium. The greatest of the Roman kingdoms disavowed the man of sin, the pope. The papacy in its turn played its required role by denouncing the French decisions and by portraying Napoleon as Antichrist as he laid waste the papal dominions in Italy.

The radical Protestant appreciation of the scene unfolding before them was almost immediate. Richard Price (1723–91), the Unitarian Presbyterian minister at Hackney in London, a former life insurance expert turned preacher, argued in a famous sermon, "A Discourse on the Love of our Country," that the English, American, and French Revolutions were rebellions against darkness, and that George III was a good king since he was the only one who owed his crown to his people, at least since the Glorious Revolution of 1688. Price sent a message of support to the French National Assembly, and his feelings were echoed by apocalyptically attuned people everywhere.[2] For such people, the millenarian signs were around them to be seen. They were taken up by James Bicheno, a very influential Dissenting schoolmaster and minister from Newbury in Berkshire. His work, which began appearing in 1793, saw the French Revolution as evidence of God fulfilling His prophecies. Bicheno continued to hold this view even after the defeat of Napoleon and the restoration of the Old Regime at the Congress of Vienna in 1815. His book *The Signs of the Times* went through five editions in the 1790s (and six in the United States). Bicheno tried to show that the symbols in the Book of Revelation—the dragon, the beasts, the horns—demonstrated that the combination of ecclesiastical and civil tyranny originated in the Roman Empire, whence it was transmitted to the papacy and to the ten successor monarchies of Rome, of which France was the most prominent. The Bourbon monarchy was therefore doubly oppressive as the promulgator of civil tyranny and the ally of religious oppression in Rome. He was convinced that the relationship between King Louis XVI and the papacy had signified the worst kind of oppressive alliance, and that the French king himself was the "beast" in the Book of Revelation. Indeed, he claimed, the Bourbons had been identified with persecution from the very beginning of their rule, the low points being the oppression of the Waldensians and the revocation of the Edict of Nantes, which had given limited freedom to French Protestants. Bicheno also pointed out that there were exactly 666 years between the reign of Hugh Capet (987) and the effective beginning of the reign of Louis XIV (1653). The only conclusion to be drawn, Bicheno argued, was that the French Revolution was more than a simple political rebellion, but was a divinely planned event of cosmic significance. Needless to say, Bicheno was somewhat more than embarrassed when God restored the Old Regime in 1815, but, undefeated, he produced another book, *The Fulfilment of Prophecy Further Illustrated*, in 1817, in which he worked this out as well, ever hopeful for a better future under the rule of the Messiah.

Bicheno, like others, claimed Isaac Newton as his great pioneer, for it was Newton who had predicted that when the Roman Antichrist declined, infidelity would take its place, which was what seemed to be happening in France. One could see that God sometimes used evil to bring about good. This is how the many-wived King Henry VIII had served God: a bad man who was responsible for the good Reformation. God might also use atheism to bring down popery, but one should not therefore conclude that He favored disbelief. The divine model was the Crucifixion: evil bringing about good.

The most important millenarian thinker during the years of the French Revolution, however, was undoubtedly Joseph Priestley (1733–1804). Clergyman, scientist, educator, Priestley would be studied alone for his discovery of oxygen, ammonia, sulfur dioxide, and for having invented soda water by working out how to inject carbon dioxide into water. He was also quick off the mark to recognize the apocalyptic significance of the French Revolution. His Fast Day sermon in 1794, "The Present State of Europe Compared with Ancient Prophecies," expressed a long preoccupation with current affairs. In a letter of 1771, Priestley had written, "I shall be looking for the downfall of Church and State together. I am really expecting some very calamitous, but finally glorious events."

Priestley supported the French Revolution absolutely, and indeed became a symbol of English sympathy for the regicides. After a dinner held in Birmingham on the second anniversary of Bastille Day, an enraged crowd attacked Dissenting meetinghouses and burned down Priestley's home and library. Priestley decamped to London, but after the execution of King Louis XVI in 1793, it was altogether too hot for him in England, and he sailed for Pennsylvania the following year. In the United States, he told John Adams that the French Revolution was the opening of a new era in the world and brought us closer to the millennium and the Second Coming of Christ, theories he developed in the following years.[3]

By 1797, Priestley was convinced that temporal power was at an end and that biblical prophecies were being fulfilled daily. Seven years later, he had already settled into a view that Jesus would personally appear on earth "in the clouds, so as to be seen by all," and would then rule until the general resurrection, governing the people of Israel. One problem was that the Jews must first convert to Christianity, and Priestley admitted that there were "no symptoms at present" of this happening. Another difficulty was that the Turkish Empire needed to fall as a precondition for the coming of the Messiah, particularly in order to prepare Palestine for receiving the newly converted Jews. Other preconditions included the breakup of the present European monarchies and the extinction of papal power. While these were daunting prospects, Priestley thought that the history of Europe during the era of the French Revolution showed that mankind was on the right track and that prophecy was being fulfilled as he wrote.

Where did these ideas come from? Many were Priestley's original elucidations of Scripture. Others came from his favorite thinkers. First among them was David Hartley (1705–57), whom he first heard about while a student in the 1750s and referred to him regularly thereafter. Hartley was the son of a diplomat friend of Benjamin Franklin's who signed the Treaty of Paris. Trying to create a scientifically up-to-date explanation of religious sentiments, he adapted Isaac Newton's notion that impressions of the senses are carried to the brain by means of vibrations along the nerves. A proper thought, then, is simply a combination of such vibrations, while passions are a mixture of simple ideas united by association. The upshot of Hartley's ideas was a denial that man was a combination of matter and spirit, and an argument that humanity was wholly material. This mechanistic interpretation was used even to posit the development of man's moral sense and his love of God. Hartley thought his associationist system actually promoted Christianity, and Priestley agreed.[4] Another influence was the American evangelist Elhanan Winchester, who also took a great interest in prophecy, fulfilled and unfulfilled.[5]

| II |

In a sense, however, all this scholarly activity was but a prelude to the practical application of messianic revolution in the notorious antics of Richard Brothers (1757–1824). This particular messiah was born in Placentia, Newfoundland, on Christmas Day 1757, where his father served as gunner in the local garrison. Anyone born in such a place on such an auspicious day was obviously destined for greatness. Brothers served in the British navy between the ages of fourteen and twenty-six, leaving it with the rank of lieutenant. Without attempting any amateur psychology, it should be obvious that this must have been the formative experience of his life, not only because of the discipline and unique circumstances of shipboard existence, but also because he must have had the opportunity to see places and cultures far removed from his own. He seems at least to have visited France, Spain, and Italy. When he turned up in London some years later, he had seen the world.[6]

He may have been a Baptist then, but in 1790, at the age of thirty-three, he underwent a profound religious conversion, which included a determination not to bear arms or swear oaths. While a relatively innocuous concession for many people, for Brothers the results were financially catastrophic, since he was thereafter unable to collect the navy pension which was due him, and which stood at the generous rate of half pay. His next port of call was the poor-house.

In 1792, Richard Brothers had a divine communication. On May 12 he wrote to King George III and other notables that God had commanded him to go to the House of Commons in five days' time to inform those present that the moment had come for the fulfillment of the seventh chapter of the Book of Daniel. Very little came of this dramatic declaration, but he followed his first communiqué with another in July, containing this time a number of important prophecies. It helps to be right in predicting the future, and Brothers was lucky that among his misses were some fairly significant hits. He predicted, for example, the violent deaths of King Louis XVI of France and the King of Sweden. By now, Richard Brothers was beginning to be noticed.

Things were going very well for him. From 1793, Richard Brothers began to describe himself as the "Nephew of the Almighty." He understood his surname as indicating that he was descended from King David through James, the brother of Jesus. In the hope that he might retain some family traits, Brothers set out to heal the blind, without success.

The following year Brothers published a book from his base at 57 Paddington Street in London, entitled *A Revealed Knowledge of the Prophecies and Times*. Much useful information was contained therein: it was a sort of diary of the future. He explained, for example, that on November 19, 1795, he himself would be revealed to be the Prince of the Hebrews, and Ruler of the World, and that the world as we know it would come to an end. This was to be the Second Coming. Three years later, in 1798, the rebuilding of Jerusalem would begin.

As might be expected, Brothers soon attracted quite a significant following. As might also be imagined, the government was unhappy about his prophetic second guessing, especially as he was sometimes right. He was arrested on March 4, 1795, under a warrant for treasonable practices and examined the next day before the Privy Council, which judged him within three weeks to be a criminal lunatic and sent him for confinement. In prison, but not forgotten, in the middle of April a famous picture of Richard Brothers was engraved by William Sharp, who had been a follower of Emanuel Swedenborg and later became a supporter of Joanna Southcott, two radical religious leaders we shall soon meet again.

Between then and 1806, Richard Brothers was kept in a private insane asylum in Islington, where he continued to write prophetic pamphlets and predict the future. Understandably, his movement suffered a blow when the Messiah apparently did not come in 1795; he had counted on the English government being severely embarrassed at having imprisoned the Messiah. Brothers was released in 1806, and continued to write, now mostly on astrology, and left off specific predictions. He died in 1824, and was buried in St. John's Wood cemetery not far from the grave of Joanna Southcott.

The life of Richard Brothers is not only entertaining but in itself also prophetic of future developments in messianic revolution. His message to the world altered the standard millenarianism he had received, and to a significant extent. For one thing, since he saw himself as the man who would lead the Jews to the Holy Land and undertake the rebuilding of Jerusalem, he drew up detailed plans for the great trek and for the new city of Jerusalem. The Jews he would lead were not merely "visible Hebrews," the sort of Jews one came across in late-eighteenth-century London, but rather "invisible Hebrews," the descendants of the Lost Ten Tribes, many of whom were living in England, he believed. Although Brothers himself was of the House of David, he identified his followers as belonging to various other tribes.

Though Richard Brothers never actively tried to establish a religious sect, he did hold court at 57 Paddington Street, and among those his works brought within the fold was Nathaniel Brassey Halhed, MP for Lymington, and an Oriental scholar. Halhed was no credulous provincial: he was ex-Christ Church, Oxford, a friend of Sheridan, a member of the East India Company, and an authority on Indian philology. Halhed converted to Brothers's views in January 1795, and twice raised the matter of the Messiah in the House of Commons, on March 31 and April 21, after Brothers had been arrested, but no one would second his motions, and this important issue was not discussed. Even Halhed, however, was shaken when November 1795 passed without supernatural incident. It seems in any case that what interested him was less Brothers's plan for leading the Jews to eternal glory than his having found scriptural proof for the necessity to make peace with revolutionary France. Like many earlier interpreters of the Bible in Cromwell's England, Halhed was keen to demonstrate divine approval for the course of action which he believed should be taken in the secular world.

Another man who fell under the spell of Brothers's writings was a lawyer from Edinburgh named John Finlayson (d. 1854), who eventually took over the publication of these works and their dissemination. Finlayson lobbied for Brothers's release, and managed to get the warrant for high treason quashed. After leaving the insane asylum, Brothers lived with him in Upper Baker Street until his death. Finlayson continued to fight for the prophet's good name until he himself died, having expended his fortune on this particular messiah.

Apart from his recommendation that peace should be made with revolutionary France, readers found comfort in Brothers's emphasis on prophecy and its use for interpreting contemporary events in a general sense. He believed in the importance of the inner light, of visions, dreams, and voices in the night. Like many of his predecessors from Savonarola to Cromwell, he also condemned the vices of modern society, and the turning away from the eternal values of religion.

In a sense, Brothers's mission was taken up by Joanna Southcott (1750–1814). She was born a farmer's daughter in Devon, and at the appropriate age went into domestic service. From the age of thirty she was involved with the Methodists, and formally joined them at Exeter in 1792, although she seems to have returned later to Anglicanism. This was the year in which she became divinely inspired, significantly, the same year that Richard Brothers received messages from on high. Between 1792 and 1814 she wrote about sixty-five pamphlets, and many unpublished manuscripts have also survived.[7] Of this body of material, about a fourth of the printed works consisted of her own history and commentary on current affairs. The remainder was commentary from the Spirit and interpretations of Scripture. Sadly, much of Southcott's material remains shrouded in mystery, since her handwriting is nearly impenetrable.

Her fame preceding her, Joanna Southcott was invited to stay in London in May 1802, where there was a small group of Richard Brothers's followers. But she refused to pay attention to Brothers's prophecies or indeed even to read them. She acknowledged one source of inspiration alone: the Holy Spirit. Indeed, she would later argue that Brothers's prophecies were blasphemous, inspired by the Devil himself. But like Brothers, she attracted a good deal of public support, and like him, she did not address public meetings, in her case because she was a very bad speaker.

Joanna Southcott honed her prophetical art to an even sharper point. She would "seal" up her prophecies with the intention that they be opened by authorized judges to see if they had come true in the meantime. These prophecies were written on half sheets of paper which she signed and gave to her followers, and the grandiose "seal" was actually a piece of bric-a-brac that she found in 1790 when sweeping up a shop after a sale, an oval seal bearing the initials IC, set off above and below by a star. It was perfect for the job. By the autumn of 1807, she had sealed up 14,000 prophecies. Some were bound to be right.

She may have learned from her experience of the Wesley brothers and Methodism that the Established Church was unsympathetic to apocalyptic movements, which had the dangerous tendency of getting out of control. It was inevitable, really, that she would be compelled to establish her own sect, even if she initially had no intention of leaving the Anglican Church. Within a short time she had three chapels in London and others at Exeter, Bath, Bristol, Leeds, Stockport, and Ashton-under-Lyme. She herself eventually settled in at Rock Cottage, in the Cotswold village of Blockley. She too had her portrait engraved by William Sharp, who did the work in January 1812.

Joanna had studied very closely the twelfth chapter of the Book of Revelation:

And there appeared a great wonder in heaven; a woman clothed with the sun, and the moon under her feet, and upon her head a crown of twelve stars:

And she being with child cried, travailing in birth, and pained to be delivered . . .

And she brought forth a man child, who was to rule all nations with a rod of iron: and her child was caught up unto God, and *to* his throne.

She became convinced that she was that woman, and in 1814, at the advanced age of sixty-five, she was informed from the heavens that she would give birth to a son, who would be named Shiloh in accordance with Genesis 49:10. Joanna Southcott revealed that it would be a virgin birth, although for form's sake she married a man improbably named John Smith, about her own age, who was steward to the earl of Darnley. Her faith was so strong that she actually developed signs of pregnancy, so convincing that six of the nine doctors consulted confirmed that she was with child.

Alas, there was no birth, and the signs of pregnancy gradually abated. Joanna Southcott died on December 27, 1814, in London. To the surprise of many of her followers, she was not resurrected on the fourth day, and was buried at St. John's Wood cemetery, where Richard Brothers would be laid to rest ten years later.

Like Richard Brothers, Joanna Southcott had a definite message and an even more clearly visible movement. She claimed that she had "sealed" about 20,000 followers by 1815, and we do have the names and addresses of about 7,000 of them. A little less than a third came from London, and more than a quarter from Yorkshire. The occupations are hard to tell, but the movement was about two-thirds women, and about two-thirds single people, men and women. In this, Southcott's sect was not so very different from millenarian sects elsewhere. The services in her group were identical to those of Anglican rite, with the addition of Southcottian hymns, and the omission of the Eucharist, but wine was passed around as a symbol.

Her followers were not very strong on organization, although she did retain hundreds of believers years after her death.

Joanna Southcott's mantle was taken up posthumously by various would-be successors. The first was Thomas Philip Foley (1758?– 1835), a Worcestershire clergyman who tried to convince Southcott's followers that it was no accident that no miraculous birth had taken place, for God intended this to be a *spiritual* rather than a carnal child. Another successor was George Turner, a merchant from Leeds who tried to turn himself into a second Richard Brothers, giving the Jews an important role in his prophecies. He suffered the same fate, being sent to an insane asylum in Yorkshire. Turner also fixed the date of the Second Coming, in his case October 14, 1820, later revised to April 10, 1821. Another would-be replacement for Joanna Southcott was Mary Book, a.k.a. Mary Joanna, the illiterate wife of a shoemaker, whose chief disciple from about 1821 was John Field, a stonemason, who commanded his followers to observe the Jewish law, including the Sabbath.

The most successful of those who carried on the Southcott torch was John Wroe (1782–1863), who had never met her personally, but came into contact with her followers. Wroe had received a divine message commanding him to become a Jew. He hurried to the synagogue in Liverpool, but was not accepted into the fold. The same disappointment followed him in London. After George Turner's death, Wroe tried to take over the entire Southcottian movement, but he remained schismatic. He also traveled extensively in Europe, visiting synagogues and trying to drum up support. Wroe's movement was centered at Bradford and Ashton-under-Lyme, but after various charges against him in 1831 he shifted his base to Wakefield, and spent more time on missionary tours to America and Australia. It was on one of these that he died in Melbourne in 1863.

| **III** |

The Southcottians became extinct and with them their distinctive and original theology, though in their time they had a good deal of success. The Swedenborgians suffered a reverse fate, since their longevity as a rather eccentric but by no means unsuccessful religious sect has had the effect of trivializing their interpretation of the Bible and of Christian metaphysics. In the long run, Emanuel Swedenborg (1688–1772) would be a decisive influence on later millenarians and mystics as diverse as Madame Blavatsky and the Reverend Sun Myung Moon. Swedenborg was a scientist and philosopher of the first rank, whose religious views were unremarkable until he was in his middle fifties. He is important for us in another way as well, for he provides a link and a channel into the world of the "radical Enlightenment," where his followers mixed with Freemasons and neo-Rosicrucians in an attempt to find the keys that would unlock the occult secrets of the universe. Margaret Jacob has argued that in order to understand the origins of "our politics and of democratic discourse" we should look back to the lodges of the eighteenth-century Freemasons: "Rather than imagining the Enlightenment as represented by the politics of Voltaire, or Gibbon, or even Rousseau, or worse as being incapable of politics, we might just as fruitfully look to the lodges for a nascent political modernity."[8] While her thesis has not met with universal acceptance, her notion of a "radical Enlightenment," centering on exclusivist societies such as the Freemasons, deserves further investigation. J. M. Roberts, in his pioneering study of secret societies, points out that in the *ancien régime* there was little scope for private activity outside the family, but that all this began to change in the early eighteenth century with the appearance in England of coffeehouses, clubs, and salons and exclusivist societies such as the Freemasons. England played a large part in this fashion, in part because England itself was fashionable in the first third of the eighteenth century. "*La prépondérance anglaise*," Roberts reminds us, was felt in a variety of spheres, in politics, in the army, and in economy, but also in the intellectual world. Newton and Locke had barely left the stage, advanced religious toleration was apparent, social mobility was a byword, and parliamentary rule a comparative reality. England's development of a lively, attractive culture and society during those years in part accounts for the success of Freemasonry, which first flourished there and then abroad, especially in France.[9]

So too can "Anglomania"—an eighteenth-century word—be used to account for the Swedish connection. Swedenborg made at least eleven visits to England, living at Cheapside but avoiding public notoriety, not so much because of his opinions as because of poor English made even more opaque by a speech impediment. By the time he died in London in 1772 and was buried in the Swedish Church there, he had delineated an impressive philosophy more suited to an intellectual school than a radical religious sect. Swedenborgianism was also out of step for another reason, in that he and his followers opposed the Newtonian synthesis because they themselves were materialists in their philosophy (albeit of a unique kind) and thought that Newton was attributing occult properties to matter which should be seen as inert.

Emanuel Swedenborg was born in Stockholm in 1688, the son of a distinguished Swedish theologian. His father changed his name from Swedberg when ennobled in 1719, for his work as court chaplain, professor of theology at Uppsala, and bishop of Skara. Emanuel studied at Uppsala until 1709, and then spent five years abroad, in England, France, and the Netherlands, where his primary aim was to learn of the latest advances in mathematics and natural science. Swedenborg seems to have come under the strong influence of Eric Benzelius, his brother-in-law, who was mystically inclined, visiting Leibniz at Hanover in 1697, moving on to Francis Mercurius van Helmont to sort out the Pythagorean Cabala, and traveling to London to meet with members of the Philadelphian Society. Returning to Sweden in 1700, Benzelius turned more seriously to the study of Hebrew, using the services of a converted Jew named Johan Kemper. The two men worked on a cabalistic interpretation of the New Testament and on annotations to Philo, and talked of founding a pansophic college in Sweden. The young Swedenborg lived in Benzelius's house from 1703 and was surrounded by this combination of arcane scholarship and mystical lore.[10]

Swedenborg came to England in 1710, despite the tense political relations between Sweden and England in the run-up to the Jacobite rebellion in Scotland, "The Fifteen." There he came under the wing of the Swedish ambassador and may have been involved in revolutionary Jacobite and Freemason circles. He had the opportunity to meet, and may have met, such luminaries as William Penn and Lord Bolingbroke. He seems to have visited Dr. Jean Esdras Edzardi, whose family had converted many Jews in Hamburg by devising a convincing mixture of cabala and the New Testament. It has sometimes been claimed that Swedenborg himself joined a Masonic lodge, but as its politics would have been Jacobite, all records of it were destroyed after the failure of the rebellion in 1715.

With perfect hindsight, Swedenborg's activities during those years do look like an ideal preparation for holding the occult views for which he became known. But here too it is possible to exaggerate. When in Hanover, he tried to pay a call on Leibniz, but found him away in Vienna. Swedenborg was following in the footsteps of Benzelius, but the discussion he and Leibniz might have had would surely not have touched only on esoteric matters. Swedenborg's relations with Rabbi Falk, the so-called Baal Shem of London, a mystical magician whose exploits made him a well-known figure in late-eighteenth-century London, are more than mystifying. In his commonplace book, Falk makes a reference to a certain "Emanuel, a servant of the king of France," which may refer to Swedenborg, with his Jacobite leanings.

In any case, it was at Wellclose Square, near Falk's house, that Swedenborg had his first vision of Christ, on April 7, 1744, and only a year later that his mission was divinely confirmed. His life was never the same. Swedenborg spent the remaining twenty-seven years dedicated to purely religious questions, publishing about thirty books, all in Latin, mostly anonymously. That in itself points to the nature of Swedenborgianism as an esoteric philosophy more than a mass movement, and his theology should be seen in a more serious context than has often been the case. We need to examine his mature philosophy in light of his claim that he received his ideas from personal visits to the spiritual world rather than from mere reflection.

Swedenborg's goal was no less than to discover the substance that held the universe together. This task was complicated by his insistence that the world had more than a simple natural or physical aspect. He tinkered with the idea of magnetism and settled on the notion that the common bond was some sort of electrical vibration or very fine indestructible substance. This latter, he believed, was the soul of man, which not only was immortal but had actual dimensions. The spiritual and natural worlds, therefore, were merely different manifestations of the same substance. (Here Swedenborg revealed himself as a student of Descartes's body/soul/mind debate, and indeed his thought is thoroughgoingly Cartesian.) Influenced by Leibniz, Swedenborg elaborated that all life derived from a single source but was organized on different levels or *series*: natural/physical, rational/living/intelligent/moral, and spiritual. Every particular object in the universe, therefore, had its own place or *degree* in each of these three series and these parallels were called *correspondences*. Swedenborg was also influenced by the platonic idea that none of the series could survive without a constant *influx* or spiritual input from God, the spiritual sun. Each degree or item in each series enjoyed a particular influx, which passed through the spiritual series, down through the rational, and finally the natural series. As a result, each item or degree on the spiritual plane had its exact counterpart with another item on the rational and natural planes, united because touched by the same influx. These axioms had platonic consequences, so that man's love and wisdom found perfect expression in the essence of God on a higher plane. Swedenborg was also anti-Trinitarian: Christ was God in human form, and at the Crucifixion, God retained some human aspects which he maintains on His highest plane, making him a sort of divine human.[11]

Swedenborg saw himself as commissioned to announce the seventh and last revelation to a New Church, the body described as the New Jerusalem in the Book of Revelation. This organization commenced in 1757 when Jesus returned to earth, not as an inferior fleshly messiah but in an interior and spiritual way, by opening the eyes of men to the true meaning of the Bible. Swedenborg's Bible was somewhat shorter than the usual version, as he excluded thirty-seven of its sixty-six books on the grounds that they were bereft of spiritual meaning. Nevertheless, he had great respect for the surviving Scriptures, and his colossal *Arcana Coelestia* was in effect an extended and unfinished commentary on Genesis and Exodus.

In his last work, *The True Christian Religion* (1771), we get the clearest epitome of his thinking on this subject, as on most others. Here Swedenborg approached the difficulties in extracting holy truth from the Bible:

> The natural man, however, cannot thus be persuaded to believe that the Word is divine truth itself, in which are divine wisdom and divine life; for he judges it by its style which reveals no such things. Yet the style of the Word is a truly divine style, with which no other however lofty and excellent can be compared. The style of the Word is such that it is holy in every sentence, in every word, and sometimes in every letter; and therefore the Word unites man to the Lord and opens heaven.

The cabalistic tincture of this sentiment needs hardly to be spelled out. Indeed, Swedenborg's theory of correspondences, when specifically applied to Scripture, takes on more than a superficial cabalistic tone:

That everything in nature and in the human body corresponds to spiritual things is shown in *Heaven and Hell*. But what correspondence is, has been hitherto unknown, although it was perfectly understood in the most ancient times; for to the men of that time the science of correspondence was the science of sciences, and was so universal that all their manuscripts and books were written by correspondences. The book of Job, a book of the ancient church, is full of correspondences. The hieroglyphics of the Egyptians and the myths of antiquity were the same. All the ancient churches were representative of spiritual things; the ceremonial laws of their worship were pure correspondences; so was everything in the Israelitish church. The burnt-offerings, sacrifices, meat-offerings and drink-offerings were correspondences in every detail; so was the tabernacle with everything in it; and also the feasts of unleavened bread, of tabernacles, and of first fruits; also the priesthood of Aaron and the Levites and their holy garments . . . Moreover, all the laws and judgments relating to their worship and life were correspondences. Now, because divine things manifest themselves in the world by correspondences, the Word was written by pure correspondences; and for the same reason, the Lord, because He spoke from the divinity, spoke from correspondences. For everything from the divinity flows into such natural things as correspond thereto; and these outward things then conceal in their depth the divine things called celestial and spiritual.

Here, in this long extract, we see some of the key elements of Swedenborg's mystical biblical interpretation. Like the cabalists, he thought that there was another parallel meaning to the scriptural word. Like the Deists and many others before them, including Maimonides, he championed the notion of "accommodation," arguing that God had adapted His message to the ability of His hearers to comprehend what He was saying, but reserving a deeper meaning for those with greater spiritual insight. Like Isaac Newton, Swedenborg advocated a prolonged close reading of biblical texts by the use of techniques which had been vouchsafed to him alone, in order to undermine the surface reading and penetrate to the divine truths lurking below.[12]

Interestingly, Swedenborg also showed some similarity to deistical biblical critics in his fascination with the contribution made by other ancient peoples to our understanding of God's word. According to Swedenborg, he had "been informed" by the spirit world that "the men of the most ancient church, which existed before the flood, were of so heavenly a genius that they conversed with the angels of heaven; and that they had the power to do so by correspondences." As a result, whenever they saw something on earth, they were able to determine its corresponding form on the spiritual plane. Swedenborg also reported that "Enoch and his associates [Genesis 5:21–24] made a glossary of correspondences from the speech of the angels, and transmitted this knowledge to posterity." This claim was to have enormous consequences. "As a result," Swedenborg explains, "the science of correspondences flourished in many kingdoms of Asia, particularly in Canaan, Egypt, Assyria, Chaldea, Syria, Arabia, Tyre, Sidon, and Nineveh, and was thence communicated to Greece, where it became mythical, as may be seen from the oldest Greek literature." We can see, therefore, he explains, that

> religion has existed from the most ancient times, and the inhabitants of the earth everywhere have a knowledge of God and some knowledge of life after death; but this is not from themselves or their own intelligence, but from the ancient Word, and afterwards from the Israelitish Word. From these two Words religion spread to India and its islands, through Egypt and Ethiopia to the kingdoms of Africa, from the maritime parts of Asia to Greece, and thence to Italy. But, as the Word could only be written symbolically, that is, by mundane

things corresponding to and therefore signifying heavenly
things, the religion of the Gentiles became idolatrous, and in
Greece mythical; and the divine properties and attributes were
looked upon as so many gods, dominated by a supreme deity
called Jove, possibly from Jehovah. And they had a knowledge
of paradise, the flood, the sacred fire, and the four ages, from
the golden age to that of iron (Daniel 2:31–35).

In orthodox fashion, if somewhat eccentrically, Swedenborg thereby
postulates the Hebrews as the source of eternal wisdom, a little
lower than the angels.[13]

Swedenborg also sought to account for the evident degeneration
of the Hebrews from purveyors of a divine monopoly to the superstitious Jews with whom his readers, we presume, were familiar. In
his view, in "the course of time the representative rites of the
church, which were correspondences, began to be turned into idolatry and also into magic." It was not by accident but by "the divine
providence of the Lord" that the Israelites lost the "science of correspondences," which eventually "amongst the Israelitish and Jewish nation [was] totally obliterated." Since their worship consisted
entirely of correspondences, this was a crucial loss, and what had
originally been a symbolic and pure worship gradually became superstition. Not only the Jews but other ancient peoples began to
confuse the symbol with the thought expressed and, for example,
worshipped images of calves and oxen, forgetting that originally
they were powerless objects which merely signified "the affections
and powers of the natural man." Fortunately, the "knowledge of
correspondences remained among many eastern nations, even till
the coming of the Lord." This is why the wise men came from the
east, bearing symbolic gifts. Indeed, the "ancient Word, which existed in Asia before the Israelitish Word, is still preserved among
the people of Great Tartary," a fact which was personally confirmed
to Swedenborg by "spirits and angels who came from that country."
"But the science of correspondences was completely unknown to

the Israelitish and Jewish nation, although all the details of their worship, and all the statutes and judgments given them by Moses, and everything contained in the Word, were pure correspondences." Apart from divine intention, the reason for this is that Jews "were at heart idolaters" and were interested more in the ceremonies than in their spiritual meaning. This is also why they were unable to recognize the messianic role of Jesus, since they were prepared for a messiah who would give them an earthly kingdom and "who should exalt them above all the nations in the world, and not one who should take care of their eternal salvation."[14]

According to Swedenborg, the "science of correspondences, which is the key to the spiritual sense of the Word, is to-day revealed, because the divine truths of the church are now being brought to light." This was a truth which he had been taught during his sojourns in the spiritual world, and his description of the Bible there was truly fantastic. In that higher place, he recalled,

the Word is kept in the shrines of the angelic temples and shines like a great star, sometimes like the sun with a halo of beautiful rainbows; this occurs when the shrine is first opened. All the truths of the Word shine, as I learnt on seeing that, when any verse is written on paper and thrown into the air, the very paper shines in the form in which it has been cut; so that spirits can by the Word produce various shining forms, even those of birds and fishes. But what is still more wonderful, if any person rubs his face, hands, or clothes against the open Word, so as to touch the writing, his face, hands, and clothes shine as if he were standing in the brilliance of a star. This I have often seen with wonder; and it showed me why the face of Moses shone when he brought down the tables of the covenant from Mount Sinai.

On the other hand, sometimes an opposite process also occurred in the spiritual world, for

> if any person obsessed by falsities looks at the Word lying in its sacred place, darkness shrouds his eyes, and the Word appears to him black and sometimes as if covered with soot; while, if he touches the Word, a loud explosion follows, and he is hurled into a corner of the room, where he lies for a time as if dead. If any one obsessed by falsity writes a passage from the Word on a piece of paper and throws it in the air, a similar explosion follows, and the paper is torn to pieces and vanishes; the same thing happens if the paper is thrown into the nearest corner. This I have often seen.

While somewhat cabalistic in flavor, then, Swedenborg's attitude toward the biblical text was, if possible, even more mystical, based on what he believed himself to have witnessed in the spiritual world.[15]

Swedenborg's view of the Hebrew language itself was original. "There was once sent down to me from heaven," he revealed,

> a piece of paper covered with Hebrew characters; the letters were curved as among the ancients, not straight as they are to-day, and had little extensions at the top. The angels with me said that each letter had a complete meaning which was largely expressed by the curves and their extensions . . . They told me that writing in the third heaven consists of letters variously curved and inflected, each of which has a special meaning; that the vowels I and E are replaced by Y and EU, and that A, O, and U have a specially rich sound; that they do not pronounce consonants roughly, but smoothly, and for this reason some Hebrew letters had dots in them to indicate a soft pronunciation. They added that hard sounds are used in the spiritual heaven because the truth of that heaven admits of hardness, whereas the good of the Lord's celestial kingdom, or third heaven, does not.

Like the cabalists, Swedenborg also thought that the very words and letters of the Bible had mystical powers which awaited deciphering by illuminati.[16]

Certainly, it is very difficult to argue with a man who claimed to "have been permitted by the Lord to be in the spiritual and natural worlds at one and the same time; thus I have conversed with angels as with men, and have become acquainted with the state of those who after death pass into that hitherto unknown world." Heaven, he revealed, was constituted as a *homo maximus*, a giant man, with the parts of his body consisting of angels. Swedenborg testified that he had "conversed with all my relatives and friends, also with departed kings, dukes and men of learning, and this continually for twenty-seven years."[17] Sometimes entrance was gained by the technique of taking one breath every thirty minutes.

Apart from spirits and angels, other sources for Swedenborg's interesting biblical theology suggest themselves. Chief among these is Jacob Boehme (1575–1624), the German mystic who became notorious for stressing the dualism of God, which required evil as a complement to His divine goodness. Boehme's most famous disciple in Swedenborg's time was William Law (1686–1762), whose influence on the Wesleys and connection with the Philadelphian Society of Jane Lead and Francis Lee are well documented. Swedenborg denied having read Boehme, but his thought showed some very obvious similarities with Law's theology. Among these was the notion that God emits an "eternal nature," His very body and being—in effect the spiritual world. This higher reality had its counterpart in a lower celestial realm made up of the opposing principles to be found in God's nature—fire/light, good/evil, and so on—this was the angelic world. Below this was an even lower existence, the material world, created by the rebellion of the angels, in which the dualities were no longer in balance. Connections and analogies among the three different levels existed and remained in operation. Man himself, originally an angel and now a denizen of the material world, was in effect a spirit trapped in a physical body. Jesus, by taking human form, injected a divine element into mankind, providing hope for his restoration to the spiritual existence. Law, unlike Boehme, was optimistic that this reunion would eventually occur, hell would be destroyed, and all mankind would be saved. Swedenborg's ideas were so similar that he appealed to many old Boehmenists, such as Thomas Hartley (1709–84), whose influence on Samuel Taylor Coleridge (1772–1834) is well known.[18]

Swedenborgianism thus began as a philosophy and only gradually mutated into a sect, largely through having been picked up by the rector of a Manchester parish named John Clowes (1734–1831), a former member of Wesley's "Holy Club" who had begun with the writings of William Law and chanced upon Swedenborg's Latin works in 1773. Clowes remained within the bosom of the Anglican Church, but he refused a bishopric in 1804 and introduced as much of Swedenborg's views into his sermons as he thought the market would bear. The new gospel spread throughout Lancashire, at the same time that the Methodists were making important inroads in this area. Both groups began within the established Anglican Church and only later, and reluctantly, declared their independence from it. Furthermore, the Methodists, like the followers of Swedenborg, placed great emphasis on nonrational religious revelation, convulsions rather than visions, but nevertheless was part of the same mixture of folk traditions and respectable religion.

John Wesley, the founder of Methodism, was himself of two minds about this strange alliance. He wrote about Swedenborg in his journal: "Any one of his visions puts his real character out of doubt. He is one of the most ingenious, lively, entertaining madmen that ever set pen to paper. But his waking dreams are so wild, so far remote both from Scripture and common sense, that one might as easily swallow the stories of 'Tom Thumb' or 'Jack the Giant-killer.'" Later on, after reading Swedenborg's *Theologia Coelestis*, Wesley added, "It surely contains many excellent things. Yet I cannot but think the fever he had twenty years ago, when he supposes he was 'introduced into the society of angels,' really introduced him to the society of lunatics; but still there is something noble, even in his ravings."[19] Similarly, a certain amount of migration took place between the two groups at the popular level, especially when the Methodist chapel became too much a symbol of respectability for many Lancashire workers. Swedenborgianism also appealed to groups outside the Methodist sphere of influence, such as those in the Huguenot community, attracted no doubt by Swedenborg's connection with Freemasonry and other European occultists, such as the French Prophets.

Like the Methodists, the Swedenborgians found themselves drawn almost inevitably into institutionalization, although one group opposed to separation gathered around Jacob Duché, chaplain of an Asylum for Female Orphans in Lambeth. Their first step was the foundation in about 1783 of the Theosophical Society, which read and discussed Swedenborg's works. The great man's manuscripts had been shipped back to Sweden after his death, where they could not be published but were now beginning to appear in greater numbers, thanks to Clowes's determination and effort. The very word "theosophical" was redolent of Freemasonry, promising a combination of biblical study and fashionable Neoplatonism. One of their prominent members, Lieutenant General Charles Rainsford, governor of Gibraltar, was involved with Cabala, Freemasonry, alchemy, and astrology. Continental Freemasonic circles were informed, aware, and excited by the existence of Swedenborgian reading groups in England, and these contacts were extended during the 1780s. Rainsford was an important link, and he promoted the Swedenborgian visitation at the Congrès du Philalethes, organized by the French speculative Freemasonic lodge of the Amis Réunis in 1784–85, and again in 1787. Swedenborgian representatives attended the meeting in 1784, which had primarily been called to unite Freemasons on the Continent and to agree on some common elements of doctrine. As a result, some of its leading lights came to England to see the new philosophy for themselves, including the Marquis de Thomé, Count Tadeusz Grabianka, and even the notorious "Count" Cagliostro, champion of "Reformed Egyptian Freemasonry," who would end his life a prisoner in a tiny Inquisition cell.[20]

This occult tinge was given a somewhat more Christian, less "pagan" motif in 1785 when, on the advice of Thomé, the group renamed itself the "Society for Promoting the Heavenly Doctrines of the New Church designed by the New Jerusalem in the Revelation of St. John." One virtue of the new name is that it preserved a key element of Swedenborgianism's attraction: its almost Romantic emphasis on spirituality, as opposed to the rationalism of the Enlightenment. Far from being a theological system opposed to empirical science, Swedenborgianism might be seen as a truly pioneering creed, extending the principle of experimentation to the spiritual realm. Most people believed that spiritual forces were at work in our material world; the Swedenborgians were the first to do something about it and, unlike the Methodists, were not so quick to ascribe these powers to the Devil.[21]

By 1788 it was clear that Swedenborg's followers would have to open their own chapel, and their society was renamed the New Church. Ordinations and baptisms soon began, and the group settled into the traditional pattern of English Dissent, without giving up the occult impulses which created it in the first place. Swedenborg's voluminous writings assumed the character of a third testament, and the man himself was increasingly venerated. The New Church underwent a crisis when Swedenborg's *Conjugal Love* was translated into English and published in 1794, for in this book he declared that a man could take a "concubine" to slake his lust or even to leave his lawful wife if he found a more fitting spiritual partner at a later stage. They were also accused, by the Abbé Barruel and others, of being, like the Deists, an illuminist sect that was indirectly responsible for the French Revolution and the political disturbances of the age. The postmillennial theology of the Swedenborgians, it was said, in claiming that Christ had already returned, also called on believers to be alert for manifestations of his renewed glory, which most obviously could include revolutionary political change. The Unitarians were also postmillennialist, and the Swedenborgians seems to have lost many followers to that less demanding sect. By the turn of the century, they were insisting that the Second Coming was spiritual rather than political, and did not involve a restructuring of national governments. But by then their period of dramatic expansion had ended.

The Swedenborgians became more respectable and even more intellectual, especially under the leadership of Samuel Noble (1779–1853), who was chiefly interested in publishing accurate translations of the founder's writings. This more philosophical inclination, which probably would have been blessed by Swedenborg himself, ensured that they would never become a truly popular sect. Not only were the books in Latin, but it took a very long time before more simplified versions of Swedenborg's writings appeared. In any case, Swedenborg's theology was contemplative, more than congregational or social, and was unsuited for the sort of passionate community that the Methodists engendered. Even if congregations in the north of England attracted locally active artisans and other people, in the south Swedenborg retained a decidedly intellectual tinge. This was not to everyone's taste, as the poet William Blake discovered.

Blake had been a follower of Swedenborg, but by 1790 he already had severe doubts. "Thus Swedenborg boasts that what he writes is new; tho' it is only the Contents or Index of already publish'd books," he complained,

> A man carried a monkey about for a shew, & because he was a little wiser than the monkey, grew vain, and conciev'd himself as much wiser than seven men. It is so with Swedenborg: he shews the folly of churches, & exposes hypocrites, till he imagines that all are religious, & himself the single one on earth that ever broke a net.

Now hear a plain fact: Swedenborg has not written one new truth. Now hear another: he has written all the old falshoods.

Blake was cross partly because in his view Swedenborg's theology was not completely original: "Thus Swedenborg's writings are a recapitulation of all superficial opinions, and an analysis of the more sublime—but no further." Indeed, he wrote, "any man of mechanical talents may, from the writings of Paracelsus or Jacob Behmen, produce ten thousand volumes of equal value with Swedenborg's, and from those of Dante or Shakespear an infinite number."[22] The fact was, that despite Swedenborg's frequent conversations with angels and other spiritual beings, his writing was in the last analysis simply an amplification and exposition of the Bible, or at least those chapters that were left after he wielded his pruning hook on the text. Yet Swedenborgianism was enormously influential on an entire group of writers and poets, not only Blake but also Balzac, Baudelaire, Emerson, Yeats, and Strindberg. Indeed, one almost hears Swedenborg talking of a "chain of signifiers" when he writes about the world of correspondences, and for that alone we should be wary of putting him too firmly *"sous rature."*

| **IV** |

Even more than these colorful individuals, however, there was no doubt that the most dominant millenarian figure of these years was Napoleon Bonaparte himself. In rapid succession, Napoleon had done such amazing prophetic things as capturing the pope, deposing the kings of this world, and appointing new rulers (mostly his relatives) in their place. But what really seized the imagination of millenarian contemporaries was the news that Napoleon intended to call the Grand Sanhedrin of Jews into session in Paris.[23]

The Sanhedrin was the ancient governing body of the Jewish world before the Roman conquest of Jerusalem in 68–70 A.D. One brief attempt to reconvene this assembly had occurred in the second century, but thereafter it was believed that it could be reestablished only by the Messiah, who, when He came, would know who might be appointed among the prescribed seventy members. Despite this prevailing belief, Napoleon on his return from a glorious victory at Austerlitz in 1805 astonished the Jewish world by announcing his intention to call a Sanhedrin into being in Paris whose brief it would be to bring about the reconciliation of Jewish and French law.

Napoleon did not enter into this task without having properly researched the question. He knew that he could not be the one to appoint delegates to a Sanhedrin, so he took the preliminary step of calling for an assembly of Jewish notables from various parts of his empire who would meet in Paris in order to select representatives to that venerable body. The Abbé Grégoire, who was in contact with various Jewish leaders, became the unofficial adviser to the leaders of French Jewry regarding the proper answers to Napoleon's questions.[24] Certainly at this early stage, it was not clear what Napoleon's motives actually were.

According to Napoleon's decree of May 1806, an assembly of Jewish notables was to meet in order to discuss how "to make the Jews useful citizens, to reconcile their beliefs with the duties of Frenchmen." The 111 delegates were to be selected by local prefects among the wealthy Jews of France and northern Italy. The two leading figures in this strange gathering were Abraham Furtado, its president, and Rabbi David Sinzheim of Strasbourg, a distinguished scholar who was immediately at odds with the spirit of religion which his colleague represented. Napoleon's representatives immediately put twelve questions to these notables, some of which touched controversial issues such as polygamy, divorce, intermarriage, and the taking of usury. They were also asked whether "Frenchmen are considered brothers or strangers," and if they "acknowledge France as their country," and if so, whether they are bound to serve in her army and obey her laws. Guided by Sinzheim, the notables managed to steer their way around the rocks and shoals of these tricky questions and to provide satisfactory answers. The Grand Sanhedrin could now go forward.

European Jewry was less enthusiastic than the Emperor about the wisdom of the enterprise. The Jews of France had no choice but to send delegates; outside of France itself, Frankfurt did send representatives, but the city was under Napoleon's direct rule. The Jews of Amsterdam were also wary, and the men who claimed to represent them at the Sanhedrin in fact represented only the reformist Felix Libertate Society rather than the mainstream synagogues. Some communities from northern Italy were also represented. In the end, the members of the Grand Sanhedrin of 1807 were very nearly the same Jews who had sat in the Assembly of Notables.

Napoleon himself opened the Grand Sanhedrin with great pomp and ceremony, presenting it as the ancient assembly revived by the Emperor to sit again as in its days of glory. The Sanhedrin ratified the decisions of the preliminary Assembly of Notables, and proclaimed them laws binding on Jews everywhere. But apart from these and other grand gestures, the delegates had no real role to play. They adjourned and never were called to sit again.

Certainly, there was much more to Napoleon's Jewish policy than the theatrical gesture of the Grand Sanhedrin of 1807. Jews in France felt directly the way he reorganized the Jewish religion into twelve regional consistories, headed by a Chief Rabbi sitting in Paris. Napoleon also compelled Jews to take surnames. He also issued his "infamous decrees," which placed limitations on Jewish economic activity. Still, the Sanhedrin was a historical moment on a messianic scale, and the effects of its summoning went far beyond the severe limitations of its achievements.

In the Jewish philosopher Martin Buber's novel *For the Sake of Heaven*, he tells the story of a small Hasidic group near Vilna in Lithuania, trying to understand the meaning of the exciting developments in France. Their messianic excitement is heightened with every new bit of information about Napoleon's success; then their hopes are dashed after Waterloo. Indeed, many people outside France saw Napoleon as a rather more diabolical than messianic figure. There is some evidence that the first version of the *Protocols of the Elders of Zion* was written by an opponent of Napoleon in his police network, who tried to demonstrate that the Emperor was in league with diabolical Jews to destroy both France and Christianity.[25] On the other hand, an Irish revolutionary who had become a high-ranking officer in Napoleon's army proposed to create a consortium of Irish radicals, French army officers, and Jewish bankers to take over the world once the Emperor was unable to do so.[26]

A most interesting if bizarre offshoot of the Paris Sanhedrin developed in the United States, where an actual attempt was made to inaugurate a Jewish state. Mordecai Noah, an American Jew who had some success as a journalist, a playwright, and a politician (he was one of the founders of Tammany Hall), was in Paris in 1815, on his way to taking up his post as American consul in Tunis. In Paris he met the Abbé Grégoire and learned about the Paris Sanhedrin. His experiences in North Africa and his firsthand observations of the dreadful conditions of the Jews there inspired him to work for his people on his return to the United States. Back in America, Noah declared himself Chief Judge of Israel, and agitated for the inauguration of a Jewish state on Grand Island, in the Niagara River, between its famous falls and Buffalo, New York. According to the plan, the members of the Paris Sanhedrin were to lend their names to this endeavor and thereby give it international legitimacy. Noah managed to get the state of New York to pass a law establishing his Jewish state, which he called Ararat, although the New York legislature insisted that the United States Constitution apply there as well, guaranteeing the rights of gentiles who wished to settle on the island. Noah made it clear that he had no intention of establishing the sole messianic Jewish state but merely a preliminary place to which Jews might come from all over the world, gathering and preparing for their deliverance and their removal to Palestine, then still under Turkish control. Noah intended to bring Jews from Europe, Africa, and Asia to Ararat, as well as the Lost Tribes of Israel among the American Indians, not to mention the Karaites, those eastern European Jews who rejected the Talmud and had been expelled from normative Judaism a thousand years earlier.

Despite all his efforts, and his declarations of modest intention, the Jewish state of Ararat collapsed just as it began. A grand ceremony was enacted at Buffalo, when the cornerstone of the state was prepared, accompanied by a parade, but no one was actually willing to move to Grand Island, not even Noah himself. The Paris Sanhedrin, meanwhile, denounced Ararat as an American real estate fraud and insisted that only the Messiah, whenever He shall come, could establish a Jewish state.[27]

Jewish opposition to the notion of a nonmessianic state remained the prevailing tendency until the beginning of the Zionist movement at the end of the nineteenth century, and indeed is still prevalent among many ultra-Orthodox Jews, even among Jews living in the present state of Israel. The memory of the Jewish false messiah Sabbatai Sevi (1626–76) and the fiasco of his messianic movement in the seventeenth century remained a frightening group trauma of what might happen if anyone tried to take on the role of Jewish savior. An offshoot of Sabbatianism led by the followers of Jacob Frank was also causing great tension among the Jews of central Europe, exacerbated after Frank and his group converted to Roman Catholicism.[28]

At the same time, many European Jews were uneasy about accepting the message and opportunities of the Enlightenment. When the French army created the Batavian Confederation in the Netherlands in 1795, Jews there were offered citizenship. In the debates that followed, both Jews and orthodox Calvinists opposed it: the Jews explained that they were happy to be legal and recognized residents of the Netherlands and they wanted to remain free from political entanglements, free to make their way to the Holy Land as soon as the Messiah called for them; the Calvinists insisted that the Jews were required to keep faithful to their mission, which was to wait until they were summoned by God at the time of the Second Coming. Both were convinced that full citizenship for Jews might lead to their assimilation, which would have the effect of interfering and even disrupting the divine plan.[29]

| V |

Napoleon's invasion of Egypt in 1798–99, and his entrance into the Holy Land in 1799, had the ultimate effect of opening Palestine and the eastern Mediterranean to European political and commercial activity. A new generation of millenarian thinkers began to interpret the events of the last decades in terms of biblical prophecies, and to look for signs of the times in current events.[30] They became especially concerned about the place of the Jews in these schemes, since the restoration of the Jews to Palestine was a crucial precondition for the return of Jesus and the onset of the millennium.[31]

Lewis Way, a wealthy English philanthropist, was a key figure in the London Society for Promoting Christianity amongst the Jews, founded in 1809 and reorganized as an Anglican mission six years later. Under Way's direction it carried on missionary activity in eastern Europe and the Middle East and advocated a kind of Protestant Zionism. Much was being written at the time about the conversion and restoration of the Jews. Joseph Wolff (b. 1796), a converted German Jew, became almost a one-man missionary movement to his former co-religionists, traveling all over the Middle East, Asia, and even the United States, meeting Jews and describing their present condition to the participants in missionary societies. These Protestant Zionists were convinced that the prophecies they saw fulfilled in the French Revolution and the Napoleonic aftermath clearly pointed to the Second Advent of Christ and the restoration of the Jews to the Holy Land.

British students of prophecy began to move away from "post-millennialism," the optimistic view that the world was continually improving and that eventually mankind would reach a millennium of perfection, *after* which time Jesus would come again. From at least the 1820s, a view began to prevail that Christ would appear *before* the onset of the millennium, and that the Jews would return to Palestine before that time. What became known as "premillennialism" was a central thesis for them, its principal tenet being the personal return of Jesus before the beginning of His thousand-year reign, and the corollary being that this glorious time would begin very soon. Interestingly enough, the premillennialists tended to be very conservative in their politics despite their radical religious beliefs, and were convinced that progress through human efforts was not possible. Only the return of Jesus would bring about the salvation of the true believers and the judgment of the world.

A number of dynamic millenarian preachers began to spread this revised word in England. One of these, Edward Irving (1792–1834), created a great stir when he preached in London in 1822 as minister of the Church of Scotland congregation at Hatton Garden. Irving was a close friend of both Thomas Carlyle and Samuel T. Coleridge. His sermons and his habit of tolerating speaking in tongues stirred up discussion about what was really behind the terms of prophecies, so he established his own Catholic Apostolic Church (also known as the Irvingites). In 1827, he published a translation of Emanuel Lacunza's *The Coming of Messiah in Glory and Majesty*, arguing for Christ's "own personal appearance in flaming fire." The author, a Jesuit who died in 1801, writing in the guise of a converted Jew, provided further ammunition for the millenarians since he stated frankly that the pope and the entire Roman Catholic leadership were the Antichrist.[32]

In view of all the exciting changes taking place during those years, it was clear that the various interpretations of events could only be clarified by having an academic conference. Henry Drummond (1786–1860), a vice president of the Jews' Society since 1823 and a Tory MP since 1810, invited twenty key figures to meet at his Surrey estate at Albury Park for eight days during the Advent season of 1826 in order to hold extended discussions regarding prophetic truth. For five years, annual conferences were held at which the leading millenarian thinkers, mostly Anglican clergymen, could trade texts about prophetic chronology, the Second Coming, and the restoration of the Jews, using only Scripture as evidence.[33]

In 1829, speaking at the Albury Conference, Drummond announced that they had concluded that the Jews would be restored to Palestine during the time of God's judgment. This judgment would fall principally on Christendom, and when the judgment was over, the millennium would begin; the Second Advent of Christ would occur sometime before the onset of this thousand-year period. Drummond was convinced that the events described in the Book of Revelation were actually taking place before his eyes in European history. He claimed that the prophecies of the first fifteen chapters had been fulfilled by 1827, and that European history around 1832 was somewhere in the middle of chapter sixteen. Some of those attending the conference announced confidently that they expected Jesus to return to earth sometime between 1843 and 1847.

This method of messianic interpretation has sometimes been called "historical millenarianism" in that its adherents believed that one could chart the progress of God's march through history in terms of the prophecies that had been fulfilled, and then keep on the lookout for further unfulfilled prophecies in the future. Joseph Wolff, also a participant at the Albury Park conference, came to America in 1837 and told President John Quincy Adams that Jesus would return in 1843, addressing Congress on the same subject. President Adams had no quarrel with the notion of a Second Coming, he said, but thought that six years hence was a bit too soon. For those who saw the French Revolution as the first sign of the coming of the Messiah, 1843 was over half a century too late.

CHAPTER 6

RAPTURE, GREAT
DISAPPOINTMENT, AND WACO

| I |

As if millenarian theory suffered from a dearth of possible alternative interpretations, in the late 1820s a quite different method of understanding the divine signs was advanced by a Protestant Irishman named John Nelson Darby (1800–82) and by various members of a religious group called the Plymouth Brethren. The Plymouth Brethren were a group of Christians who could not find spiritual satisfaction in any of the organized churches, which they found to be unacceptably corrupt. They would meet together outside current church circles, at first in Dublin, and then in Plymouth, England. Darby was especially interested in the issue of prophecy, and, inspired by the meetings at Albury Park, he began to organize similar events in Dublin, called the Powerscourt Conferences.[1]

In 1833, at the third such conference, Darby and other Plymouth Brethren advanced a "futurist" rather than a "historical" millenarian view. Darby promoted the theory that the premillennial world could be seen as falling into several different divine "dispensations," or phases, as God moved through human history up to its climax. Employing a somewhat peculiar interpretation of a prophecy in Daniel 9:24–27 about "seventy weeks," Darby began with an axiom from Ezekiel 4:6 whereby a single day was equivalent to a year for calculating purposes. Seventy weeks, or 490 days, was therefore in actuality 490 *years*, the divine unit of millenarian history. Darby reckoned that this period of time began with the rebuilding of the Temple in Jerusalem after the return of the Jews from Babylonian Captivity, a marvelous event which occurred exactly 483 years before the birth of Jesus Christ. Unfortunately, instead of the birth of the Messiah ushering in the final act of mankind seven years after His appearance on earth, the divine clock stopped and eternal history was unable to proceed, thanks to the fact that the Jews rejected Christ. The rejection by God's Chosen People of His son prevented the final seven-year period from taking place in human history. Divine history came to a halt, and the entire interval between the birth of Jesus and modern times and beyond was a sort of historical pause, or long parenthesis, which might explain why the world had become so corrupt.

But there was also a bright side to this interpretation, for Darby believed that his generation was standing at the threshold of this final seven-year period, after which time the Messiah would come and change history forever. They were about to reenter divine history, for in this last phase many remaining prophecies would be fulfilled. The final "dispensation" was this seven-year period, leading up to the Battle of Armageddon and the Second Coming. Saying that the prevalent "day for a year" system of ready reckoning was not always valid in every individual case, Darby argued that the 1,260 days of the Beast's rule prophesied in Daniel would be exactly as written, three and a half years. Since it was inevitable that this last phase would be accompanied by many violent and unpleasant external circumstances, Darby suggested that the faithful would be spared these discomforts by being "raptured"—that is, taken up and spiritualized in heaven until the finale of human history took place, at which time they would return to earth with Jesus.

The restoration of the Jews in the Holy Land was a key element in these last years, as Darby and the dispensationalists turned their prophetic spotlight on the Jews. The promised restoration of the Jews to Palestine was therefore a key issue in American prophecy conferences held between 1878 and 1918.[2] The dispensationalists saw the collapse of the Ottoman Empire as opening the door for the Jews to be restored in actuality to their ancient land in Palestine.[3]

In Darby's view, the events predicted in the Book of Revelation were not historical occurrences which had taken place in past times. He argued instead that *all* the events in that critical text would happen in the future as the final dispensation takes place.[4] Darby's vision of premillennialism rejected the study of past and present human events as a way of finding where we are on the divine time-table, which was the strategy of the historical millennialists. Newton's disciple William Whiston, as we have seen, thought that one could count up all the fulfilled prophecies, calculate how long it took to fulfill them, and then project how long it would take for the rest to be accomplished. Darby, on the contrary, argued for a complete and total break between the very exciting divine history from the time of the rebuilt Temple until the birth of Jesus, and the final seven-year dispensation, separated by a hiatus of more than eighteen centuries. One interesting corollary of Darby's view was that it denied the possibility of predicting when the time of the end would actually take place. Nothing in human history over the past 1,800 years provided any basis for future assessment.

Darby wrote an enormous amount, most of which was found to be too dense for ordinary readers. He was also a difficult personality and had stormy relations with his associates. He therefore never became the leader of a church or sect, but contented himself with traveling through England, America, Europe, and the British colonial world promoting his divine theory. He never enjoyed much success in Britain itself beyond the immediate circle of the Plymouth Brethren, a group which kept splintering into subfactions. On the other hand, dispensationalism enjoyed a stupendous flourishing in the United States, where it remains until today the dominant method of prophetic interpretation, championed by such Fundamentalist icons as Pat Robertson, Jerry Falwell, Hal Lindsey, and many others.

Darbyites were also active in trying to help Jews to fulfill their divine role and to return to Palestine. Napoleon had succeeded in opening up the Middle East to European contacts, and soon British missionaries made their way to Jerusalem as well. In 1841 a bishopric of the Anglican Church was established in Jerusalem, and Michael Alexander, a convert from Judaism, was installed as the first Anglican bishop there. The British Society for the Conversion of the Jews sent missionaries across Europe into the most obscure *shtetlach* of Poland, Russia, and the Balkans, urging Jews to convert and to move to Palestine. What may be the first overt Zionist action occurred when these missionaries encountered the English Sir Moses Montefiore in Jerusalem. Montefiore was distributing alms to poor Jews who did little but pray for the coming of the Messiah. The missionaries encouraged him instead to get the Jews to do something toward establishing themselves in the Holy Land, to build a house, clear a field, anything. Soon afterward Montefiore built the first edifice outside the walls of Jerusalem, which in a sense was the beginning of the rebuilding of Palestine.[5] Another important figure in these early years was Warder Cresson, an American Quaker who moved to Palestine in the 1850s and had himself appointed American consul so that he could greet the Messiah when He came on behalf of the government of the United States. Cresson gathered stones in preparation for the rebuilding of the Temple as well.

Christian Zionism therefore moved from theory to practice during the late nineteenth and early twentieth centuries, especially among English and American millenarians. There is no doubt that Darby's mission was very influential in spreading a certain practicality with millenarian teaching. From 1837, Darby was on the move, and found willing ears especially in Canada, Australia, New Zealand, the British West Indies, and, of course, the United States, which he visited at least six times between 1859 and 1877.[6] He had much greater success after the Civil War was over, when many churches began to fear the growth of liberal theology and the rumors of Higher Biblical Criticism which were coming out of Germany. Theologians looked for a new ideology that could transport them over these winds of religious change. Darby's dispensationalism seemed almost heaven-sent.

Darby's personal influence in the United States came mostly from his individual meetings with ministers there, especially in the Midwest. In St. Louis he encountered James H. Brookes, a Presbyterian clergyman who would become a leader of millenarianism and dispensational theology. Brookes edited the first major American Fundamentalist periodical, *The Truth for Christ*, which appeared from 1875 until his death in 1897. He was the president and principal speaker at the Niagara Bible Conference from 1878, which was the main vehicle for Fundamentalist views.[7] It was at these meetings that Brookes began to formulate the two basic tenets of premillennialism: (1) the belief in the literal Second Coming of Jesus Christ on earth; and (2) the faith that Jews will be literally restored to their own land in Palestine.[8] Brookes and his followers also insisted that the Bible is accurate in all of its factual details and should be taken literally wherever possible.[9]

Like Darby, Brookes was very interested in the Jews and wrote a good deal about them. What is most interesting is his consistent stand against anti-Semitism. Again and again he chastised Christians for their attitude toward both ancient and modern Jews. He emphasized that "salvation is from the Jews" and maintained that there was no evidence in the Gospel story for rejecting them. Even in the present day, he insisted, there was no excuse for the persecution of contemporary Jews in eastern Europe or elsewhere, or for the contempt that most Christian Americans displayed toward the Chosen People. As Brookes put it:

Nine tenths of the Americans say that the Jews are a mean race, and if they are meaner than the Gentiles, considering the blessings and privileges the latter have received, they must be mean indeed. It is probable that if our ancestors had been banished and expelled, kicked and cuffed, robbed and murdered for centuries the world over, we too would feel like raising our hand against every man. The Gentiles in view of the past, and what they ought to know of themselves at present, should be slow to speak of the meanness of the Jews.[10]

Brookes died just as the Zionist movement was beginning, but he was always very excited to hear any news about Jews going back to Palestine or about the work of various missionary societies among the Jews there or in the United States.

Brookes played a further key role in the history of messianism by bringing Cyrus I. Scofield (1843–1921) into the movement. Scofield had been a soldier from Tennessee in the Confederate army during the Civil War, a man with a somewhat scandalous past involving drunkenness and marital difficulties. This did not stop him from becoming a lawyer in Kansas and a political figure there, but this glory did not last long, and he was soon accused of stealing political funds. He was jailed in St. Louis for forgery in 1879, and it was while he was in prison that Scofield experienced a remarkable religious conversion. He was released and began to practice law in St. Louis, where he met Brookes and became a devoted disciple. Scofield took on a ministry at the Dallas First Congregational Church, and started a publication called *The Believer*. He also became a key figure in the activities of the Moody Bible Institute and a participant in the various Bible and prophecy conferences.[11]

Scofield's most important contribution to the messianic world was an edition of Scripture that became known as the Scofield Reference Bible (published today by no less than Oxford University Press), which he began work on from about 1901. He had as his purpose to guide readers to the prophetic themes contained within the Bible and to give them the proper messianic interpretation. Using the Authorized King James Version as his text, Scofield employed section headings, lucid footnote explanations, and cross-references to other biblical texts, so that readers could find for themselves the way to the millenarian message. The Scofield Reference Bible was first published in 1909, and has been in print ever since, being perhaps the single most influential publication in the history of messianic theology.[12] For the more naive reader, there was little to distinguish the word of God from that of Scofield, and his footnotes easily acquired almost canonical status. Most importantly, Scofield adopted Darby's dispensationalist interpretation in its entirety. Scofield himself, having produced the monument which still bears his name, became leader of the Dallas Seminary, the institution where Hal Lindsey and many other Fundamentalist millenarians were trained.

| II |

Scofield's Reference Bible became the key text for Fundamentalist Christians, who truly can be said to be called by that name only after the appearance of a collection of twelve pamphlets known as *The Fundamentals*, three million copies of which were published between 1910 and 1915. This project was the brainchild of Lyman and Milton Stewart, California oilmen who had heard a preacher in Los Angeles storming against the infidel professors of theology at the University of Chicago Divinity School. The Stewarts convinced the preacher, A. C. Dixon, to supervise putting the case forward to the general public in a series of small works championing the dispensationalist interpretation of Scripture and underwritten by the brothers to the amount of $300,000. A committee of "Fundamentalists" was formed, most of whom were already involved with the Moody Bible Institute in Chicago. One of these men, Louis Meyer, was a converted Jew who ran a ministry for Jews there and who became the second editor of the series.

The pamphlets dealt with the key issues of the inerrancy, inviolability and authenticity of the Bible, but with much else as well. The authors of *The Fundamentals* attacked German biblical criticism, contending that the ancient Hebrew records had to be authentic, since God had chosen the Jews as the people to hear and convey His message. They stressed that recent archaeological findings, or some of them at least, tended to confirm the accuracy of biblical history. As one of the authors, William G. Moorhead, put it: "Ancient Judaism has one supreme voice for the chosen people, and its voice was prophetic . . . If any man deny the inspiration of the Old Testament, sooner or later he will deny that of the New."[13]

As with other dispensationalists, the Jews were not neglected by the authors of *The Fundamentals*. They stressed four topics: the importance of Jewish history, the fact that Jesus and His first followers were Jews, the important theological problems within Judaism, and the certainty that the Jews would play a vital role in God's future plan for human history. Interestingly enough, these early Fundamentalists used nonbiblical Jewish sources, such as the Mishnah, the Talmud, and other Jewish exegetical writings, to show how carefully Jews had tended the Old Testament over the centuries. Because of this it was not at all improbable that the original Mosaic text of the Bible had been preserved over millennia.[14]

As had been the case in the earlier years of dispensationalism, various firm believers in the imminent Second Coming at the end of the nineteenth century and the beginning of the twentieth did much to encourage the return of Jews to Zion. The return might not actually bring forth the coming of the Messiah, but it might lessen the burden of His task once He appeared on earth. These goals were made quite clear, for example, at a Prophecy Conference held in New York in 1878. One of the guest speakers from England was the Earl of Shaftesbury, who since the late 1830s had been trying to interest the British government and public in creating in Palestine a homeland for Jews from all over the world. Shaftesbury told his excited listeners that there were signs that this work was one of the preconditions for the Second Coming.

One interesting late-nineteenth-century figure was Arno C. Gaebelein (1861–1945), a German immigrant to the United States, who went to the trouble of learning Yiddish and set up a mission on New York's Lower East Side to inform Jews of what lay ahead. Gaebelein established newspapers in both Yiddish and English which combined information about the Messiah and the growing Zionist movement. These papers, *The Hope of Israel* (for Jews) and *Our Hope* (for Christians), became important vehicles for spreading the millenarian message. In 1900, he declared that of all the signs of our times, Zionism was the most startling. Gaebelein's goal was not to convert the Jews, but rather to make them aware of their part in the dynamic future ahead. He was soon joined by a professor from Denver named Ernest Stroeter, who had heard Gaebelein preach and joined him in his missionary and publication work. Gaebelein in 1895 traveled to Europe, studying firsthand the situation of the Jews in Russia, Germany, Poland, Romania, Galicia, and England. Wherever he went, he spoke of his fervent support for the national restoration of the Jewish people in Palestine. He also became fast friends with a leader of the Hebrew Christians in Russia, Joseph Rabinowitz. Stroeter for his part made several trips to Europe beginning in 1896, and even traveled to Palestine to see how Jewish colonization was progressing.[15]

Another Fundamentalist millenarian leader in the United States during those years was William Blackstone of Chicago, whose bestseller *Jesus Is Coming* (1878) made him rather well known. Blackstone convened a meeting of Jews and Christians in Chicago to discuss the establishment of a Jewish state in Palestine. The Jews, mostly Reformed rabbis, saw no point in this, and replied that they wanted Jews to live in the United States as full citizens. Blackstone in 1891 sent a proclamation to President Benjamin Harrison urging him to use his influence to convene an international conference to help establish a Jewish state in Palestine and to urge the Jews of eastern Europe to settle there. Among those who signed his petition were William P. McKinley, the next President of the United States, John D. Rockefeller, J. P. Morgan, Cyrus McCormick, and many other eminent persons. Later on, Blackstone sent Theodor Herzl a copy of the Old Testament in which he had marked the passages that ensured the restoration of the Jews to Palestine. At least for Christian Zionists, Blackstone's influence was seen to be decisive. As S. Maxwell Coder, sometime academic dean of Chicago's Moody Bible Institute, declared: "It has been claimed with some reason that Zionism, humanly speaking, owed its origin largely to the efforts of a Christian student of prophecy and lover of Israel, William E. Blackstone."[16]

When Herzl's *Der Judenstaat* was published in 1897, proposing the establishment of a Jewish state as a solution to the misery and persecution of European Jewry, one of his first disciples was the Anglican minister in Vienna, William Hechler, who had been putting out broadsides proclaiming that the millennium was imminent. Hechler became a chief supporter of the fledgling Zionist movement. He attended the first Zionist Congress in Basel; he helped put Herzl in contact with the Kaiser, the Sultan, and eminent people in England, thereby transforming the wild vision of a Viennese journalist into a plausible international movement. Hechler remained active in Zionist affairs for the rest of his life. He accompanied Herzl on the great man's one and only trip to Palestine, when he met the Kaiser. (Hechler was also looking for the lost Ark of Noah.) Herzl actually died in Hechler's arms, while Hechler himself passed out of this life in Palestine in 1925.[17]

For many millenarians, the Balfour Declaration of 1917 expressing the British government's support in principle for the establishment of a Jewish homeland in Palestine seemed like the most important sign of the imminent coming of the Messiah. The creation of the British Mandate for Palestine after the First World War gave England a special responsibility toward paving the way for the arrival of Jesus Christ, they believed.

And so too in the United States did recent events seem to signal great cosmic changes. Isaac Haldeman, minister at Manhattan's First Baptist Church, in an influential book published in 1910, argued that the only genuinely positive sign of the times was the "rise of the Jewish people in world leadership" and the progress of the Zionist movement.[18] As the Great War came to an end, a number of important conferences were held in which the prophetic implications of the war and its conclusion were hammered out. A critical one was convened in Philadelphia in May 1918. One speaker, A. E. Thompson, pastor of the American church in Jerusalem until he had been expelled by the Turks during the war, pondered the prophetic meaning of General Allenby's conquest of Jerusalem—the "capture of Jerusalem is one of those events to which students of prophecy have been looking forward for many years"—and another discussed "The Regathering of Israel in Unbelief," arguing that the Jews could be returned to Palestine even before their inevitable conversion to Christianity.[19] Another conference on prophecy took place in Carnegie Hall in New York in November, immediately after the end of the war, where Gaebelein made similar claims about the significance of the British capture of Jerusalem.[20]

A decade later, David L. Cooper, of the Biblical Research Society of Los Angeles, wrote in his best-selling book on the eternal God that now that the Balfour Declaration had been proclaimed, "whenever, in the opinion of the League of Nations, conditions justify, the Palestinian Government will be recognized as one of the family of nations. When that time comes, the times of the Gentiles will have run their course. This fact means that God will again resume His dealings with the Hebrew people." God would deal with them for seven years, a period that would begin "when the Hebrew people are in full possession of Palestine." Cooper believed that since events were moving toward the reestablishment of the Jews in their homeland, "it is most probable from this point of view that the time is approaching very rapidly for Messiah to return and to inaugurate that glorious reign of righteousness."[21] Cooper kept faith with his beliefs. In a preface to the 1953 edition, five years after the state of Israel was established, he noted that now "we may be certain that the times of the Gentiles have run their course, and that God will begin again to deal with the Jew in fulfillment of Old Testament predictions."[22]

Gaebelein was worried that Zionist Jews were too secular, and were returning to the Land of Israel as unbelievers. He was concerned about whether they would see the light and convert before the Second Coming. He and other Protestant Zionists like him considered that Hitler's persecution of the Jews was also part of the divine plan, God acting through the enemies of the Jews in order to prepare them for the awful punishments that they would have to undergo during the seven-year Times of Tribulation and at the Battle of Armageddon.[23] This sort of "positive" interpretation of the Holocaust continued to appear, both in Fundamentalist writings and in some Orthodox Jewish interpretations, where the *Shoah* is presented as a punishment for religious backsliding which had the beneficial effect of directing many Jews to Palestine, where they could contribute to crucial divine developments connected to the birth pangs of the Messiah.[24]

| III |

Another influential millenarian interpreter of the nineteenth century was William Miller (1782–1849), a farmer from upstate New York who had fought as a captain in the War of 1812, before having a deep religious crisis which changed his life and that of messianic believers everywhere. Miller had gone through a skeptical phase, studying Voltaire, Paine, and Hume, but dedicated his life to Christ in 1816. At first he joined the Baptists, but careful perusal of Scripture changed his mind.[25]

Many of the prophecies Miller studied in the Bible had been, he believed, already fulfilled, and this convinced him that the rest of them concerning the Second Coming were soon to be realized. "Finding all the signs of the times and the present condition of the world to compare harmoniously with the prophetic descriptions of the last days," he wrote, "I was compelled to believe that this world had about reached the limits of the period allotted for its continuance. As I regarded the evidence, I could arrive at no other conclusion." He slowly became convinced that the popular post-millennial view—that the temporal millennium would occur *before* the Second Advent—was false; that Scripture did not support the theory of the return of the Jews; that Jesus would return and establish the Kingdom of God; and that the earth would perish and there would be a new heaven and new earth. The prophecies in the Book of Daniel showed that all this would be fulfilled when Jesus returned on or before the "Jewish year, 1843."[26] As Miller preached all over New England, he and his followers put on more than 120 camp meetings during 1842–43, but his views met with considerable hostility.[27]

The Millerites were the only significant millenarian movement in the English-speaking world that did not see the Jews as major participants in the great events to come. The chief element in Miller's theology, influenced by Isaac Newton, G. S. Faber, and Thomas Newton, was that Christ would return in about 1843 to judge the wicked and cleanse the world by fire. Nonbelievers, including Jews, would be destroyed in this judgmental conflagration, and there would be no Jews left to restore to Palestine or anywhere else. "The Jew has had his day," he believed, and saw no role for them in the Second Coming.[28]

One interesting manifestation of the Millerite phenomenon was his representation in contemporary literature.[29] In February 1843 Nathaniel Hawthorne wrote a story entitled "The New Adam and Eve," in which he imagines the "good Father Miller's interpretations of the prophecies to have proved true. The Day of Doom has burst upon the globe, and swept away the whole race of men." In Hawthorne's tale, the new Adam and Eve view the destruction and "pass unconscious judgment upon the works and ways of the vanished race." There were other references to Miller and his followers in Hawthorne's works during this period.[30] Ralph Waldo Emerson was said to have informed a Millerite that mankind would be better off without the world.[31] John Greenleaf Whittier, a Quaker and an Abolitionist, discussed the Millerites in an essay entitled "The World's End." He did not oppose the Millerites on theological grounds, noting that such prophecies had always been a part of Christianity, but objected to their social impact, since "the effect of this belief in the speedy destruction of the world and the personal coming of the Messiah, acting upon a class of uncultivated, and, in some cases, gross minds, is not always in keeping with the enlightened Christian's ideal of the better day." In his opinion those who thought the world was about to end were not likely to work to improve it.[32]

Conservative American writers were more uncompromising in their denunciation. James Fenimore Cooper introduced a condemnation of "Miller's interpretations of the prophecies" in his novel *Wyandotté* (1843).[33] So too did a novel published by Henry Wadsworth Longfellow in 1849 include a description of a Millerite camp meeting and of the special gowns they wore on The Day. In Longfellow's story, the Millerite preacher so distresses a young orphan girl that she drowns herself in a river rather than face the wrath of God on His imminent Second Coming.[34] Oliver Wendell Holmes made fun of the Millerites in *The Autocrat of the Breakfast-Table* (1857–58), referring to their excitement over the comet of 1843, noting that, as for himself, he would have been worried "if I had thought the world was ripe. But it is very green yet, if I am not mistaken; and besides, there is a great deal of coal to use up, which I cannot bring myself to think was made for nothing. If certain things, which seem to me essential to a millennium, had come to pass I should have been frightened."[35] Curiously, Holmes used the argument about the earth's coal, which was exploited by Thomas Burnet in the seventeenth century, in reverse: Burnet had argued that it would be England which would burn brightest at the End of Days when the coal underneath was ignited by divine fire.

Many other authors had a go at the easy target of the Millerites, and this only spread their fame further. One might also note the novel written a century later by Robert Coover, published in 1966. In *The Origin of the Brunists*, the character of Miller is rather clumsily called "Giovanni Bruno," but the story is clearly based on the tale of what happened to the Millerites after 1843. What gives a spooky quality to Coover's novel is the Day of Doom he assigns to his group: the last day under the astrological sign of Aries—April 19, the very day of the events in both Waco and Oklahoma City.[36]

Miller had prophesied that the world would come to an end sometime between March 21, 1843, and March 21, 1844. In fact, his system of prophetic chronology was hardly different from that used by Johannes Alsted two hundred years before. He was heartened by the appearance in the sky of a spectacular comet on February 27, 1843, which remained visible in both hemispheres for weeks, but when nothing came to pass, most Millerites remained undaunted. Then, examining the Hebrew calendar and its differences from that of the Karaites, they proposed that the actual date for the end of the world should be recalibrated to October 22, 1844: the failure of this final date became known in Adventist lore as the "Great Disappointment."

| **IV** |

The Great Disappointment did not lead to the dissolution of the Millerites, who had invested far too much exegetical effort into determining the Last Day. Miller himself had five years in which to contemplate his mistakes before he passed on to a Better Place. Within a short time, he and his followers concluded that, in a sense, they had not been incorrect in positing 1843–44 as the time of the

Second Coming, but in defining the Second Coming too dramatically. What had actually happened at that time, they argued, was that Jesus had commenced the judging process, reviewing the eternal files of the saints and sinners on earth; the results of His findings would be revealed at some unspecified point in the future, when the judgment in heaven was completed.

One group that emerged as a result of William Miller's failed prophecy was the Jehovah's Witnesses. Their founder was Charles Taze Russell (1852–1916) of Pennsylvania, who revised Miller's millennial date to 1874 but argued that Christ's return to earth would be invisible. His failure to convince the local clergy led him to begin issuing in the late 1870s a series of books and magazines himself, which were sold by his followers. In 1881, he founded the Zion's Watch Tower Tract Society, which in 1931 changed its name to the Jehovah's Witnesses. Despite Miller's embarrassing failure, Russell had great success, and his movement spread to England, Germany, and Australia.

Like Miller, Russell was not above revising his millennial arithmetic. His new date was 1914, when Russell decreed the heavenly Kingdom of God would be established and Christ would begin to select the saintly group of 144,000 souls who, according to Revelation 14:1–3, were destined to be saved. Russell seems to have expected the Messiah to come during his own lifetime, but the movement thrived even after his death under the leadership of "Judge" Joseph Franklin Rutherford (1869–1942), who not only gave the Jehovah's Witnesses their name and their slogan, "Millions now living will never die," but also ironed out the fine points of their messianic theology. The movement continues to thrive with almost a million believers even today. There were some whispers about great events scheduled for 1975, but setting dates seems to have gone out of fashion with these particular spiritual descendants of William Miller.

The theology of the Jehovah's Witnesses is interesting in its own right. They argue that "Jehovah God" created both heaven and earth, but that Satan rebelled against Him and has managed to gain control over the world through the evil manipulation of temporal economic, political, and religious organizations. The struggle between Jehovah God and Satan is sharpened by the Witnesses' Arianism—that is, they reject the notion of the Trinity and see Christ as a figure fully distinct from God Himself. This will become clear at the Battle of Armageddon, they believe, when Jesus will lead His angels and Jehovah's Witnesses against mankind's evildoers, especially but not exclusively devils, demons, Catholic priests, orthodox clergymen, capitalists, and the United Nations. A new heaven will appear for the lucky 144,000, and the thousand-year millennium of peace and everlasting life will begin for Jehovah's Witnesses and other worthy and resurrected dead. Fortunately, at the end of this long period there will be a further judgment of those who never had the opportunity of hearing the message of the Jehovah's Witnesses, a sort of divine appeals court at which extenuating circumstances may be pleaded.

Apart from this distinctive theology, the Jehovah's Witnesses have adopted special practices of their own. They have their own translation of the Bible, and regard communion as purely ceremonial, baptism being practiced for reasons of fellowship rather than sanctification. They reject the use of tobacco and alcohol, and will not accept blood transfusions. Witnesses are scarcely noted for their allegiance to social causes, since there is no point in trying to patch up a doomed world. They also deny loyalty to nation-states and reject military service. About six thousand Jehovah's Witnesses were murdered in the Nazi death camps. This particular lifestyle is thought to prepare the way for Christ's return, and toward that end the Jehovah's Witnesses have prepared a house in California owned officially by Abraham, Isaac, and King David, who have rooms prepared for their imminent arrival.[37]

| v |

Perhaps the more fruitful branch of the movement which passed over the watershed of the Great Disappointment became known at first as the Adventists, later the Seventh-day Adventists. Its original adherents were all refugees from the trauma of 1844. One key figure was Ellen Harmon White (1827–1915), who had visions of what was transpiring in heaven and how this related to the situation of the saints on earth; her visions, written down and disseminated, became the defining text of the new group. Among these revelations was the picture of the heavenly copy of the Ten Commandments, from which she understood that the Fourth Commandment was still in force, and that the Jewish Saturday Sabbath was still to be observed, not the Christian Sunday. As she herself put it in 1847, "The holy Sabbath is, and will be, the separating wall between the true Israel of God and unbelievers; and that the Sabbath is the great question to unite the hearts of God's dear waiting saints."[38]

Seventh-day observance became the defining characteristic of the Adventists, and part of their apocalyptic theology. Christians who observed Sunday were the forces of evil, beginning with the Roman Catholics, who had first distorted true Christianity, followed by Lutherans and their successors, and finally even the government of the United States, which promulgated laws for Sunday observance. The Seventh-day Adventists, however, were truly God's servants, His elect, the surviving remnant who had the seal of God, and who would be lifted up to heaven at the time of the Second Advent. At this time, the saints would begin their sojourn in heaven for a thousand years, while the earth was ruled by evil forces. After this millennium, Jesus would return to earth, put an end to the Battle of Armageddon, destroy the evil forces, and then make a new Jerusalem on earth.

The Seventh-day Adventists organized themselves into an official church in 1863, with all the accoutrements of schools, Bible study groups, and health-oriented activities. This last feature was also the result of a vision received by White, according to which true believers should lead an exemplary life of good health based on proper nutrition and medicine, staunch morality, vegetarianism, and abstinence from the use of tobacco or alcohol. Among their chief institutions was a great health clinic in Battle Creek, Michigan, established in 1879 and run by Dr. John Harvey Kellogg. Adventism and health were practiced there, although Kellogg eventually came into conflict with Ellen White and was expelled from the church in 1907. But Kellogg's brother William, who invented the cornflake as the paradigm of healthy food for the clinic at Battle Creek, and C. W. Post, another giant in the burgeoning breakfast-food industry, who was an employee there, made some of these precepts an everyday part of American life. The Seventh-day Adventist hospital at Loma Linda, California, also had a bright future, becoming an advanced center for medical treatment and research.

The Seventh-day Adventists might be described as passively revolutionary. Many other millenarians (such as the dispensationalists whose theology was adopted by most groups today which we would call Fundamentalist) see a clear divine plan in human historical development, and it leads up to the Second Coming. The Adventists, on the other hand, view the return of the Messiah as more of a relationship between God and themselves (the remnant, God's emissaries on earth). It is therefore necessary to improve themselves, morally and medically, and to bring knowledge of God's word as told to Ellen Harmon White to the apocalyptically deprived throughout the world. This has remained the principal basis of their activity until our own time. Their doctrines have encountered difficulty and even danger, notably because of their pacifism: although they are willing to work in hospitals and serve in medical capacities in wartime, they will not take on combat roles. An arresting painting on the wall of the Seventh-day Adventist headquarters in Takoma Park, Maryland, called "The March of the Reformers" depicts a line of figures beginning with Daniel, followed by John Hippolytus, Joachim of Fiore, John Wyclif, Luther, John Knox, and Isaac Newton, who passes the torch on to John Wesley, standing alongside a man in a modern business suit labeled "Today." He is the Seventh-day Adventist, who is the special witness to God's mission. More than 8 million people belong to the Seventh-day Adventist Church, about 750,000 of whom live in the United States.

| VI |

As the Seventh-day Adventists expanded, they inevitably took on many of the characteristics of mainstream Protestant churches, with institutions to train missionaries and medical workers. Yet they never had a clearly defined official creed, which led to splinter groups and prophets who had better ideas on how to prepare mankind for the Second Coming. One of these splinters was the Branch Davidians.

The origin of this group can be found in the sect established by a Bulgarian immigrant to the United States named Victor Houteff (1886–1955), who left the Orthodox Church and joined the Seventh-day Adventists in 1918. Houteff was given the task of running the church schools in Los Angeles, where he preached about the need for a stricter moral life and a more intense preparation for the Second Coming. In 1929 he began to reveal his own personal interpretation of Scripture in a periodical which he called *The Shepherd's Rod*, based on a passage from Micah 6:9, "hear ye the rod."

Houteff's message was that the normative teachings of the Seventh-day Adventists were not adequate. Even though Houteff insisted that he kept close to the basic message of the church, including devotion to the visions of Ellen Harmon White, Saturday Sabbath observance, and special nutritional and health codes, the church leaders opposed his teachings and accused him of heresy and of disrupting their work. The key problem was that he insisted that there is a progressive revelation of truth, that the visionary stage was still in progress, and that new prophets will arise, such as himself. Inevitably, Houteff in 1930 was barred from teaching in the church schools, and his supporters were threatened with ejection.

Houteff shifted to teaching in the home of a friendly supporter. He insisted throughout that he had no intention of bringing his message to any but Seventh-day Adventists and that he saw himself as part of that world alone. His mission was to enhance and to reform that revelation. Christ Himself was delaying His return because His church of Adventists had become worldly and apathetic, taking more interest in their mundane activities such as establishing sanatoria and schools than in those spiritual ones which would bring forward the Great Day.

In 1935, a year after Houteff was expelled from the Seventh-day Adventists, he set up a communal group, called the Davidian Seventh-day Adventists, near Waco, Texas, on a couple of hundred acres of land, later expanded to a settlement of 375 acres. He gathered around him fewer than a hundred people, who accepted him as a prophet and named his community Mount Carmel. The families who came to live with him dedicated themselves to intense Bible study, communal fellowship, and farming. Houteff promised that their center in Texas was only temporary, and that within a year or so they would be divinely transported to Palestine, where they would become the leaders of the elect as the Second Advent began, after which time they would arise into heaven and live there for a thousand years.[39]

Houteff's community in Waco was a sort of Seventh-day Adventist world in miniature. It had a rest home, a dispensary, a publication center (which produced the leader's voluminous writings in great quantities), and a school. His followers were devoted to vegetarianism and Sabbath observance, and had Bible study every day and full religious services on Friday and Saturday. They regarded themselves as members of the Seventh-day Adventist fold, even though they had been expelled from the official church, and they proselytized solely within that world. Only in 1942, during the Second World War, did they organize themselves as a separate sect.

Adventists were exempt from the draft, and in order to protect their pacifist beliefs they had to declare themselves a breakaway sect from the parent group.[40]

Despite their efforts, the Branch Davidians failed to expand, and in 1952–53 they took the step of sending missionaries to Seventh-day Adventist communities in other parts of North America, Britain, India, Australia, and the West Indies. There seems to have been some success but this paled with the death of Houteff himself in February 1955. Many of his followers saw him as the Elijah who would usher in the Kingdom of God, and his passing left the group in disarray.

After an initial period of uncertainty, Houteff's widow, Florence, his second wife, assumed leadership of the Davidians. In December 1957 they sold Mount Carmel for $700,000 and bought a second site over twice as big nearby for only $85,000; with the rest of the money they built an impressive spread of houses and farm buildings at a new Mount Carmel. Perhaps as a way of asserting her prophetic powers, she took the bold step of announcing on November 5, 1955, that in exactly 1,260 days (an allusion to the Book of Daniel) the Kingdom of God would be established, during Passover 1959. According to Florence Houteff, the scene for the Second Advent would be set by another war in the Middle East in April 1959 (the Sinai campaign of 1956 showed that such an occurrence was likely), after which time the Seventh-day Adventists would be purified and the Kingdom of God established in Jerusalem. What transpired was a sort of replay of the Great Disappointment of 1844. Hundreds flocked to Mount Carmel, selling their homes, giving away their worldly goods, and settling down in tents to await King Jesus.

Soon after April 22, 1959, it was clear that "disappointment" had struck again, and the Davidians began to splinter. Some rejoined the normative Seventh-day Adventist Church. Florence Houteff herself admitted that she must have been mistaken, and with the community down to under fifty members, she sold most of the Mount Carmel property and retired to California.

In the leadership struggle that ensued, the key figures who emerged were transient members of the Davidians named Ben and Lois Roden. The two Rodens went to court to gain control of the remaining property at Mount Carmel and, having accomplished this, assumed prophetic authority as well. Ben Roden announced that his prophetical status should be confirmed by understanding that he and his group were the "branch" of the root of Jesse, the spirit revived by King David, spoken of by the prophet Zechariah (3:8 and 6:12), and confirmed by Jesus's announcement: "I am the vine, ye *are* the branches" (John 15:5). Roden thereupon renamed the group the Branch Davidians and proclaimed himself the third prophet in chronological succession after Ellen Harmon White (who had unraveled the mysteries of the gospel, set up the true church, and made the Saturday Sabbath the central day for divine worship) and Victor Houteff (who had insisted on progressive revelation, the imminence of the millennium, and the importance of the remnant). Roden pressed for perfecting the elect by trying to reproduce the character of Christ in each member of the group as preparatory to the Second Advent.

Breaking with the Millerite tradition, Roden saw contemporary developments among Jews in the new State of Israel as among the signs that the Second Coming was nigh. He even managed to persuade Israeli officials to allow him to set up a Branch Davidian center at Amirim in the Galilee. Roden believed that his vision was confirmed in the Six-Day War of 1967, which he claimed was prophesied in the Bible. Toward that end, Roden added to the Saturday Sabbath other Jewish ceremonial festivals for the Branch Davidians, such as Passover, Pentecost, and Tabernacles, which he thought were crucial for setting the time scale for the Last Days.

His wife, Lois, added a further feminist element to the Branch Davidian theology following a vision in 1977 in which she was visited by the "Holy Spirit Mother," who revealed to her that the Holy Spirit was in fact feminine. Indeed, the Messiah at the Second Coming would be a woman. Lois Roden believed it was her role to teach the femininity of God, and she began a magazine called *SHE-kinah*, the Hebrew word for the godhead, which is a feminine noun. Ben Roden died in 1978 and four years later was buried on the Mount of Olives in Jerusalem. Lois was buried beside him after her death in November 1986, but meanwhile she found herself forced to defend her leadership against a challenge posed by her son George. She took support from a Seventh-day Adventist from Tyler, Texas, a local handyman named Vernon Wayne Howell (1959–93), who joined the group in 1981. Nine years later, Howell changed his name to David Koresh, but in the meantime allied himself with Lois Roden against her son. Lois, for her part, announced that Howell/Koresh was her designated successor, and they traveled to Israel together in 1983. Howell/Koresh almost certainly had a sexual relationship with Lois Roden, which she herself confirmed, long after her son and many others had suggested that their desire was to conceive a child who would embody the prophetic succession. In any case, she was very upset when Howell/Koresh married the fourteen-year-old daughter of a Branch Davidian elder in January 1984. They had three children, all of whom died on April 19, 1993, with their parents.

In January 1985, Howell/Koresh and his pregnant wife visited Israel, where he had a vision designating himself as a "Cyrus" figure who would lead the elect back from exile to the Promised Land. On his return to Waco, however, he found that George Roden had taken control. Armed with a gun, George Roden drove Howell/Koresh out of Mount Carmel in June, and changed the name of the community to Rodenville, Texas. This seems to have been the moment when firearms were introduced to the pacifist community of Branch Davidians. Howell/Koresh and his supporters took to living in basic conditions near a town appropriately named Palestine, Texas. Howell/Koresh also began contracting polygamous "marriages" with teenage girls, all of whom produced children. But the struggle was far from over. In November 1987, George Roden dug up the body of a Branch Davidian woman who had died twenty years before, put the coffin in the chapel, and challenged Howell/Koresh to raise the dead. Howell/Koresh tried to get him arrested for grave desecration, but he needed a photograph to prove his story. This particular dispute culminated in a gunfight, when Howell/Koresh appeared at Mount Carmel dressed in camouflage and backed by seven young male followers armed with assault rifles. George Roden was shot in the chest and hands, and the authorities were forced to intervene. Howell/Koresh was tried for attempted murder, but it ended in a mistrial, and some of the jurors hugged him when he was released. All the guns and ammunition were returned to him. Roden somewhat spoiled his case by informing the judge that he had divine powers with which to punish him, and after actually murdering someone six months later in an unrelated incident, was incarcerated as criminally insane. Now without any challenges to his leadership, Howell/Koresh took control over the property at Mount Carmel.

In many respects, the group led by Howell/Koresh was not very different from many other splinter Seventh-day Adventist communities. Many others were also grouped around charismatic prophetic figures who tried to make sense of Scripture, preparing themselves for the Second Advent. The circumstances of his having taken control were somewhat dramatic, but even the proliferation of firearms at Mount Carmel was not unusual: in their case it was part of a small business buying and selling guns. They also repaired expensive automobiles for resale in California. Otherwise, Mount Carmel was a sort of self-subsistence commune, oiled by large sums of money donated by the families of members. Membership was voluntary: people joined and then dropped out, and some members had jobs outside, repairing cars or farm equipment. Others stayed only part of the time in Waco, otherwise living in California or England, and regarding Mount Carmel as a place of pilgrimage. At the time of the siege, about 130 people were living there, equally divided among men, women, and children and between whites and others (blacks, Asians, Hispanics).

What made the compound at Waco somewhat different was the

character of Vernon Howell himself. In August 1990 he changed his name legally to David Koresh, the first name linking him with the biblical king and the second name the Hebrew for Cyrus, the Persian king who returned the Jews to Palestine after the Babylonian Captivity, earning for himself an almost messianic place in Jewish history. Koresh combined Bible study with rock music, and his proselytization bore fruit with members from Seventh-day Adventist communities not only in the United States but also in Australia and England.

Inside the compound, a kind of intensive theocratic preparation for the Second Advent was going on. Koresh preached that he and his followers were crucial players in mankind's quest for salvation. Jesus Christ had died only for the salvation of those who lived prior to His time, and the implication was that Koresh himself was a sinful messiah whose mission it was to open the seven seals described in the Book of Revelation, as a prelude to the End of the World. His followers would be among the 144,000 faithful who, according to Revelation, would ascend to heaven and reign with the Messiah for a thousand years.[41]

In view of this idea of their divine role, the group life of the people in Mount Carmel took on exceptional importance: everything they did was part of a plan for saving the world. Koresh had their lives regimented down to the smallest detail. After working all day, Koresh would regale them at night with sermons about how wondrous their existence would be, and how horrendous would be the lot of the unfaithful, especially the Seventh-day Adventists who refused to recognize his ministry. Koresh told them that they were truly in the Last of Days, and that soon they would emigrate to Israel, where they would begin by converting the Jews, leading to world disorder and finally war, and the Battle of Armageddon. The cleansing angel who would prepare the world for the New Jerusalem would be none other than David Koresh himself.

Another factor which made Koresh's leadership problematic was his sexual theology. He asserted that his own polygamous marriages to both young and older women in Mount Carmel had theological significance. He seems to have had six other "wives" apart from his legal spouse, and a total of twelve children, four of whom have survived, including a daughter born before he joined the Branch Davidians. His argument was that since he was a messiah, his offspring would become part of a new saintly group, the House of David, which would rule in heaven after the Advent. Yet despite the scandal which this aspect of his theology caused at the congressional hearings into the Waco disaster in 1995, apart from one case, the parents or husbands of the chosen women had acquiesced, because they agreed with Koresh about the cosmic importance of what was about to occur. As far as one can tell, if Mount Carmel and David Koresh had been left to themselves, they would have studied more of the Bible and deciphered more texts in the Book of Revelation about the seven seals and the preconditions for the coming of the Messiah. Koresh would have impregnated more women and might have produced the twenty-four pure youths whom he thought were necessary to rule in the heavenly millennial world. Some parents might have rebelled and taken themselves and their children out of the group, but many more might have lived on quietly in Waco for years.

This rather plausible viewpoint has led many commentators to see the roots of the tragedy at Waco in the politics of the civil authorities, especially the Bureau of Alcohol, Tobacco, and Firearms (BATF), and in the exposé of the Branch Davidians published in the local Waco newspaper. Yet despite the congressional investigation into what happened, it is still difficult to establish the precise sequence of events.[42] Certainly it is true that Koresh refused to accept a summons from the BATF, which led to a gun battle on February 28, 1993, and the death of four government officers and six Branch Davidians. Yet it is also clear that the federal and state authorities refused to listen to the Branch Davidians and, in negotiations between the FBI (called in to replace the BATF) and Koresh, angrily brushed aside his musings on Revelation, seeing his appeal to theology as irrelevant to the question of his stockpiling of firearms. It is surely apparent that there was no necessity for resolving the fifty-one-day standoff between the government authorities and the "saints" at Waco at the particular moment when the fiery denouement took place. In this second bungled raid, on April 19, the entire compound was burned to the ground, killing at least seventy-four Branch Davidians, including Koresh himself and twenty-one children under the age of fifteen.[43] Janet Reno, who had just been appointed Attorney General at that time, said she made the decision on the basis of the information and advice which had been given to her, but some of this was later deemed misleading or even false.[44] Her more careful behavior in 1996, when she allowed a similar standoff in Jordan, Montana, with the Freemen to drag on for two and a half months until a peaceful conclusion could be reached, showed that some learning had taken place. At Waco itself, the site has become a place of pilgrimage for right-wing survivalist groups, among whom there was some hope that Koresh might be resurrected about December 13, 1996 (1,335 days after his death, as per Daniel 12:12).[45] The date of the conflagration also took on a new significance when Timothy McVeigh decided to blow up the federal building in Oklahoma City on April 19, 1995, two years to the day after Waco. Even the date of issue of his forged South Dakota driver's license, which he used to hire the fatal truck, was April 19, 1993.[46] Like Joachim of Fiore, McVeigh knew the importance of cosmic dates.

CHAPTER 7

FROM BRITISH ISRAEL TO CHRISTIAN IDENTITY AND ARYAN NATION

Perhaps the most fertile messianic theory to emerge during the nineteenth century was the one usually known by the name of British Israelism. The concept was, in brief, that the British, or perhaps the Anglo-Saxon races in general, were the literal descendants of the Lost Ten Tribes of Israel, and therefore all of God's biblical promises applied to them and not to the modern Jews. It was the Anglo-Saxons who were the Chosen People, and this was demonstrated not only by evidence in Scripture but also by anthropological investigations of the historical migrations of the tribes since the Babylonian Captivity in the sixth century before Christ. The modern Jews, offspring of those who rejected Christ, were therefore excluded from God's grace, while the British, descendants of the Jews who did not have the opportunity to hear the message of Jesus, had the best of both Jewish and gentile worlds: they were the heirs of promise and saved by Christ's blood as well. As we shall see, British Israelism provided the ideological underpinning for a number of key Christian Identity groups that are still active in the United States today.

| **I** |

As early as 1649, John Sadler of Cambridge argued that the English were descendants of the Israelites and gave what he considered scriptural and linguistic evidence for this.[1] As we have seen, the self-proclaimed "Nephew of the Almighty" Richard Brothers made similar claims in the eighteenth century, although later British Israelites stoutly rejected him as a founding father, saying that he "got hold of the true facts regarding our origin, but being a person of weak intellect, he ended his days in the mad-house. This was not caused by his opinions."[2]

British Israelites recognized Ralph Wedgwood, a contemporary of Brothers, as a true precursor, however. Wedgwood wrote a *Book of Remembrance*, which he described as "the outline of an Almanack constructed on the ancient cycles of time, and proving, by an harmony of prophetic numbers, that this is the predicted era of new things, the final restitution of all things; the fulness of the Gentiles." He, too, was inspired by Napoleon's great victory over the pope, and argued that "great Babylon is now fallen, and Satan binding, in the empire and person of Napoleon." In the course of his interpretation of these contemporary events, he insisted that the prophecies of Daniel and Revelation demonstrated that "the British Empire is the Bow of Ephraim, which has bode in strength—Messiah's promised Possession and Naval Dominion." Wedgwood also argued that there was "Evidence that the British Empire is the peculiar possession of the Messiah."[3]

But it was John Wilson (d. 1871) who was the true ideological founding father of British Israelism. The son of a weaver from Kilmarnock, Ireland, Wilson, having developed the notion that the English were the true and literal descendants of the Lost Ten Tribes of Israel, promulgated it in lectures he gave in Dublin and elsewhere in Ireland between about 1840 and his death thirty-one years later. Wilson seems to have met with great success, peppering his lectures with other fashionable subjects, especially the skull-measuring techniques of phrenology. Wilson tried to start a couple of monthly magazines, but these failed within a short time.[4] Much more successful was the published version of his lectures, which went through five editions between 1840 and 1876.[5]

Wilson's ideas were clearly expressed and easily explained. His thesis, in brief, was that

> the prophecies must be literally fulfilled, and that Judah must mean Judah, and Israel mean literally Israel. At the same time, he agrees with those who apply to these Christian nations many of the prophecies respecting Israel, believing, as he does, that these nations have not merely come into the place of ancient Israel, but are truly the seed of Abraham according to the flesh—are of the so-called "lost house of Israel," the leading tribe of which was Ephraim. These nations have been brought forth at the time and in the place predicted; they are the modern nations of Europe, and especially those of Saxon race, whose glorious privilege it now is to "preach the gospel for a witness unto all nations ere the end come."

In the early editions of his lectures, Wilson claimed that the British were only one of the Israelitish heirs, along with the Germans and the Scandinavians, but by the fifth edition in 1876, England had moved up to a unique position, demonstrated not only by her extraordinary maritime skills, but also by the rise of America as her brother Manasseh.[6] He explained that after "considering the subject for more than a quarter of a century,"

> and having the truth of his views tried in many ways, [he] sees nothing to shake his confidence in that which he has so long maintained, that "Israel's grave was the Saxon's birthplace"; that the English, although not Jews, are yet sprung from the outcasts of Israel, after whom the Word of God was sent to the

north country, and to these "isles afar off." He still holds that
the Christian people of these islands are of that "fulness of
the Gentiles" promised to come of Ephraim, unto whom,
through the cross, was appointed the birthright and the power
of ministering blessing to all the nations of the earth.[7]

Wilson proved his thesis that the English were the lineal descendants of the lost tribe of Ephraim in various ways. Like the
Spanish theologians who thought that Native Americans were biblical Jews, Wilson laid greatest stress on cultural comparison and
linguistic analysis. The name "Britain" itself derived from the Hebrew word for covenant, *brit*. Other traces of the Lost Israelites
could be found elsewhere in Europe, he claimed, such as the remnants of the tribe of Dan, whose legacy survived in places like Don,
Dnieper, Dniester, and, of course, the river Danube. The word "Cos-
sack" was a corruption of "Goi-Izak." Even the title of the song
"Yankee Doodle" was not originally American: "The name seems
to be a Hebraic nursery epithet of endearment, and it would be
interesting to trace the history of the tune, still more remotely." As
if part of a dark prophecy, Wilson also demonstrated the veracity
of British Israelism with a large dose of racial reasoning, which
gave pride of place to "the European branch of the SEMITIC race"
in England and America. As we shall see, this racist element of
British Israelism became dominant when the theory was transmog-
rified in the United States.[8]

Not content with merely identifying the whereabouts of some of
the Lost Ten Tribes, Wilson also tried to develop a practical program for retaking the Land of His Fathers, promoting a sort of British Israelite Zionism. "The land of Israel is a rich epitome of all
lands," he wrote with the confidence of a man who had never been
to the Middle East,

and of all countries it is the most centrally placed in respect
to both land and water. Especially is this the case with regard

to the different offshoots of the British Empire; so that in going there, we are, as already noticed, only removing into the midst of our family, to invite its several members to draw more closely around us. When the people are there who can take advantage of the capabilities and position of that Land so distinctly pointed out by the finger of God throughout all time; and now from the influence of the Old and New Testament, so much looked to from "all the ends of the earth"—when the people are there whose wants require the most extensive railway and telegraphic communication, these will be provided . . . They will come from America, India, Australia, New Zealand, and the Cape; young, as well as old and middle aged. Very soon many of our people will find it more convenient to send their children thither for education, when more facilities are provided, and such as are already being implanted in the Land of our fathers.

"What was regarded a few years ago as a wild dream," he noted, "is now merely a rational expectation."9

Wilson believed that the world was in the midst of God's divine program, as revealed in Scripture:

The Time has fully come when the Restoration of All Israel should take effect. The appointed "Seven Times" have run their course. The two prophetic half weeks, each consisting of three and a half times 360, or 1260 years, making together 2520 years, during which Israel were to be punished by being excluded from the Land, are more than ended. The threatened desolations have been accomplished in the east, the west, the north, and the south. In the Land itself, and in the surrounding countries, matters are exactly as predicted by the prophets. We are now invited to go and see how truthful God has been in the accomplishment of His threatenings; and to experience

in the Land as we have done so wonderfully *out* of it, how
faithful our God is in the fulfilment of His promises.

All that was required was for the British to conquer Palestine from
the Turks. "There is no time to be lost," he warned.[10]

Although Wilson spread his ideas as a paid lecturer, he made
no attempt at first to establish a sect or even a group of fellow
believers. After all, he promoted a historical theory which by itself
did little to threaten the mainly middle-class Victorians who came
to see the show. Even those who were convinced by his exegesis
were not really required to do anything, merely to appreciate the
demonstrated fact that they were the descendants of the Lost Ten
Tribes and that God had promised to them His love and protection.
Joining a club would not bring forward the Second Coming by a
single day. Nevertheless, from the early 1870s a number of small
associations of like-minded believers did emerge, and British Israelism was launched as a movement. In 1871–72 the Anglo-
Ephraim Association was founded at meetings presided over by
Bishop Gobat of Jerusalem.

Wilson's reluctance to form an organized movement makes Edward Hine (1825–91) the first proper Anglo-Israelite. He had left
school at age twelve and worked his way up to deputy manager in
the late 1860s of the "Penny Bank." But the key event in his life
occurred in 1839 at the age of fourteen when he heard Wilson
lecture in Aldersgate Street and became convinced about the truth
of British Israelism.[11] He gave his first lecture on the subject thirty
years later, two years before Wilson's death, making him in a sense
the man to whom the torch was passed.[12] Hine was a fervent believer
that the British alone were the heirs of Israel, and he violently
opposed the "Teutonists" who would share the honor with other
Anglo-Saxon peoples. Hine pointed to Britain's supremacy on the
seas and her extensive colonial empire as proof of the manifestation
of God's promises to Abraham. Conversely, he argued that these

demonstrations of God's will also provide "an over-whelming wit-ness to the truth of scripture"; British Israelite theory in general "unsealed the sealed book." He encouraged Britain to take posses-sion of the Holy Land and to motivate her poor people to seek a better life by returning to their country of ultimate origin, Palestine. He even thought of buying land in Palestine, but nothing came of this scheme.[13]

Like Wilson before him, Edward Hine was also very successful as a lecturer and public speaker. He offered to lecture anywhere in the United Kingdom without charge if his hosts could guarantee a reasonable attendance and pay expenses.[14] Part of the reason for this generosity may have been that lectures provided him with the opportunity of selling his books. According to Hine's own reckon-ing, between October 1870 and July 1871 he sold 30,000 copies of his *Seventeen Positive Identifications* without the need to adver-tise, to solicit reviews, or to give away free copies to influential people. By 1873 he was ready to launch a magazine, the point of which was to provide a center for British Israelite activity in lieu of the sort of organization that goes with sectarian religion, and that Hine refused to allow. As with other such groups, the editorship of the magazine provided de facto leadership of the group itself.[15] A weekly and a monthly periodical were soon unleashed on the British public.[16]

Hine had his ear to the ground, and in March 1875 while lec-turing near Peterborough, he suddenly announced that he was mov-ing to Liverpool to be near "the North West, being the first to be spiritually moved by the Identity knowledge." It may be that Liv-erpool was receptive to the British Israelite message because of the large Roman Catholic Irish immigration to that city. But whatever the reason, by 1876 Liverpool had three "Israel Identification" as-sociations, while London had only two.[17] These groups were quite separate from the Anglo-Ephraim Association in London, which was rather more Teutonist in orientation, as its publication, *The Stan-dard of Israel*, made clear. Hine's movement thrived in the north, but in other parts of England as well. From the early 1870s, annual conferences were held, and soon there were unconnected but substantially similar associations in Dublin, Southampton, and Bristol. Hine made a great push in the summer of 1877, speaking to more than 40,000 people in three months, but he failed to hold his band together, losing control to local people and others who were not so disposed to cut off so entirely the rest of the Anglo-Saxon peoples from the promises made to Abraham. In any case, like Wilson, Edward Hine's forte was charismatic lecturing in an era before the mass media, and he was happy to speak to anyone who would listen, not only to those who were willing to climb aboard the British Israelite flagship.

After John Wilson and Edward Hine, the torch passed to Edward Wheler Bird (b. 1823), born in India, the son of a well-known provincial judge. Bird worked in the Indian Civil Service, and retired to Bristol in 1868 from a senior position. There he quickly became involved in various evangelical activities, including the London Society for Promoting Christianity amongst the Jews, the Bible Society, and others. In 1874 he came upon one of John Wilson's books, and became an enthusiastic supporter of British Israelism, becoming chairman of the Bristol and Clifton Anglo-Israel Association in April 1875.

Bird saw his mission as bringing a certain organization and systematization to the British Israel message according to the interpretation of Edward Hine. In 1874, he helped to found the Anglo-Israel Association in London, which was expressly created to combat the teachings of the Teutonists. Bird even invited Hine to be vice president of the new Association, but he declined, preferring to go his own way. This was a shame, since Bird and his new group swept all before them, only four years later swallowing whole the rival Teutonist Anglo-Ephraim Association, incorporating with them into a new Metropolitan Anglo-Israel Association, with Bird as president and Viscount Folkestone as patron.

As we have seen, movements such as British Israelism require a publication as a center, and their history is crucial to understanding the entire phenomenon. Bird had been a regular contributor to Hine's magazines before branching out on his own in 1875.[18] Hine's *Israel's Identity Standard* began to appear in 1876 edited by William Cookson at Liverpool. Bird applied to be editor, and Cookson agreed; the name was changed to *Banner of Israel*, a monthly, the first issue of which appeared in January 1877. Bird's editorship of this publication set the seal on his leadership, especially as the Teutonist *The Standard of Israel* failed in 1875.

Bird was careful not to confront Hine directly, but after all he worked in London and Bristol and had the most influential and important patrons and followers, while Hine, isolated in the more humble north, became more isolated and extreme. Hine further alienated Bird and others when he published an article suggesting that he himself was "Joseph, the Shepherd of the State of Israel."

Another subject on which Bird and Hine differed was the Jewish question. Bird was treasurer of the Bristol branch of the London Society for Promoting Christianity amongst the Jews, and in 1887 was appointed to Honorary Life Governorship of the Society. Hine, on the other hand, boasted that since he had begun lecturing, the income to the SPCJ had fallen by £15,000, which was desirable from his point of view since he did not think that modern Jews should convert to Christianity at all: "it would be utterly against all Scripture teaching for their body to accept Christ, that God promised to accept them under Moses." Furthermore, he wrote, it "is not enough for the British to see that they are identical with Israel, but we have to labour to make the Jews see it also; and we are not likely readily to gain their co-operation if we go to them with obnoxious prejudices." As Hine looked around him, he noted, "We sadly fear that the nonsense taught by some who have espoused the Identity cause, that God wills the conversation of the Jews to Christ, has been the great difficulty in the way of the Jews publicly acknowledging our Identification with Israel."[19]

From 1878, then, it was impossible for Hine to compete with the

Metropolitan Anglo-Israel Association under Bird's leadership. Refusing to accept the inevitable, Hine set up the British-Israel Identity Corporation at the beginning of 1880 with himself as manager, with the aim of publishing a daily and a weekly from London, as well as buying up the copyrights in British Israel works. He did manage to establish yet another magazine, *British-Israel and Judah's Prophetic Messenger* (1880–86), edited by John Unwin, a Sheffield manufacturer. But now he had new ambitions, and expressed his intention of entering national politics under the British Israel banner. On April 8 Hine held a meeting at Exeter Hall to show how British Israelism was congruent with the ideology of the Tory party under Benjamin Disraeli.

Hine's political career was short-lived, however, as he was soon sacked from his post as manager of the corporation for having disappeared without paying his debts. The British-Israel Identity Corporation issued an appeal for funds on his behalf, and even though Hine was eventually reinstated as leader, this was only after the president and secretary resigned in protest. In any case, Hine's new corporation collapsed in 1881, a year after its foundation; the *Messenger* continued to appear under the editorship of Unwin and later of his wife, but with a circulation of no more than 1,400 it was not profitable and ceased publication in early 1886. Hine himself moved to the United States.

Bird now publicly disassociated himself from Hine and said so both in his *Banner of Israel* and in the local press. His own Metropolitan Anglo-Israel Association was flourishing, with three hundred subscribing members in London and about twenty-seven affiliated groups. By the middle of the 1880s, Bird had established doctrinal unity as well, defining Teutonism as unacceptable British Israelite heresy.

British Israelism was always primarily an ideology, a particular understanding of English and biblical history, and one did not have to become a formal member of any organization in order to be an Anglo-Israelite. Nevertheless, like-minded believers did tend to come together in affiliated societies. British Israelites were mainly respectable middle-class people with an intellectual bent, a clearly recognizable part of the English religious scene.

After the First World War, all those who believed in the basic tenets of the movement were invited to join a new British Israel World Federation, replacing a loosely organized group of the same name (apart from the significant postwar difference that the word "British" replaced the term "Imperial"). It is clear that they had a substantial following and could draw a crowd. In 1929, they filled the Albert Hall, and two years later, more than 20,000 people attended the weeklong annual congress. Thousands of pounds were raised, and hundreds of meetings of the BIWF were held at the 239 branches which they commanded at one time. There was a significant decline in the late 1930s, parallel to the decay of other societies connected with the fading notion of British Empire; a brief Indian summer on the eve of the Second World War, when attendance at meetings increased tenfold; and by 1945 the grand days were clearly over.

Since British Israelism was an ideological conception more than a religious belief, it is no surprise to learn that the BIWF failed to unite all those people who accepted the notion that the British are the literal descendants of the people of Israel. Other organizations appeared after the war, such as the Society for Proclaiming Britain Is Israel (1945) and the Crown Covenanters Society (1961). As was true in the United States, these groups tended to support right-wing political positions. The predominance of women and the elderly was marked. The supporters were mostly middle-class, although in its heyday a significant number of peers, overseas bishops, and high-ranking military officers were also members.[20]

| II |

While British Israelism degenerated in England to yet another eccentric fringe movement, its transplantation to the United States in the 1880s not only ensured its survival but enabled it to merge with other groups that favored extravagant biblical interpretations, such as Millerism, dispensationalism, and Christian Aryanism. If Britain was Ephraim, then the United States was Manasseh, another Lost Tribe and heir to the promises of Abraham. The same themes which had been discussed by Wilson, Hine, and Bird on an exegetical level took on greater meaning in the New World. More details were hammered out: the British royal family, it was claimed, were lineal descendants of David, king of Israel; the Church of England/Episcopalian Church was the church of the covenant people; and the British and their American brethren were chosen by God to rule the world.[21]

But there was more evidence as well. Take the prophet Jeremiah, for example. Further American research revealed that Jeremiah did not die in Egypt, but instead made a voyage to Spain with two princesses of royal birth, the daughters of Zedekiah. The younger princess married in Spain, but Jeremiah took the older one with him to Ireland, where he settled, and married her off to the ruler of that Anglo-Saxon kingdom. She was Tea Tephi of Irish lore, and through her the Davidic succession on the throne of Israel was maintained, and passed to the kings of Britain and her empire. Jeremiah also brought the Stone of Scone to Ireland, the very stone used by Jacob as a pillow at Bethel, captured by the English in Scotland in 1298, and returned to the Scots only in 1996.[22]

There was further etymological evidence as well, a favorite proto-anthropological technique since the days of Columbus. The word "British" was probably a corruption of the Hebrew "*brit-ish*," "man of the covenant." The promise to Israel was through Abraham's son Isaac, and his descendants became known as "Isaac-sons," later abbreviated to "Saxons." The name of the city of London shows traces of the tribe of Dan, which settled there. The name "America" is merely the Hebrew words "*am-erik*," "the country of [Leif] Erik[son]." The Scottish plaid derives from Joseph's coat of many colors. Looking at all of this evidence together, who could not conclude that the British and Americans were the true Chosen People of God, and that the biblical promises applied to them alone?

But most fascinating of all was the introduction of pyramidology to the British Israelite scheme at the time of its transplantation to the United States, and thus a key issue from its inception there. The basic idea was that the Great Pyramid was God's original record of revelation, presented in symbols and terms of modern science and preserved in the stones of the pyramid itself. Just as God recorded His revelation in the form of words in the Bible, so too did He give us the same information in stone, which can be deciphered by mathematics, understanding the measurements of the Great Pyramid. Since biblical interpretation is never perfectly clear, we are almost compelled to seek further information in the dimensions of the Great Pyramid.

In practice, what this meant was understanding that there is such a thing as a "pyramid inch," 1.00106 British inches, exactly one twenty-fifth of the Sacred Cubit (25.0265 British inches), which conveniently is precisely one ten-millionth of the earth's mean polar radius. The builders of the Great Pyramid constructed that massive edifice so that each pyramid inch (especially in the ascending and descending interior chambers) would signify a single year in the history of mankind. Thus in it we can trace the entire history of the world from the beginning of the "Adamic race," in about 4000 B.C., to its conclusion, in about 2000 A.D., when man will become extinct in the millennial Sabbath. The Great Pyramid documents the dates of the Flood (2352 B.C.), the Exodus (1513 B.C.), the life of Christ in great detail, the war between the United States and Mexico (1846), the repeal of the British Corn Laws (also 1846), the First World War, and the abdication of Edward VIII (1936). The Pyramid can also be used to predict future events efficiently. Adam Rutherford, a great pyramidologist of the 1930s, predicted the creation of the State of Israel "after 1941," and the establishment of Christ's millennial reign on earth at September 21, 1994, on the autumnal equinox.[23] Peter Lemesurier, Rutherford's successor, has since corrected that happy date to July 2, 2989.[24]

Who built the Great Pyramid? It was named for the Pharaoh Cheops, but perhaps the builder was Enoch, who led the Shepherd Kings to Egypt and lived for 365 years, symbolically the same number of days in a single year. Perhaps the builder was Melchizedek, who was really Job. But two things are clear, as Rutherford put it: "that the Great Pyramid in Egypt is a Divinely designed monument and that it is truth in structural form." In other words, he says, "the teaching of the Bible and that of the Pyramid are identical in every particular, the one in words, the other in stone."[25]

One of the first Americans to promulgate the British Israelite view was the pastor of a Congregationalist church in Brooklyn named Joseph Wild, who claimed that he gave 130 sermons on that subject between 1876 and 1879. Significantly, he first came across the theory by reading a book by John Wilson in the 1850s. In his own book, *The Lost Tribes and 1882*, first published in 1879, he wrote:

> The main idea I wish to convey in this book, is that God is conducting his Providence through his ancient people, Israel, whom I believe are found in the Saxon race. And his throne on earth, through which flow the purpose of Providence, is David's throne, which I believe to be at present the English throne. Queen Victoria (and God bless her) I believe to be David's seed. The United States fulfills the role of the tribe of Manasseh. Therefore to understand the prophecies, Providence, and the present movements of nations, as well as the future lot and destiny of each, we must read the Scriptures in this light.

One of the many signs that the end was at hand, he thought, was that Jews were moving to return to Palestine.[26]

Wild was followed by a number of others, the most important of whom for the link with the British Israelites in England was Lieutenant Charles A. L. Totten, an artillery officer in charge of military instruction at Yale in 1889–92, who wrote a number of texts on this subject. His first British Israelite work, which appeared in 1883, entranced C. Piazzi Smyth (1819–1900), the Astronomer-Royal for Scotland, who was also an ardent pyramidologist.[27] In Totten's next book, which included a preface by Smith, he declared, "It is a startling statement, and yet one founded upon ample evidence, that the Anglo-Saxon Race is the literal, lineal, and blood descendant of the Ten Tribes of Israel, whom Shalmanesar deported in Media *circa* 721 B.C., and who thereafter, and hitherto, have been so completely *lost!*" Totten stressed how wondrous it was that, in an age of disbelief spawned of modern science and secular Enlightenment ideas, a few people "of the Anglo-Saxons should awaken to the demonstrable conviction that we ourselves are the actual descendants of Israel, literal sons of Abraham, of Isaac, and of Jacob." He pressed the theme that the promised finale of human history was at hand, to be led by the Anglo-Israelites. One sign of the fast approach of the culmination was the "natural anticipation of Judah [i.e., the modern Jews] for her promised return" to Palestine.[28]

When Edward Hine came to the United States in 1884, he linked up with Charles Totten and stayed with him in New Haven. Hine enjoyed the chance to re-create himself in this virgin land and made a new career lecturing about the true destiny of the British people and their American brethren up and down the eastern seaboard and into Canada and the upper Midwest, returning to England in February 1888. He also had more to say now about the role of the tribe of Judah, the modern Jews, in the divine plan. Eventually, groups devoted to the ideology were formed in the western United States and Canada, clustering around Vancouver, Portland (Oregon), and Los Angeles.

A key figure in the move westward was J. H. Allen (1847–1930), a Methodist from Illinois who founded a "Holiness" church in Missouri, one of the precursors of the Pentecostalist revival which broke out in Los Angeles in 1906. Allen eventually moved to California and settled in Pasadena, helping to fuse his own British Israelism with other religious movements and to promote the rise of Christian Identity in the West, which has remained its center.[29] Allen's popular work *Judah's Sceptre and Joseph's Birthright*, first published in 1902, included a map on the front flyleaf of Europe and the Middle East showing a direct line from Jerusalem to the British Isles. Allen insisted in this work that most Christians had erred in not expecting a physical return of the Messiah King on earth among His Chosen People. Britain held first place among the Chosen, the United States the second rank. The recent rapid expansion of the British Empire and the westward expansion of the United States were obvious signs of the chosenness of these two countries and of the imminent climax of the drama of world history in which the lead role would be played by these two Anglo-Saxon nations.[30]

Another important American Christian Israelite was Professor F. Odum, who had been raised in the Anglican and Methodist traditions, but whose university studies had led him to have doubts about the teachings of the Bible. "To my mind either the Book was a fraud or the teaching from the pulpit was false," he proclaimed. Fortunately, he encountered the views of the British Israelites and, despite initial doubts, soon "found that my judgment was captured by the straight and marvellous array of facts." In a text published in the midst of the First World War, Odum wrote that "the proofs that we, the Anglo-Saxon peoples, are the ancient Ten-tribed House of Israel, in *a national and official sense*, is as clear to my mind as the noon-day sun is to the eyes of mortals," or even as manifest as geometrical theorems. He thought one could therefore dispense with the Higher Criticism of the Bible, which was so prominent in Germany and was making its way in the United States, for it was merely "that devil's, German, atheistic process of human speculation." Clearly the biblical Israel was not represented by modern Jews, since the House of Judah was never part of that chosen group.[31]

The first chapter of Odum's book produced data about the extent of the British Empire in 1916 in population and area, its wealth, its trade—statistics intended to demonstrate that "Great Britain is the only nation in the world's history that is in the full enjoyment of all the national and material blessings promised to ancient Israel" in the Bible itself. The recent rapid expansion of British control in the Middle East and Africa was further evidence that Britain was God's covenant people. Odum agreed that the "Saxons" were really "Isaac's sons" and that the Angles were the sons of Joseph through Ephraim. In the Kurdish area of Iraq, the biblical Ur of the Chaldees, there is a river called "Engl" and a town named "Angl," he told his readers, and the English language derives its structure from Hebrew. The tribes of Israel were dispersed but joined together in the British Isles under a sovereign of the Davidic line, who adopted the Union Jack (Jacob) as their flag. "One thing that is sure," Odum concluded, "all the above Hebrew Scripture names, the history connected therewith, and the prophecies concerning them, are found in Britain, the covenant isles, and are found nowhere else on this round globe." The British were "God's saviours to mankind. We must rule all nations."

Odum concluded that the British Empire and its rapid growth can only be providential. "Britain, the STONE KINGDOM [the fifth kingdom of Daniel], will own Palestine; bring back the Jews in safety; control the world from Jerusalem and be the only worldpower of all future time." This in itself was an interesting prophecy in that Odum wrote those words before British forces under General Allenby actually conquered Jerusalem. The great news, he wrote, was: "The time is at hand when the nations shall be made to see that God had and has ONLY ONE PLAN through the ages, viz., TO SAVE MANKIND THROUGH HIS KINGDOM OF PRIESTS, HIS CHOSEN RACE, HIS PECULIAR PEOPLE, HIS ELECT, HIS ROYAL PRIESTHOOD, HIS Anglo-Saxons, or the Joseph sons of Isaac." Needless to say, Britain's role in the war was as the force of God fighting against Germany, agent of Satan. Reading Odum, it is hard to remember that there was a time when British Israelites believed that the German peoples might be part of the Anglo-Saxon race that was destined to receive God's promises to the Chosen People.[32]

While many British Israelites regarded the tribe of Judah, the modern Jews, as having no part in God's inheritance, not all groups were openly anti-Semitic. Among those who regarded the Jews as dangerous impostors was Reuben H. Sawyer, a minister in Portland, Oregon, who led an active Anglo-Israel Research Society there. Sawyer lectured throughout the Northwest and helped establish the British Israel World Federation in London in 1920. At the same time, Sawyer found the time to serve as a leader of the Ku Klux Klan in Oregon in 1921–24.[33]

Like Sawyer, many others saw the Jews as virulent opponents who were trying to usurp the role of Chosen People from its rightful representative, the British and Anglo-American white Christians. Others adhered to the medieval notion of the Jews as, literally, children of Satan. An important center of such beliefs was to be found in the heart of the Ford Motor Company. The company's spokesman, William J. Cameron (1878–1955), a key American British Israelite and the promoter of an anti-Semitic attitude based on the *Protocols of the Elders of Zion*, was Ford's right-hand man in the company and served him from 1918 until 1946, the year before Ford's death. Henry Ford himself had been involved in the publication of a book entitled *The International Jew* (1920), which amounted to a collection of articles from Ford's newspaper, the *Dearborn Independent*. It was a sort of annotated version of the *Protocols*, showing how the Jews had begun taking over America as early as 1492 when some of them arrived with Columbus. After a libel suit was filed in 1925, Ford was eventually to make the rational business decision of withdrawing his book and apologizing to the American business community in July 1927, but the issue refused to die.[34]

Its liveliness was due in part to the efforts of Gerald L. K. Smith

(d. 1976), a former associate of Huey Long, the governor of Louisiana, who was assassinated there in 1935. By the Second World War, Smith was the most notorious anti-Semite in America, and in the early 1950s, Smith moved his operation to Los Angeles and pushed Anglo-Israelism into more overt anti-Semitism, merging it with the growing Christian Identity movement. Smith reissued Ford's *International Jew*, and in a new preface reported that he and his wife had visited Henry Ford, who insisted not only that he had never made any apology to the Jews but that his signature on the document that said so had been forged by an associate at the company.[35] In any case, Los Angeles became a center of the British Israel movement in the 1930s and 1940s, with conferences held there in 1945, 1946, and 1947. Gradually the California movement lost its links with the organizations in England and even with followers on the East Coast, fusing instead with the very anti-Semitic Christian Identity movement, a process actively encouraged by Smith.[36]

Some of this anti-Semitism was muted during the Second World War, especially after the entry of the United States into the conflict in 1941. Nevertheless, a number of anti-Jewish Anglo-Israelite works did appear, such as the pseudonymous *When? A Prophetical Novel of the Very Near Future*, issued by the British-Israel Association of Greater Vancouver in 1944, in which it was claimed that the Jews were the offspring of Satan. The Anglo-Saxon Christian World Movement of Vancouver published *When Gog Attacks* in the same year by one C. F. Parker, who treated the *Protocols of the Elders of Zion* as historical fact, and Cain as the founder of the Synagogue of Satan. The author also tried to show that Ashkenazi Jews were not the descendants of the biblical Hebrews but instead of Turko-Mongol descent, a point that would be emphasized as time went on.[37]

In the 1950s, new people connected with Gerald L. K. Smith and the racist interpretation of British Israelite views appeared on the scene in the Los Angeles area, such as William Potter Gale (1917–

88) and Wesley Swift (1913–70). Swift was the son of a Methodist minister in New Jersey, and had begun his career in the (Pentecostalist) International Church of the Four Square Gospel of Aimee Semple McPherson. Swift set up his own church on the outskirts of Los Angeles, calling it at first the Anglo-Saxon Christian Congregation, then changing its name to the Church of Jesus Christ Christian, emphasizing the position that Jesus was not a Jew.[38] William Potter Gale also had a lasting influence. His background was military, since he had been a colonel on General Douglas MacArthur's staff during the Second World War, later on serving in the Philippines. Gale came across Christian Identity writings in the early 1950s, and helped to found the Christian Defense League (CDL) in the early 1960s, a group whose first president was Richard Grint Butler. After Wesley Swift's death in 1970, Butler was to set up a church with the identical name in Idaho, the Church of Jesus Christ Christian, and unite it with a movement known as Aryan Nation, as we shall see. Gale was also one of the founders of the Posse Comitatus in the 1970s, a loosely organized movement based on the concept that no governmental unit above the level of the county sheriff's posse has any standing in the United States Constitution.

| III |

The British Israelite movement in the United States received its greatest boost from the conversion of Herbert W. Armstrong (1896–1986), a businessman who founded the Worldwide Church of God at Eugene, Oregon, in 1933. Armstrong testified that his theological mission began when his wife had a dream in which God commanded him (through her) to observe the Sabbath on Saturday (like the Seventh-day Adventists). Armstrong studied the Bible looking for justification for this belief, and became a Sabbatarian. He read the works of J. H. Allen and others, and his studies led him to conclude further that since the messianic king of Israel had not yet arrived it was blasphemous to celebrate either Christmas or Easter.[39] The

Worldwide Church of God was Armstrong's alternative to established religion, and Ambassador College, incorporated at Pasadena in 1947, was the seminary in which his doctrine was taught, boosted by his frequent radio broadcasts and his publication, *Plain Truth*, the vehicle for disseminating it further. His ritual followed biblical Israelite practice, including worshipping on Saturday. He also celebrated the major Jewish religious festivals, adding three features of Christian practice: baptism by immersion, a celebration of the Lord's supper, and foot washing.

Armstrong was a British Israelite in the literal sense of the term. He claimed that he was related to Quakers who had come to America with William Penn in the seventeenth century, and that he himself was descended from King Edward I of England, and therefore from King David himself, albeit on only one side of his family.[40] In theology, he was naturally an anti-Trinitarian, regarding the doctrine of the Trinity as a pagan accretion. In its place, he offered a sort of Arian thesis that the Deity consists of the Eternal (Yahweh) and Jesus. The Holy Spirit is a power, not a person. Armstrong also talked about the Family of God, composed of Yahweh, Jesus, and the human community of believers, the members of the Worldwide Church of God. These latter would be saved if they believed in Jesus, and would be rewarded in heaven according to how well they followed the Ten Commandments, the biblical dietary laws, and the celebration of the holy days specified in the Bible. The Worldwide Church of God itself was the "Philadelphia" Church referred to in Revelation 3:7.

In his last work, *Mystery of the Ages*, Armstrong offered a scenario about the end of the world, which would be preceded by the emergence of the fourth kingdom of Daniel's dream—manifested in our world by the European Union. This infernal organization would be crushed by the returning Jesus, followed by the Battle of Armageddon, and the final saving of the true believers. Armstrong was also convinced that events that occurred in the Middle East between the time of General Allenby's entrance into Jerusalem in

1918 and the founding of the State of Israel were indications that the end was at hand. Indeed, he insisted, "Israel is God's timepiece." Unlike many British Israelites who harbored anti-Semitic views, Armstrong was an enthusiastic supporter of the state of Israel despite the Zionist wish to be free of the British Mandate.

The Worldwide Church of God suffered bad times after the death of Herbert W. Armstrong in 1986. Indeed, it fractured into various groups, one of which has been trying to jettison the founder's millenarianism and thereby to become an ordinary evangelical Protestant church.[41] Ambassador College in Pasadena went bankrupt and closed, but there is an Ambassador University in Big Sandy, Texas. The mainstream Armstrong doctrine is now carried on by the Philadelphia Church based in Edmond, Oklahoma, whose magazine, *The Trumpet*, claims a circulation of 60,000. Their views concerning Israel coincide with those of the most nationalist Jewish groups, supporting the suppression of Palestinians and the invasion of Lebanon. The Philadelphia Church also opposed the return of the Stone of Scone to Scotland in November 1996, urging that the English keep this important artifact ready for the coronation of King Jesus.

| IV |

Various strands of millenarian theorizing were brought together in postwar America. Fusing new versions of anti-Semitism, pre-Adamite racism, British Israelism, neo-Nazi Aryanism, and other ideologies, they formed the central tenets of militant revolutionary messianism. Those attracted to such ideologies were distressed to see the United States change from a society dominated by white male Christians to one incorporating people of color, Jews, and women in positions of power and authority. They believed that the Communist menace abroad was looking for any opportunity to destroy American society already weakened from within. Their amalgam of various theories and ideologies combined existing ideas with conspiracy theories about the subversive activities of Jews, Free-masons, and Communists. The civil rights movement and its successes made them feel even more dispossessed, and they imagined they would have to fight for the survival of the Christian white American world they thought they knew against the government of the United States, which they considered was no longer legitimate, since it had given itself over to those who by rights should not have power at all. Military survivalist groups, militias, the Posse Comitatus, the Freemen, and others began to prepare for the Battle of Armageddon, or something like it, on American soil.[42] Many of the militia groups are primarily survivalist, and interested more in opposing gun control than in promulgating a political ideology.[43] But others adhered to ideas based on a combination of British Israelism, dispensationalism, and other concepts found in the writings of people like Nesta Webster and Eustice Mullins, or in the works of groups like the Christian Reconstructionists, who advocate promulgating God's law as the law of the land.

In the writings of these militant groups we hear the echo of earlier, more benign theories. Consider, for example, the statement by Richard Grint Butler, leader of the Aryan Nation: "We believe that the true, literal children of the Bible are the 12 tribes of Israel, which are now scattered throughout the world and are known as the Anglo-Saxon, Celtic, Scandinavian and Teutonic people of the earth . . . All races did not descend from Adam. Adam is the father of the White Race only [and] the Jew is the adversary of our race and God." So the children of Satan are alive and pose a variety of dangers. In the end, there will be an accounting by Yahweh: those who have followed His Law will be redeemed, and the rest will be sent to eternal damnation.[44] We find similar sentiments expressed in the credo of the Church of Israel at Schell City, Missouri, which pledges, "We believe that Adam is the father and beginning of the Caucasian race and of no other race. We believe that all of the non-white races were on earth before Adam." The Chosen People, the Israelites, are "today identified among the Anglo-Saxon-Germanic-

Scandinavian-Slavonic kindred peoples," while the "Jews of today are the Canaanite, Edemite, Amalekites and other related peoples identified in the world today as Zionists, Khazars and other related terms."[45]

A further example is the Posse Comitatus, founded in about 1969 in Portland, Oregon, by Henry "Mike" Beach, a former member of the Anglo-Israelite Silver Shirts movement of William Dudley Pelley and William Potter Gale.[46] By 1984, leading Aryan Nation figures were active in the group.[47] According to the Posse Comitatus, Jews are the children of Satan and blacks are "mud people." They believe that since the United States was founded as a Christian commonwealth, it should be run as a Christian country for Christians alone; its highest legitimate governmental unit is the county, and the highest official the sheriff; common-law courts should try all disputes. The group remained obscure until 1975, when the FBI was informed that they intended to assassinate Nelson Rockefeller. Their investigation discovered that the group was active in twenty-three states; one of their leaders, James Wickstrom, had a Christian Identity ministry in Wisconsin.[48]

One important element in this kind of Christian Aryanism is the pre-Adamic theory, which originated in the seventeenth century and became part of later British Israelism in the 1920s; since that time it has appeared in almost all the racial Aryan representations as a way of both accounting for and eliminating the theological importance of nonwhites.

In the general Judeo-Christian biblical frameworks, the entire human race in all its forms and diversities is descended from Adam, the first man, and from Noah and his family, sole survivors of the Flood. But after the discovery of the Americas, European explorers and colonizers pondered the question of the origin of the peoples whom they found there. One interesting answer to this question came with the publication in 1655 of *Prae-Adamitae* (Men Before Adam), a book by Isaac La Peyrère, a Calvinist, probably of Marrano origins, who was secretary to the prince of Condé, the most powerful nobleman in France. La Peyrère had long been worried about certain passages in Scripture which seemed to suggest another source for mankind besides Adam. Who was Cain's wife, and who were the people among whom Cain and his wife settled when they were expelled from Adam and Eve's company after his murder of Abel? La Peyrère noted that St. Paul in Romans postulated that sin came into the world with Adam, and this seemed to suggest that there had been a world before Adam where sin was unknown. La Peyrère offered the theory that this pre-Adamite world had existed from the beginning of time, a world with the characteristics of what Thomas Hobbes called the "state of nature," a lawless place where people fought one another without end. Not liking what He saw, God then established a lawful world by creating Adam; it was this second world of Adamites that provided the characters in the divine drama recorded in the Bible. Meanwhile, the world of pre-Adamites, the rest of the globe apart from the tribes of Israel, continued its meaningless existence.[49]

La Peyrère offered his theory as a way of accounting for all the different peoples in the world, including the Native Americans. He coupled it with a revolutionary messianic concept: that the biblical Jews, whom God had rejected when they refused to accept Jesus, would be recalled to Christ when Jesus returned as the Jewish Messiah. In order to prepare for this great day, the Jews should be invited to France, where a Jewish Christian church should be established entirely for them, free of any offensive practices or doctrines that Jews had abhorred in the past. Then, when Jesus returned, which would occur in the very near future, He could gather them up and take them and the king of France to Jerusalem, where the Temple would be rebuilt. King Jesus and the king of France as His earthly regent would henceforth rule the millennial world, the recalled Jews serving as courtiers in the new divine government. Thus would the world be saved, Adamites and pre-Adamites alike.

La Peyrère's pre-Adamite theory attracted few followers in his own time. When he tried to get his book published as early as 1643, it was banned, and was circulated at first only in manuscript form, achieving a certain notoriety among eminent contemporaries. Queen Christina of Sweden met La Peyrère in Antwerp in 1655, soon after her abdication, and offered to pay for the publication of his interesting manuscript; La Peyrère took the text to Amsterdam, where it was published in 1655 in several editions that were almost immediately banned and burned as heretical and blasphemous. The author himself was arrested and released only upon promising to convert to Catholicism and to apologize personally to the pope, both of which he duly performed. La Peyrère retired to a monastery and spent the rest of his life clandestinely gathering further evidence for his pre-Adamite theory in the vain hope of venturing into print once again.

In many ways, La Peyrère's greatest success occurred long after his death. Planters in Virginia saw the "pre-Adamite whimsy" as a brilliant theory which might keep black people in slavery forever.[50] La Peyrère himself may have been a benign universalist, but his theory lent itself to justifying distinctions between races, and explaining why European whites should dominate over all the other peoples of the world. His polygenetic thesis of human origins was further developed by early anthropologists, biologists, and others to account for the varieties of mankind and the superiority of some kinds of people over others. By the early nineteenth century, American ethnologists were busy measuring skull size, brain capacity, and other features in order to prove the inferiority of nonwhites and the biological hopelessness of blacks. Before the Civil War, they were using their polygenetic findings in order to justify slavery and the withholding of education from black people.[51] A geologist at the University of Michigan, Alexander Winchell, incorporated La Peyrère into his analysis of the latest scientific findings.[52] The most racist version of the pre-Adamite theory was provided by Charles Carroll in his sensational book published in 1900, *The Negro a Beast*.[53]

The British Israelites did not at first seem particularly interested in polygenetic racist reasoning. Their immediate concerns were with the Great Pyramid, the perfect expression of God's message in stone. They wanted to understand how this divine creation operated, since it could have been built only from God's instructions which posited the ordained units of construction and measurement. It was probably the brainchild of the Patriarchs, or of Hiram the Phoenician, since the Egyptians themselves, as polytheists, could not have comprehended the divine message. David Davidson, an early-twentieth-century British Israelite, introduced La Peyrère into the equation: he argued that the Adamites were the progenitors of the white British Israelites whose ancestors had built the Great Pyramid; the non-Adamites were dark-skinned, inferior beings.[54] From Davidson onward, this racist form of pre-Adamism was infused into British Israelism and carried forward into the theories we call Christian Aryanism.

The status of the Jews was progressively devalued and demonized: first, the British Israelite tribes were separated from the tribe of Judah; then it was denied that the Jews were a biblical tribe at all, and proclaimed that they had a different role in divine history. It was suggested that the Jews were in fact descended from Cain, and Cain from Satan, who impregnated Eve with demonic offspring, which would account for the endlessly hostile role the Jews were thought to have played throughout history, including the present.[55]

Another line of reasoning that became popular among Christian Aryans took the Jews out of the Bible entirely, insisting that they were an Asiatic race of impostors claiming to be the Chosen People, but in reality were merely the descendants of Khazars, from southern Russia. It was known even in the Middle Ages that the Khazar kingdom had converted to Judaism in the late ninth century, or at least that its leaders had done so. Indeed, this story led Judah ha-Levi to write his famous *Kuzari* in Spain in the eleventh century, portraying the conversion as the result of a public dispute among a Christian, a Muslim, and a Jew, each presenting the merits of his respective religion, at the end of which the king of the Khazars chose Judaism as the state religion.

The Khazar theory had a long history, for it was championed not only by Christian Aryans but also by some Jews who sought a better historical explanation of the origins of Ashkenazi Jewry. Perhaps the most famous modern Jewish exponent was Arthur Koestler, whose book *The Thirteenth Tribe* (1976) was a popular account of the hypothesis. More recently, linguists have discussed whether Yiddish should not be considered a Slavic language with many German words rather than the other way around, perhaps pointing to a connection with the ancient Khazar kingdom.[56] Another view has it that the Khazar theory explains all Jewish history, showing how the Jews were driven to the west by the Mongol and Turkish invasions of Aryan Europe, where they caused so many difficulties that they had to be driven east again, toward Poland and Russia.[57]

These were some of the ideas that were in the air and available to the theoreticians of Christian Aryanism. Chief among them was Richard Grint Butler, who in the 1970s set up the Church of Jesus Christ Christian Aryan Nation at Hayden Lake, Idaho, in a fortified compound. This center serves as the base for meetings and conferences also attended by ideological supporters from outside the church such as Eustace Mullins and Larry Pratt.[58] All these groups oppose large political units, which suggests that there is no overarching structure uniting their activities, but the meetings at Hayden Lake loosely connect people with similar inclinations. They also support more militant groups like the Posse Comitatus, which adds to the ideology of Christian Aryanism and Christian Identity a deep hatred of the federal government and all political entities above the county level. The fact that many of its members are veterans of the American armed forces and have fought in Korea or Vietnam makes them more immediately dangerous.[59] Members of the Posse Comitatus refuse to pay federal income taxes or to obtain driver's licenses or social security cards. One member of the group, Gordon Kahl, a farmer from North Dakota, stopped paying taxes in

1967 and organized a Posse group in his area as a sort of shadow government. After a meeting of his group in 1983, a disturbance occurred during which two federal marshals were killed, and Kahl himself was soon located by the FBI in Arkansas and shot dead. He became a martyr for the Christian Identity movement as a whole.[60]

One interesting Christian Identity group is called The Order, and is the project of Robert Matthews, an Arizona man and sometime Mormon convert who gravitated from the John Birch Society to survivalist groups in the Northwest. Matthews attended meetings of the Church of Jesus Christ Christian, and was encouraged in his work by Butler and others. Soon he gathered together a band of a few dozen people to prepare for the Great War against the Zionist Occupation Government (ZOG) of the United States, which would save the white Christian Aryans who would participate in the Second Coming. During the 1980s, The Order established headquarters in various isolated locations in Idaho, Montana, and Washington, creating large arms caches and offering training in survivalist techniques. Its members commonly refer to The Order as the Silent Brotherhood, or the Bruders Schweigen. To obtain the necessary funds for their existence and struggle against the federal government, they began with small-scale holdups and robberies—of a pornography shop, a number of banks, and in July 1984 a Brinks truck in California transporting nearly $4 million. Matthews was so pleased with the results that he distributed some of his newfound wealth among other groups that he visited throughout the country. It was the Brinks robbery, and the murder in Denver in 1984 of Alan Berg, a left-wing Jewish television talk-show host, that roused the FBI to action, culminating in a shoot-out on Whidbey Island, Washington, on December 8, during which Matthews and others were killed; a number of his followers were jailed.[61]

Another group in the same tradition that has attracted some media attention is the Christian Identity community of about a hundred people at Elohim City, Oklahoma. The spiritual leader there is a

Canadian-born former Mennonite named Robert G. Millar (b. 1926), who founded the little Ozark village in 1973 and called it after the Hebrew name for God, Elohim. "I believe that the inheritors of the promises of the 12 tribes of Israel," Millar explains, "are primarily the Celtic tribes, the Germanic people and the Scandinavian people, not inclusively and not exclusively, but primarily." His proof is economic as well as religious, since this "people represents 9 percent of the population of the world. They control 50 percent of the wealth of the world. So it's evident that the promises of God have come to pass."[62] Millar's granddaughter married James D. Ellison, another Identity leader who was arrested by the FBI in 1985, and helped to negotiate his surrender to the federal authorities. Ellison had been leader of a group in northwestern Arkansas called the Covenant, Sword and Arm of the Lord, but he went to prison on racketeering and weapons charges. Timothy McVeigh telephoned someone who lived at Elohim City, a German citizen named Andreas Strassmier, on April 5, 1995, two weeks before the bombing at Oklahoma City. Millar was also the spiritual guide of Richard Snell, the white supremacist who was executed in Arkansas on April 19, 1995, the day the federal building in Oklahoma City was bombed and the second anniversary of the conflagration at Waco. Indeed, Millar witnessed the execution, claimed Snell's body, and had him buried at Elohim City.

A new twist to traditional interpretations of Scripture came to public attention with the appearance of the Phineas Priesthood, which seeks justification for its violent actions in the biblical story of Phinehas told in Numbers 25. According to this instructive tale, Phinehas was justified in having murdered a "son of Israel" who had married a foreigner, and in having killed the bride as well; God praised him for saving the people of Israel from sinfulness and the plague. A Reverend Paul Hill, who in March 1993 shot and killed an abortion doctor in Pensacola, Florida, offered the Phinehas defense, but the court where he was convicted of murder disregarded this.[63] The Phineas Priesthood has also been active in northern

Idaho, home ground of Christian Identity. Three men from Sand-point, Idaho, were arrested in 1996 and charged with a campaign of crime apparently inspired by their beliefs: on April 1 they were said to have exploded a pipe bomb outside the office of a newspaper in Spokane, Washington, and then to have robbed $50,000 from a bank there. On July 12, 1996, they were charged with bombing the Spokane Planned Parenthood Clinic as a diversion, and then robbing the same bank branch once again. The FBI caught up with them on October 8, when they stopped for gas after a planned bank robbery in Portland was foiled after a tip-off. Bank-robbing equipment was found in their cars, and evidence has linked them to the Phineas Priesthood.[64]

A key text for these Christian Aryan groups is *The Turner Diaries*, by William Luther Pierce (b. 1933), a former physics professor at Oregon State University and aide to George Lincoln Rockwell of the American Nazi Party. Rockwell was assassinated in 1967 by one of his own former followers, and Pierce stayed with the American Nazis for three more years and then in 1970 founded his own National Youth Alliance in Hillsboro, West Virginia, which through inexorable force of time eventually dropped the middle word from its title, becoming in 1974 the National Alliance. Pierce in earlier days had been a follower of Robert Welch, president of the John Birch Society, who had introduced him to *The John Franklin Letters*, an anti-utopian novel that describes the United States under Russian control.[65] Pierce wrote his own contribution to this genre as *The Turner Diaries*, which appeared in serial form in its magazine *Attack!* between 1975 and 1978, and was published as a paperback book in 1978.[66] Robert Matthews claimed that he was merely carrying out the plan described in *The Turner Diaries*, and Timothy McVeigh had the book in his possession when he was arrested for the bombing in Oklahoma, which killed 168 people, including fifteen children in a day-care center, and injured more than four hundred others.[67]

The Turner Diaries is a clumsily written fictional account of the white Aryans' "Great Revolution" of 1991–99 against the Zionist Occupation Government in Washington, D.C.[68] The narrator is Earl Turner ("1956–93"), who comes on board at the very beginning of the action. In the story, Congress passes the Cohen Act, according to which white Aryans become second-class citizens, and preference is given to Jews, blacks, and Hispanics. The underground Aryans make weapons, blow up the FBI headquarters in Washington (using the same sort of homemade dynamite-detonated truck bomb made of ammonium nitrate fertilizer and fuel oil that was used to destroy the federal building in Oklahoma City), attack the Capitol with mortar shells, and destroy communications and utility centers. They also manage to steal weapons and armaments from military bases where they have secret allies. Eventually the rebellion spreads until the white Aryans establish an independent state for themselves in the West. Once in power, they expel the "clearly distinguishable nonwhites" in order "to increase racial pressure on the whites outside California." The "almost-white mongrels," on the other hand, who might constitute a "danger that will later 'pass' as white," are force-marched out of the city. "I have a suspicion their trip into that canyon north of here will be a one-way affair!" the narrator suggests. As for "white women who were married to or living with blacks, with Jews, or with other nonwhite males," they are lynched on lampposts, power poles, and trees at every intersection on a solemn "Day of the Rope": a "whole batch are apparently faculty members from the nearby UCLA campus." As for Earl Turner, his martyrdom is achieved on November 9, 1993, in a kamikaze attack on the Pentagon, which eliminates effective opposition to the revolution. Israel, New York, Toronto, Russia, and China are destroyed by nuclear bombardment, and the fifty million surviving white Americans begin to rebuild a racially pure society. And so it was, "in the year 1999, according to the chronology of the Old Era—just 110 years after the birth of the Great One—that the dream of a White world finally became a certainty." Hitler was born in 1889, so one may assume that he is "the Great One." *The*

Turner Diaries comes with an "Epilog," supposedly written in the year 2099, the Year 100 by the new chronology, assuring everyone that the revolution was successful "and that the Order would spread its wise and benevolent rule over the earth for all time to come."

Although some commentators have seen *The Turner Diaries* as a sort of Christian Aryan militia version of *Mein Kampf*, in fact the ideology is rarely spelled out and brought in only between the lines of what is meant to be an exciting action adventure. "There is no way a society based on Aryan values and an Aryan outlook can evolve peacefully from a society which has succumbed to Jewish spiritual corruption," Pierce's narrator insists. "Your day is coming, Jews, your day is coming." The book also includes detailed instructions on how to blow up bridges, make pipe bombs, destroy communications systems, and generally cause complete chaos.

William Pierce sees himself as being in great personal danger. He built a steel house in West Virginia with funds given to him by Robert Matthews, and hopes to ward off his enemies while protected within. His benign appearance on *60 Minutes* while he expressed his extreme views only reinforces his dangerous image. In the meantime, he publishes articles in his journal, *Free Speech*, available on the Internet, on such subjects as "Disney and the Jews," railing against the fact that since the "Jewish" takeover of the Disney company, "they" have made such films as *Pocahontas*, which advocates interracial marriage.[69] According to Pierce, his National Alliance group intends to achieve "a thorough rooting out of Semitic and other non-Aryan values and customs everywhere," and to create in North America and western Europe "a racially clean area of the earth for further development of our people." Yet his book was taken seriously by the FBI only in 1985 when The Order came to their attention.[70]

It is clear that there are many such groups throughout the United States, sharing a common view of the sad state of the world and the necessity for true believers to take an active part in the struggle. In October 1995, an Amtrak train was derailed in the Arizona desert. A typewritten letter found at the scene, signed by a group calling themselves Sons of the Gestapo, proclaimed their motivation for this act as rage toward the BATF and the FBI: "It is time for an independent federal agency to police the law enforcement agencies and other government employees."[71] The group also argues that the fire at Waco was set deliberately, and condemns the federal authorities for the deaths of the wife and teenage son of a survivalist named Randy Weaver, who were shot and killed by the FBI in August 1992 at Ruby Ridge, Idaho.[72]

Another recent demonstration of the potent mixture of British Israelite ideology and American militia survivalism occurred during the eighty-one-day standoff between the Montana Freemen and the FBI, which came to a peaceful end on June 13, 1996. The origins of the dispute combined the troubles of the Clark family of Jordan, Montana, with larger and more dangerous organizations and individuals. The elder Emmett Clark and his brother Ralph and his son Richard were all struggling to make a living as farmers, and were easy targets for four Freemen who arrived in Montana and began to spread the word. In 1994, armed men stormed the county courthouse in Jordan and held a "common-law meeting" regarding a farm subsidy check. Like the Posse Comitatus, they rejected the authority of the federal government, and like the Christian Identity movement, they were white supremacists who claimed biblical authority for their beliefs. Within a short time, the Freemen began issuing arrest and death warrants for government officials; they also were free with bogus checks and money orders to the tune of $1.8 million.

In early 1995, the two older Clarks lost their farm in a foreclosure, and Emmett's grandson, Dean Clark, managed to buy 2,300 acres of their property in an attempt to keep some of the land in the family. The other Clarks refused to accept the transaction, and on September 28 the Freemen moved their headquarters from Roundup, Montana, to Dean Clark's new ranch, without his permission, and reinstalled the two older Clarks. Others joined, and when the FBI lured one of the leaders to the edge of the compound and arrested him on March 25, 1996, the rest of the group holed up at the ranch with their families and children, over twenty people against the law enforcement agencies of the United States. The FBI and Attorney General Janet Reno waited patiently until the protest ran out of steam in June, spending about $7.5 million in maintaining the siege.

In court, the Freemen proclaimed that their only law was the Bible. One of the accused said that "my only lawgiver is Yahweh." According to documents examined by the authorities and others who have spoken with the Freemen, they believe that only white Christian males have special "Freemen" status, equivalent to full citizenship, while all the rest are in a second-class status. The Montana Freemen, like other militia groups, argue that since the federal government is controlled by "Zionists," it has no authority to tax Freemen or compel them to submit to their laws, and they ignore the charge that some of them have defrauded businesses and others of nearly $2 million. Others say they need not repay any bank loans since the currency of the United States has no real value.[73]

The Montana Freemen who made news in 1996 for refusing to recognize the authority of the state or of the federal government held views that are identical to those we have seen in other groups of a similar nature. Their inspiration comes from Hayden Lake, from books such as *The Turner Diaries*, and from the mythology surrounding the deaths of martyrs like Gordon Kahl, Robert Matthews, and the victims at Waco. Behind these sources is a long line of messianic speculation beginning with Joachim of Fiore and wending its way through seventeenth-century England to British Israelism and its transplantation to the United States more than a hundred years ago. James "Bo" Gritz, a retired Green Beret colonel who is a prominent figure in the militia world, said that the Montana Freemen were a "potpourri circus of over-the-hill outlaws, people with no past or future." But he could not have been more mistaken.

CHAPTER 8

THE END OF THE WORLD AND
THE NUCLEAR MESSIAH

| I |

One of the most influential writings concerning the fulfillment of prophecy in modern times is *The Late Great Planet Earth* by Hal Lindsey (b. 1929), first published in 1970, with undefined assistance from Carole C. Carlson. Its author and publisher announce on the book jacket that it has sold nearly twenty million copies, making it by far the best-selling book in the messianic tradition, apart from the Bible itself. Lindsey was born in Houston, Texas, and attended the university there. He then worked as a tugboat captain on the Mississippi River but gave it up in order to study at the Dallas Theological Seminary, a center for Fundamentalist dispensationalist thought.[1] Lindsey went on to become a leader in the Campus Crusade for Christ, and today serves a church in the Los Angeles area.

Lindsey's book has been so influential in part because of his clear exposition of the dispensationalist scheme and his dynamic description of how the Book of Revelation has come to life before our very eyes, beginning with the establishment of the State of Israel in 1948. As he put it, "the prophetic countdown began!" The Cold War, so important to Fundamentalism, is portrayed as the fulfillment of the biblical prophecies of what would happen immediately before the final End. The culmination of history, Lindsey explained, will be the Battle of Armageddon, in the Jezreel Valley of northern Israel, at which time the damned will be destroyed, the just will be saved, and Christ will reappear on earth and rule for a thousand years.

One key to Lindsey's popularity is that he refrained from trying to build on millenarian writings that appeared before 1948. Instead, he made events in Israel in that year and during the Six-Day War in 1967 central to reading history backward and forward. In a documentary film, *The Return*, he insisted that the Hebrew prophets predicted that as human history nears its end, a precise pattern of events would occur, the most important of which "is the Jew returning to the Land of Israel after thousands of years of being dispersed. The Jew is the most important sign to this generation." Lindsey was certainly not the first millenarian commentator to place emphasis on events in Palestine. As we have seen, at least from the time of Napoleon's invasion of the Middle East, and from the growth of the Zionist movement, Christian messianic observers appreciated that the final times might well be near at hand, and signs of this became clearer to them after General Allenby conquered Jerusalem for the British in 1917, and once the Balfour Declaration defined British support for the establishment of a Jewish state in Palestine. But Hal Lindsey's vision further focused on the establishment of a Jewish state in Palestine in 1948 and the reconquest of the holy sites in Jerusalem in 1967. According to Lindsey, the third and final precondition for the coming of the Messiah would be the rebuilding of the Temple on its original site. The Dome of the Rock on the Temple Mount, a place holy to Islam, was an obstacle, he admitted, but "obstacle or no obstacle, it is certain that the Temple will be rebuilt. Prophecy demands it." Perhaps an earthquake would clear the site for construction. "The most important prophetic sign of Jesus Christ's soon coming is before us," he insisted.[2]

In general terms, Lindsey said, the seven years preceding the Second Coming of Christ would be years of wars, disasters, and catastrophes before the climactic end at Armageddon. "The new State of Israel will be plagued by a certain pattern of events that has been clearly forecasted." One pattern involved Russia, which Lindsey believed has been prophesied in Ezekiel 38 and 39, where it is said that a northern nation would arise and oppose Israel. Other Hebrew texts, Bible commentaries, and contemporary conduct show that the prophet must have been referring to Russia. The Hebrew word *rosh* (head), which appears in Ezekiel 38:17, is thought to be a reference to Russia, which is also the "Gog" so frighteningly described, and Lindsey also identified the allies of Ezekiel's Gog— Russia's satellites behind the Iron Curtain and client states in the Arab world. Yet although Russia is arming and equipping her allies in the Middle East, who will attack the newly restored Jewish state, they are doomed to be defeated "by an act that Israel will acknowledge as being from their God. This will bring many in Israel to believe in their true Messiah." Unfortunately, this Middle Eastern conflict is predestined to escalate into the Third World War, at which point Jesus will return "to prevent the annihilation of all mankind." The Cold War is thus part of the divine plan, as described in the Bible, that leads to the Battle of Armageddon and the Second Coming. "We have seen how current events are fitting together simultaneously into the precise pattern of predicted events." Indeed, "it's happening. God is putting it all together" in such a way that it will have "a greater effect on mankind than anything since Genesis 1."[3]

Lindsey's scenario included China and the European Community (the last incarnation of the Roman Empire), being led by a Führer, the biblically forecasted Antichrist who will pretend to be the long-awaited Messiah, propounding a false global religion deceiving the masses of people, for many Christians will apostasize and embrace this new world order and false religion of ecumenical unity.[4]

Hal Lindsey is a classic dispensationalist, accepting the general timeline as revealed by John Nelson Darby. The most important aspect of this view is the "Rapture," which will allow the faithful to be spared the tribulations of the last seven-year period of woe. "Rapture," as Lindsey defined it, means that "someday, a day that only God knows, Jesus Christ is coming to take away all those who believe in Him." These true believers will be lifted off the planet without the need of space suits, UFOs, or rockets, and will be kept in heaven until the final terrible events have taken place. No one knows exactly when this will occur, yet "we believe that according to all the signs, we are in the general time of His coming." All true believers are advised to live in a sense of general anticipation of the Second Coming of Christ.

The Rapture will be of great advantage to the faithful, because events on earth will be devastating indeed. Lindsey noted that the establishment of the State of Israel created a necessary but insoluble problem between Jews and Arabs; a local conflict destined to escalate into another world war. The Israelis will make a compact with the Antichrist, leader of the European Community, which will allow them to reinstitute divine sacrifice, as they had in biblical times. They will then have to rebuild the Temple, at which point the Divine timepiece will begin marking off the final seven years, the times of tribulation. The Antichrist will take over the entire world, claiming that he can bring peace and security. At exactly the halfway point, this new-modeled Roman emperor will go to Jerusalem and have himself proclaimed God Incarnate—a warning sign to "the believers of that day that Armageddon is about to begin." Israelis who recognize Jesus as the Messiah will flee and hide themselves in the mountains and canyons of Petra, across the Jordan River in the Hashemite Kingdom.[5]

Lindsey seemed to be privy to information about the exact nature of the imminent war against Israel. He knew that Russia would invade Israel simultaneously with the Arab countries, and a map in his book shows the tactical challenge this will pose. Another map details the course of the war, showing the arrival of Russian and European armies in Israel.[6] Ezekiel revealed that there would be a tremendous shaking of the land, with torrents of fire and brimstone. Lindsey interpreted this biblical text as a reference to nuclear war: "this could be a direct judgment from God, or God could allow the various countries to launch a nuclear exchange of ballistic missiles on each other." China would also be involved. Vast numbers of peoples and cities would be destroyed. While all of this is going on, Lindsey predicted, about a third of the Jews in Israel will finally see the light and accept Christ, being rewarded by miraculous preservation. (He cited two biblical texts as proof: Ezekiel 39:6–8 and Zechariah 13:8–9, which although they fail to mention Jesus by name, are concerned with the Jews recognizing God.) "As the battle of Armageddon reaches its awful climax and it appears that all life will be destroyed on earth—in this very moment Jesus Christ will return and save man from self-extinction."[7]

Lindsey's book has a number of obvious subtexts. One is that true believers should keep fast to the premillennialist interpretation of events, even if mainstream churches tend to treat the dispensationalist schema as verging on heretical. They should keep track of events in Israel in order to know when the messianic "countdown" will begin with the rebuilding of the Temple in Jerusalem. A second implied theme is that the United States will lose its leadership of the Western nations unless it accepts Christ. Failure to do so will propel it into the abyss with the rest of the Western nations, overwhelmed by drugs, satanic witchcraft, and Oriental religions. Indeed, Lindsey warned, it is very possible that "drug addicts will run for high political offices and win through the support of young adults."[8]

Lindsey's more recent work updated some of his prophecies, but nothing significant altered his original predictions of 1970, though the end of the Cold War was a blow to his interpretation, and the

Gulf War and the emergence of radical Islamic movements provided interpretative challenges. But Lindsey still believes that an invasion of Israel will take place, driven among other reasons by the necessity to have access to that country's potash resources.[9] The present period of calm before the Rapture has also given him time to consider the implications of his views for Jewish history. In another book, entitled *The Road to Holocaust* (1989), Lindsey has suggested that anti-Semitism began with a misreading of Scripture from Origen and Augustine onward, Church Fathers who either did not understand premillennialism or rejected it outright. Lindsey makes Luther a chief villain in excluding the Jews from divine history and in formulating the very perversion of Christianity that helped make Nazism possible. He also cites many books about the Holocaust, especially those by Raul Hilberg. As he sees it, the biological Jews are the ones who will bring about the fulfillment of God's prophecies at the End of Days. They have been in a sort of limbo for centuries, awaiting the moment. Once Israel was established, they became critical actors in the world-historical drama. Those who tried to destroy the saving remnant of the Jews were acting against God's plan for mankind.[10]

Curiously, the theology of Louis Farrakhan's Nation of Islam includes elements that are very similar to Lindsey's divine plan, with the crucial difference that God is a black man and black people can recognize the black God within themselves. This God has temporarily given the Devil the power to rule the world through the white man, who promotes slavery, colonialism, and other forms of oppression. This era is about to end, when black people will be redeemed and the white world destroyed. In the meantime, Farrakhan insists, black people should be compensated for slavery through the payment of reparations and the establishment of an independent black nation in either America or Africa, to be ruled by Islamic law.[11]

On the other hand, the beliefs of the Heaven's Gate cult are no more than a science-fiction version of the "Rapture." On March 26,

1997, thirty-nine members of this group committed mass suicide in the belief that they would be taken aboard a space ship from the "Kingdom Level Above Human" which lurked behind the Hale-Bopp comet. Marshall Herff Applewhite (1932–97), their leader, claimed that he and his deceased former associate Bonnie Lu Trousdale Nettles (1928–85) were in fact aliens from that Level, presently inhabiting human containers, as was Jesus Himself two thousand years ago.[12] A similar group is the Renewed Order of the Solar Temple, formerly under the leadership of a Belgian homeopath named Luc Jouret and a Canadian named Joseph Di Mambro, both of whom were among the seventy-four cult members who have committed suicide in Switzerland and Canada since 1994. They claim that their deaths enable them to ascend to the star Sirius.[13]

But it is Hal Lindsey who has remained the most well-known and popular of the millenarian interpreters of the Bible and current events. Unlike many others, however, he has never tried to create an organized movement around himself or his ideas. He broadcasts his message not only in inexpensive paperbacks but also in videotape presentations and prophetic newsletters which help adjust his basic schema to current events. He has also led tours to Israel, so that believers can see the actual places where the great events will shortly take place. His views, meanwhile, have been taken up by many others, such as Randy Weaver, whose wife and son were killed by FBI agents in the well-publicized standoff at Ruby Ridge, Idaho, in 1992. We know that Weaver and his wife were inspired by *The Late Great Planet Earth* to join the survivalist movement and to establish the isolated shelter in Idaho where their tragedy was enacted.

| II |

Another of Hal Lindsey's admirers was former President Ronald Reagan. Many of the Christian Fundamentalists' views have become mainstream, so it is not surprising that Reagan reflected such beliefs. As Gore Vidal put it, Reagan "has come among us to dispense not only good news for the usual purposes of election, but Good News. Reagan is nothing so mundane as an American president. Rather, he is here to prepare us for the coming war between the Christ and the Antichrist. A war, to be specific, between the United States and Russia, to take place in Israel."[14]

Much of the evidence for Reagan's holding these apocalyptic views comes from the testimony of others. Reagan told William Rose in 1968 that when he was in the hospital he was visited by his pastor from Bel Air, California, the Reverend Donn Moomaw, and by the Reverend Billy Graham, the famous evangelist. According to Reagan himself:

> We got into a conversation about how many of the prophecies concerning the Second Coming seemed to be having their fulfillment at this particular time. Graham told me how world leaders who are students of the Bible and others who have studied it have come to the same conclusion—that apparently never in history have so many of the prophecies come true in such a relatively short time. After the conversation I asked Donn to send me some more material on prophecy so I could check them out in the Bible for myself.[15]

Three years later, when governor of California, Reagan asked Graham to deliver a spiritual "State of the State" address to the California legislature, during which he admonished the politicians that the only alternative to Communism was the biblical plan. Reagan asked Graham if Jesus would be here soon. Graham, giving his standard reply, assured him that "Jesus Christ is at the very door" and could be here any moment . . . or not.[16]

Reagan read Lindsey's *The Late Great Planet Earth* in 1971, and was soon discussing it with many people and recommending that they read it. When Reagan became President, he had Hal Lindsey give a talk about "theological" plans for a nuclear war to the chief planners in the Pentagon.[17] But the most interesting account of Reagan's views during those years comes from James Mills, at that time president pro tem of the California State Senate, who published his account of their conversation in the *San Diego Magazine* in August 1985. According to Mills, "each and every conversation I've ever had with Ronald Reagan finally became so stirring that recalling it revives in me a degree of internal unrest. This is particularly true of our dialogue about Armageddon."

Mills was seated next to Governor Reagan at a banquet when a fiery dessert, cherries jubilee, was served. Reagan suddenly began talking about the biblical prophecies, especially those in Ezekiel 38–39, which he thought had best "foreseen the carnage that would destroy our age." He insisted that Libya's becoming a Communist state is "a sign that the day of Armageddon isn't far off." He also noted that Ezekiel foretold that Israel would come under attack from the ungodly nations, Libya among them. Mills, who had been raised as a Fundamentalist, reminded Reagan that this passage in Ezekiel also said that Ethiopia would become an evil power, but that Haile Selassie had not become a Communist or joined forces against the Chosen People. Reagan agreed, but insisted that "there is only one thing left that has to happen. The Reds have to take over Ethiopia." When Mills expressed his doubts, the President pressed his point, insisting that "it's inevitable. It is necessary to fulfill the prophecy." (Mills noted in 1985 that Haile Selassie was indeed deposed by the Communists three years after their conversation.) Reagan was sure that the End of the World was on the horizon, and assured Mills:

All of the prophecies that had to be fulfilled before Armageddon have come to pass. In the 38th chapter of Ezekiel it says God will take the children of Israel from among the heathen, where they'd been scattered, and will gather them again in the promised land. That has finally come about after 2,000 years. For the first time ever, everything is in place for the battle of Armageddon and the Second Coming of Christ.

When Mills answered that according to Scripture no man can know when this will happen, Reagan replied firmly, "Everything is falling into place. It can't be too long now. Ezekiel says that fire and brimstone will be rained upon the enemies of God's people. That must mean that they'll be destroyed by nuclear weapons. They exist now, and they never did in the past."

Reagan followed up these general views by giving Mills a strategic picture of the Third World War, probably based on Lindsey and his book. Gog from the north would lead all the powers of darkness against Israel. Bible scholars have been saying that Gog must be Russia, since there is no other powerful nation north of Israel, a prophecy about Gog that made no sense before the Russian Revolution, when Russia was a Christian country, but now that Russia is both Communist and atheistic and has set itself against God, "it fits the description of Gog perfectly."

Mills was so impressed by what Reagan had told him that he immediately made extensive notes of what had been said, on the basis of which he wrote up his magazine article published in 1985. Mills knew President Reagan fairly well, although he himself was a Democrat, and was convinced that Reagan's foreign and military policies stemmed from his apocalyptic views. Mills even believed that Reagan's fiscal policies were "in harmony with a literal interpretation of Biblical prophecies. There is no reason to get wrought up about the national debt if God is soon going to foreclose on the whole world." Mills argued that all Reagan's domestic policies were based on the conception that the end of the United States and the world was imminent. "It is only by keeping such considerations in mind that we can appreciate where our President may be coming from and possibly may be taking us."[18]

Ronald Reagan made no secret of his belief in the coming Apocalypse. Speaking in 1980 on Jim Bakker's *Praise the Lord* television show, he suggested, "We may be the generation that sees Armageddon." He told the televangelist Jerry Falwell, "I sometimes believe we're heading very fast for Armageddon." When Reagan became President in 1981, he had Falwell attend a National Security Council meeting and speak about the relevance of the Bible for nuclear war. Falwell apparently also had some influence in drafting the Republican Party planks against abortion and the Equal Rights Amendment. Reagan went into some detail with Thomas Dine, head of the American Israel Public Affairs Committee (AIPAC), a pro-Israel lobby: "You know, I turn back to your ancient prophets in the Old Testament and the signs foretelling Armageddon, and I find myself wondering if—if we're the generation that's going to see that come about. I don't know if you've noted any of those prophecies lately, but believe me, they certainly describe the times we're going through."[19]

Reagan's views about the Apocalypse very nearly became an issue in his campaign for reelection in 1984. During the presidential debates with Walter Mondale, the Democratic challenger, Reagan was asked a very pointed question by Marvin Kalb of NBC:

> You've been quoted as saying that you believe deep down that we are heading for some kind of biblical Armageddon. Your Pentagon and your Secretary of Defense have plans for the United States to fight and prevail in a nuclear war. Do you feel that we are now heading, perhaps, for some kind of nuclear Armageddon? And do you feel that this country and the world could survive that kind of calamity?

According to *Time* magazine, Nancy Reagan gasped, "Oh, no!" But the President himself answered judiciously that he had talked with various people about the biblical prophecies "of what would portend the coming of Armageddon," and that he knew that a number of theologians during the last decade believed that the prophecies are being fulfilled. Nevertheless, he said, "no one knows whether those prophecies mean that Armageddon is a thousand years away or the day after tomorrow. So I have never seriously warned and said we must plan according to Armageddon."[20] On national television, Reagan adhered to Billy Graham's party line on Armageddon.[21]

It is not inconceivable, however, that Reagan's flirtation with the notion of a divinely inspired nuclear holocaust may have been a factor in influencing Gorbachev to call the Iceland summit in October 1986 at very short notice, the purpose of which was to offer complete mutual disarmament. Ironically, perhaps one result of Hal Lindsey's prophecy of a nuclear apocalypse was the end of the Cold War and the consequent elimination of one of the theoretical underpinnings of the dispensationalist Armageddon.

| III |

Another important conduit of the messianic message has been the Reverend Jerry Falwell, born in 1933 in Lynchburg, Virginia. Falwell had his born-again experience at the age of eighteen and studied at the Baptist Bible College in Springfield, Missouri. After his ordination in the Baptist Bible Fellowship, he founded the Thomas Road Baptist Church in Lynchburg, and still remains the pastor of that church in the town in which he was born. Falwell's church has grown to have more than 18,000 members, and although it remained independent until 1966, since then it has been allied with the Southern Baptists, the largest Protestant group in the United States. The message of Falwell's church is also spread through its attached institution of higher learning, Liberty University.[22]

Falwell's fame comes from his mass media missionary work, however. His *Old Time Gospel Hour* television program has had an audience of millions of people, and has been the basis of his fundraising for various religious activities. The most famous among these is the Moral Majority movement, which he founded and which galvanized many Fundamentalists, Evangelicals, and passive Christian believers into national political activities for a very conservative agenda. Falwell has also been at the forefront of American Christian supporters of Israel during the last two decades.

Falwell comes out of a rather different background than Hal Lindsey, and his millenarianism has a distinct slant. Falwell lacks the excited, almost frenzied messianic expectation of Lindsey and does not see contemporary events as evidence of a "countdown to Armageddon." Unlike Pat Robertson, he is not worried about conspiratorial forces which are supposedly working to undermine the American world and its destiny. He sees himself as the champion of a return to *sola scriptura* in the tradition of the seventeenth-century English Independent Baptists, while at the same time accepting the dispensationalist scheme of history so common among American Fundamentalists.

Falwell's Moral Majority is a more recent version of Fundamentalist involvement in American politics. Early Fundamentalist efforts to oppose the teaching of Darwinism in schools declined after the 1920s, but the urge to influence current affairs remained important.[23] The presidential campaign of the conservative Republican Barry Goldwater in 1964 propelled many Fundamentalists into political activity. A dozen years later, many of them entered political life in support of Jimmy Carter, a Southern Baptist.[24] Then, in 1979, the Moral Majority was organized by Falwell at the urging of three secular conservative figures: Howard Phillips, a Jew who had headed the Office of Economic Opportunity in the Nixon administration; Paul Weyrich; and Richard Viguerie, a political consultant who developed a direct-mail campaign for the conservatives. Among them, they had computerized mailing lists of about 10 to 20 million names to which they sent material explaining their religious and political standpoint. The Moral Majority was very active during the Reagan presidency, lobbying for federal support for prayers in public schools, for religious schooling, and for outlawing abortion and pornography.[25]

Falwell dissolved the Moral Majority in 1989, the year when Pat

Robertson founded his Christian Coalition. It may be that Falwell was disappointed that none of his major political planks was enacted into law or even supported actively by most Republicans in Congress. Since the end of the Moral Majority, he has struggled to keep the rest of his empire in operation, especially Liberty University, which sank into debt. His television campaign was also damaged by the sex and financial scandals that brought down his fellow evangelists Jim Bakker and Jimmy Swaggart. When his empire collapsed in 1987, Bakker turned over his Praise the Lord (PTL) ministry to Falwell, who for a few months tried to breathe life into that bankrupt leviathan. Oral Roberts (b. 1918), the Pentecostalist television minister of Tulsa, Oklahoma, also suffered hard times, especially at his university, where he was forced to close the dental school and give the law school to Pat Robertson.[26] In the meantime, Falwell spread the word by selling videotapes, which make rather extreme charges against those in power, especially President Bill Clinton.[27]

A closer look at Falwell's theology reveals his contribution to be rather more interesting than others who have had more lasting success. In a book he edited, two of his supporters define Fundamentalism on the basis of the following five points: the inspiration and infallibility of Scripture; the deity of Christ (including His virgin birth); the atonement of Christ's death; the literal resurrection of Christ from the dead; and the literal return of Christ in the Second Advent. In the explanation of the fifth point no mention at all is made of the possible connection between the return of Jesus and events taking place in Palestine. Falwell holds that the return of Jesus will be independent of antecedent events and is entirely determined by the divine will: "I do not believe anything has to happen before what we call the Second Coming or the Second Advent of Christ occurs. Neither the salvation of the Jewish people in Israel nor the creation of a one world church or a one world government." Falwell's silence about the Jewish role in the Second Coming is intriguing, especially in light of the paramount importance of the formulations offered by earlier American dispensationalist Fundamentalists about the restoration of the Jews to the Holy Land. Indeed, of the twelve original pamphlets which appeared under the title of *The Fundamentals* and which gave the name to the entire movement, two dealt with the restoration of the Jews.

Falwell's description of the rise of modern American Fundamentalism is concerned mostly with its opposition to Protestant liberalism, and as a way of combating the decline of American morals. The function of the Moral Majority was to energize Fundamentalists who had become so disillusioned with politics that they despaired of change and, by their withdrawal, were actually contributing to contemporary developments. Falwell managed to forge a coalition of Southern Baptists and many others even from the conservative Catholic and Jewish camps, in his efforts to find political and legal solutions for their shared social and moral concerns. According to his fourfold program, he proclaimed, they were looking for candidates "who are pro-life, pro-American, pro-Bible morality and pro-family from either party." Of the twelve issues with which the Moral Majority was initially concerned, the tenth dealt with America's unswerving support for the State of Israel. No millenarian reason was cited.

This decentralization of the millenarian role of the Jews was also apparent in Falwell's more extended statements about the Moral Majority. In one document, after listing five moral principles, the sixth point declared, "We support the state of Israel and Jewish people everywhere." This is followed by the statement: "It is impossible to separate the state of Israel from the Jewish family internationally. Many Moral Majority members, because of their theological convictions, are committed to the Jewish people . . . Support of Israel is one of the essential commitments of the Moral Majority. No anti-Semite influence is allowed in the Moral Majority." Falwell gave his reasons for supporting Israel: God promised a blessing to those who bless Israel, and a curse for those who do not; second, "To stand against Israel is to stand against God." He explained that he loves Jews because God does, and history (that is to say, the Bible) has shown that God deals with countries on the basis of how they treat Jews: "My deep conviction is that America will not remain a free nation unless we defend the freedom of Israel." His third point was almost Zionist in flavor: "The land and people of Israel are important because, as members of the human family, they have a right to exist." He cited the text of Genesis 15 as setting the boundaries of Israel and giving support to its claim to the land: "We believe that the Jews have the historical, theological, and legal right to the land called Israel."

Falwell's fourth reason for supporting Israel was more curious, and offered as the most important justification both for Israel's survival and for Christian support of it: "Our Savior came from a Jewish family and the Lord Jesus Christ was a Jew." Both Testaments of the Bible were written by Jews and since God gave His message to the Jews, we as Christians stand in debt to them. Therefore: "Any who do not support Israel are inviting the judgment of God upon themselves," especially since "God keeps His word to punish those who punish the Jews." Not to be misunderstood, Falwell ended this part of his discussion by asserting that he did not oppose Arabs, but they must understand that Israel had the right to exist as a nation.

In an interview, Falwell explained that he hardly knew about Jews outside of the Bible until he started his ministry. Jews were not a common phenomenon in Lynchburg, Virginia, yet in accordance with the standard practice among dispensationalist Fundamentalists, Falwell preached an Armageddon theology, and since first visiting Israel in the late 1960s, conducted personal tours of the Holy Land for his followers.[28]

In an interview in 1981, Falwell spelled out what he saw as the future events in the Middle East. These would begin with a nuclear war against Russia, leading to the Battle of Armageddon and the return of Jesus. Russia would attack Israel because of its need for oil and its hatred of Jews, at which point "all hell will break out," culminating in an atomic holocaust. Falwell's description kept faith with the dispensationalist scheme, including a Rapture of the faithful and rivers of blood terminating the history of mankind and bringing the return of Christ, who would reign for a thousand years on earth. Unlike Lindsey's, Falwell's future involved only Russia as an attacker of Israel and confined the conflict to the Middle East. Asked if Russia might be destroyed with nuclear weapons in a devastating first strike, Falwell replied that we should take into consideration that good Russians would not actually be eliminated in such an attack, since they would have already been raptured beforehand. He would not be pinned down as to the exact timing of the Second Coming, but noted, "I don't think my children will live their full lives out."[29] Two years later, he expounded his views on this subject in a pamphlet, making it clear that (like Lindsey) he believed that the conflict in the Middle East would begin when Israelis start construction of the Third Temple on the site of the Dome of the Rock.[30]

Further clues about Falwell's plans for the future come from his videotapes. In one of them, "Jerry Falwell Teaches Bible Prophecy," he states cheerfully that Armageddon is an actual reality. "Thank God, it's the End of Days for the gentiles," he explains, "for it then sets the stage for the introduction of the King, the Lord Jesus, in power and in great glory." Falwell was happy to declare that "we are part of that terminal generation, that last generation, that shall not pass until our Lord comes." He saw recent developments in Russia as further manifestations of the prophecies of Ezekiel, giving the usual Fundamentalist gloss that the *rosh* referred to in Ezekiel stands for "Russia," land of Antichrist which would invade Israel "in the latter days" aided and abetted by countries in Africa and Asia. Peace would come only when Jesus returned to His throne in Jerusalem. Falwell ended the video on a happy note by telling his viewers, "That day is coming. And, for sure, you and I are going to be part of it."[31] Similarly, in a sermon given in December 1984, Falwell gave full and frightening details of what would happen at the Battle of Armageddon, when millions of people would be killed. Like Lindsey, Falwell believes that many Jews would be hidden and saved: "I don't know how, but God will keep them because the Jews are the Chosen People of God." Here too, after describing the carnage of the End of Days, he ended cheerfully, shouting, "Hey, it's great being a Christian. We have a wonderful future ahead!"[32]

Ironically, Falwell's lack of emphasis on the role of the Jews at the End of Days has made him more concerned about the political situation in Israel than other dispensationalist Fundamentalists such as Hal Lindsey. According to one member of his group, on tours that Falwell conducted in Israel in the 1980s the ratio was about 30:1 between the time spent on briefings with Israel political and military leaders and visiting or discussing the meaning of Christian holy places. Presumably, his hope was that the pilgrims would pressure American political leaders to help fulfill Israeli military and economic requirements. For this reason he established a "Christian Embassy" in Jerusalem, when nearly all foreign governments moved their embassies to Tel Aviv after Jerusalem was declared the eternal capital of Israel in a flag-waving parliamentary session. In February 1986, he led a National Prayer Breakfast in honor of Israel in Washington, along with Jimmy Swaggart, Oral Roberts, and Pat Robertson. Falwell was rewarded for all his efforts: he met Prime Minister Menachem Begin at Kennedy Airport in New York with a limousine, and drove with him to the Waldorf-Astoria Hotel, where Begin awarded him the Jabotinsky Medal for service to Zionism, "the highest honor an Israeli prime minister can bestow on friends of Israel for their friendship and service to that land," as Falwell put it.[33] "I am personally a Zionist," Falwell proclaimed, "having gained that perspective from my belief in Old Testament Scriptures."[34] Yet his Zion seems to be rather more America than Israel, an America made pure and holy through projects like the Moral Majority.[35]

| IV |

Another apocalyptic end might be mass suicide, especially when ordered by a charismatic leader, even a "living God." One example of a religious group centered on a figure who claimed to be the Messiah or a living God is that of the Reverend James Warren Jones (1931–78), who committed suicide with 913 of his followers on November 18, 1978, at their community of Jonestown in northern Guyana.[36]

Jim Jones was born near Lynn, Indiana, the child of a man who had suffered serious health problems since being gassed in combat in the Second World War. After their divorce in 1945, his mother, Lynetta, helped support the family by working in a factory and as a waitress. After graduating from high school, Jones married a nurse and studied at Indiana University in 1950. He soon left after turning more seriously to religion, and enrolled in Butler University in 1951, which was then run by the Disciples of Christ. By 1953, Jones had founded his own congregation within the Christian Assembly of God. Seven years later, his People's Temple Full Gospel Church was listed as a congregation within the fellowship of the Christian Church (Disciples of Christ) of Indianapolis. The Disciples are a dissenting Protestant umbrella organization dating from the nineteenth century which accepts fellowship from any Bible-based church and grants autonomy to each of its member congregations.

Jones had been raised in the atmosphere of Pentecostal Christianity and was excited by its emotionalism, its expressions of the spirit, faith healing, and ethos of mutual help and support. It was also from this background that he became a committed opponent of racism and a crusader for integration, principles which were put into practice at his own church and within his family. Jones and his wife had one child, a son named Stephan born in 1959, and adopted eight others, including blacks and Koreans, one of whom was killed in a car accident. Throughout the 1950s, Jim Jones succeeded in building up a following among the black population of Indianapolis and the towns nearby.

But it was the ministry of the black evangelist Father Divine that caught Jones's attention. Father Divine, as George Baker (d. 1965) called himself, was the leader of the interracial Harlem-based Peace Mission movement, predominantly made up of black worshippers.[37] Their calling was to help the poor with free food and clothing, and to a great extent they were inspired by the eighteenth-century Shakers, who under their leader Mother Ann Lee (1736–84) lived together in a celibate pacifist commune near Albany, New York. Mother Ann was known as "the female principle in Christ" who personally fulfilled the Second Coming.[38] Father Divine's followers went a bit further, regarding him as the "living God," but Jones initially was skeptical of such grandiose claims. In 1959 he explained his involvement with Father Divine's movement: "I had heard the usual opinions that it was supposed to be a harem run by a demonically possessed immoral person; in fact, I was almost convinced that it was a complete fraud. I had always been extremely opposed to adulation or worship of religious leaders."[39] Jones persisted, and he and his wife went to a Peace Mission hotel in Philadelphia, which they immediately left when informed that couples could not occupy the same room since celibacy was a central tenet in Father Divine's teaching. Jones returned alone a few days later to attend one of Father Divine's informal services, which was partly a free feast of food and partly a gathering to sing songs of praise to their leader.

Eventually, Jones became convinced that Father Divine had created an integrated communal society that could serve as a model for the rest of America. On his return to Indianapolis, he tried to duplicate many of the things he had seen, establishing a soup kitchen, a free grocery store, a free clothing shop, and other such institutions. At his People's Temple Full Gospel Church, he tried to follow Father Divine's message of faith healing and public confession for moral and spiritual improvement. By the late 1950s, he was trying to convince Father Divine himself to declare Jim Jones his designated heir apparent of the entire Peace Mission movement.

Jones's success in this aspiration was put to the test in 1965, when Father Divine died and Jones tried to persuade the widow of the living God to bless his succession. It was to no avail. In 1971, he arrived at the Peace Mission estate near Philadelphia with 160 followers, demanding that Jim Jones be acknowledged to be the new Father Divine, as demonstrated by his miraculous achievements. Mother Divine, for her part, rejected Jones and his crew: "How can you possibly think FATHER DIVINE would reincarnate HIMSELF in these last days of mortality in a human likeness, much less in one born in sin and shaped up in iniquity, according to his own testimony and now married, having one child according to the flesh? The Sonship Decree came through a virgin birth, and the FATHERSHIP came with the beginning of days or the end of life."[40] The following year, Jim Jones tried once again to take over the Peace Mission, met with Mother Divine, but eventually had to admit defeat. Jones later claimed that more than a hundred of Father Divine's people defected and joined him at the People's Temple.[41]

By that time, Jones had a new worry, nuclear war. In this Jones was no different from many other Americans, who built fallout shelters in their backyards and agonized during the Cuban Missile Crisis of October 1962. Jones read an article in *Esquire* magazine that mentioned a claim that there were still a few safe places in the world, such as the city of Belo Horizonte, Brazil, so Jones went there in April 1962 and worked for two years among the poor in Rio de Janeiro, until a military government took power. On the way to Brazil he visited Guyana, and the basic idea of Jonestown was born.[42]

Jones returned to America and began establishing branches of the People's Temple up and down California. He had plans to create a worldwide ministry as well, bringing his message to unfortunates living outside of the United States. He was continuing to try to be recognized as Father Divine's successor and his theology developed in the direction of the claim that he was a "living God." Jones convinced his followers that he not only could heal the sick but had raised no fewer than forty-three people from the dead. The competition was a manifestation he called the "Sky God," the deity of Judaism, Christianity, and Islam, who was "guilty of criminal offenses against humanity" and of having caused all of the misery on earth, most especially that suffered by poor people and black Americans. Jim Jones was the savior "who would make a heaven out of the hell created by the Sky God."

This Jones promised to accomplish by the apotheosis of socialist principles. "I am the only fully socialist; I am the only fully God. So I am now on the scene." He was, he said, the reincarnation of Akhnaton, Jesus, the Buddha, Lenin, and Father Divine. In his sermons, filled with a mixture of biblical phraseology and socialist ideas, along with proof texts from the Bible, he referred to himself as a "Christian atheist," in the sense that he rejected any "Sky God," Jesus, God the Father, or any other supernatural being. As an "apostolic socialist," Jones, like Father Divine, could heal the sick, make prophecy, and bring about the Kingdom of God on earth.[43]

Despite the more outlandish elements in his theology, Jim Jones's People's Temple was accepted in 1960 as a congregation in the Christian Church (Disciples of Christ). It thus gained tax-exempt status for its activities both in the United States and in Guyana, and Jones's substantial donations to the Disciples kept the People's Temple members in good standing.

The members of the various People's Temples were very prominent for their good works. Jones's integrated church membership proved attractive to inner-city black people, as did his extensive charity efforts and the establishment of (noncelibate) communes. Father Divine had supported his own movement by establishing businesses that then gave jobs to his members and showed profits as well. Jones preferred to rely on federal and state assistance to the poor and the aged, topped up by donations and the sale of religious souvenirs. Although in both cases a considerable amount of money was generated, neither Father Divine nor Jim Jones overtly used the cash in order to enrich themselves. Another feature which Jones learned from Father Divine was the necessity of removing the dying from the others in the congregation, or the church's "heaven on earth." Terminally ill congregants were taken to separate apartments or hospitals so that there were no actual deaths within the fellowship.

At the same time, Jones began to accumulate political power. In October 1976 he was appointed to the San Francisco Housing Authority by Mayor George Moscone (who would be murdered in his office by a disgruntled employee nine days after Jones died) and became its chairman the following February. He received numerous humanitarian awards and was a prominent member of the religious community in San Francisco at least until July 1977, when *New West* magazine published an exposé of his activities which hastened his decline. Jim Jones resigned from the Housing Authority the next month, in a letter dictated by shortwave radio from Guyana. By the time the August issue of *New West* was on the stands, he had left the United States forever.

In December 1973, Jim Jones had founded the People's Temple colony on 27,000 acres of leased land in Guyana, to be called Jonestown. Guyana's socialist government and the large black population there seemed, he thought, to provide a sympathetic milieu. By 1975, fifty members of the People's Temple were living there, and within two years, as pressure on Jones grew in California, nearly a thousand people joined them, including the "Father" himself. Jones saw his colony as a revolutionary challenge to a corrupt world. Education and health care were provided at Jonestown, and at first very few members of the group made any attempt to leave.

The very existence of Jonestown was made much more precarious when Deborah Layton Blakey swore out an affidavit on June 15, 1978. Blakey "had grown up in affluent circumstances in the permissive atmosphere of Berkeley, California," according to her own account. Her marriage to an English Fundamentalist led to eventual membership in the People's Temple in August 1971, for which she became financial secretary. Blakey moved to Jonestown in December 1977 and stayed there until, while on assignment in Georgetown in May 1978, she escaped. Her document describes the poor working and living conditions at Jonestown, the beatings and sexual perversions. She also told of practice drills in mass suicide and of the fear Jones instilled that the colony would be invaded by American law-enforcement agencies. Blakey also knew the details of the crisis over John Victor Stoen, who seems to have been a child of Jim Jones and a former Temple member named Grace Stoen, whose husband, Timothy, was a former assistant district attorney in Mendocino and San Francisco counties. The child was in Jonestown, and the Stoens wanted him back.

Their efforts caught the attention of Congressman Leo Ryan of California, who flew down to Jonestown on November 14, 1978, as a member of the House International Affairs Committee, accompanied by two aides, thirteen members of a "Concerned Relatives" group, an NBC film crew, and other journalists. When the party arrived at Jonestown on November 17, they found that Jim Jones had his lawyers in place, the well-known radical attorneys Charles Garry and Mark Lane, who had made a name for himself hunting up conspiracies in the Kennedy and Martin Luther King assassinations. Although their visit was conducted calmly and the achievements at the colony seemed impressive, Congressman Ryan was slipped notes from community members who wanted to leave Jonestown.

The next day, Saturday, November 18, while preparing to depart, Congressman Ryan was attacked by a Jonestown man who held a knife to his throat, but who was persuaded to desist. Later that afternoon, as Ryan's group was boarding two airplanes at the nearby Port Kaituma airport, they were attacked and shot at by members of the settlement, who killed Congressman Ryan, three reporters, and one escaping church member, and wounded eleven others. An hour later, Jones gave the order for the "White Night," and 914 people committed mass suicide, most by drinking a mixture of flavored water and cyanide, although a few were also shot, including Jim Jones himself, who had apparently committed suicide as well.

After his death, reports began to appear about a vast hidden fortune left behind at Jonestown. Lane claimed that he knew the secret bank numbers of an $11 million fund in a foreign bank. On the day of the suicides, Tim Carter, one of Jones's inner circle, had been ordered to go with two other men to the Russian Embassy, taking with them a suitcase containing half a million dollars in small bills. They had instead buried the money in the jungle, where it was later recovered. This Russian connection was one of Jones's last delusions: earlier, a delegation from Jonestown had met twice with the Soviet press attaché in Georgetown about the possibility of moving the entire settlement to Russia and Soviet consular officials had visited Jonestown. Jones in the last few months held Russian-language classes at Jonestown, where members had to say "good morning" in Russian before receiving their breakfast. Ironically, despite Russia's status as the Kingdom of Satan for most Fundamentalist groups, at Jamestown it was slated to be the next "heaven on earth."

| V |

There is no doubt that the events at Jonestown gave living messiahs a bad name. One victim of the backlash against religious leaders with messianic claims was Sun Myung Moon (b. 1920).[44] Moon was convicted in 1982 by a United States federal court of conspiracy to evade the payment of taxes, and was sentenced to eighteen months' imprisonment and ordered to pay a $25,000 fine, plus legal costs. He served thirteen months in a Connecticut jail.

Moon's church had been founded in 1954 in Korea under the name of the Holy Spirit Association for the Unification of World Christianity (HSA-UWC), based on a theology set forth in his book

Divine Principle, which has appeared in English in various translations. Moon had been brought up in a family that converted to Presbyterianism when he was ten years old, and when Jesus Christ appeared to him on Easter Day 1936, he wrote, the direction of his life became apparent. Korea was occupied by Japan between 1905 and 1945, so it is not surprising that Moon studied electrical engineering at a Japanese university for two years beginning in 1941. He returned to Korea in 1943 and was arrested by the Japanese there for some reason, but after the war, in June 1946, he had another revelation, which led him to desert his wife and two-month-old child for a religious mission to North Korea. Two years later, Moon was sentenced to five years in a prison camp, but he was liberated by United Nations forces during the Korean War after serving only half his term.

Moon returned to South Korea, and established his church in Seoul in 1954. He was soon joined by Dr. Young Oon Kim (b. 1915), "Miss Kim" in Moon parlance, a professor at a Methodist women's university in Seoul, who brought a number of her students with her. Miss Kim had spent three years at the University of Toronto, where she wrote a thesis on Swedenborgianism. She translated *Divine Principle* into English, and in 1959 became the first Moon missionary to the United States, settling at the University of Oregon. Others in America came into the movement, mostly but not all Koreans. Among them was Colonel Bo Hi Pak, then assistant military attaché at the South Korean Embassy in Washington, who became Moon's chief interpreter. Another key figure was Sang Ik Choi, who spent seven years in Japan in the early 1960s and there became familiar with Japanese systematic training programs and communal living, which he would introduce into the Moon movement on his return to the United States. Choi and Miss Kim led two complementary Moon movements that lived together in relative harmony.

Moon made his first world tour in 1965, when he established 120 "Holy Grounds," 55 of which were in the United States. He repeated this in 1969 and again in 1971, when he spoke publicly in the West for the first time, and when he adopted the name Unification Church for his movement, with a base in America. His followers were often full-time workers for the movement, earning money by selling peanuts, candles, flowers, and dried-flower arrangements. With income thus generated, Moon took part in various business ventures in Korea, especially factories for machine parts, ginseng tea, and paints. His rallies, such as those in 1976 in Yankee Stadium and at the Washington Monument, attracted a good deal of attention, as did his conducting mass weddings of hundreds of followers at a time. Moon's holdings in the United States soon included the New Yorker Hotel (bought for $5 million) and Tiffany's ($2.4 million). His News World Communications, Inc., owns the *Washington Times* and other papers.

The theology of the Unification Church is interesting in its own right, although not nearly so original as Moon would have his followers believe. Moon claims that he received the "divine principle" from God Himself by means of hints and clues, but that its final construction was Moon's alone. Apart from God and the Bible, Moon also recognizes the authority of communication from the spirit world, sometimes achieved with the aid of a medium.[45] The emphasis in Moon's theology is on the unification of all religions. Even his God is composed of both male and female elements (sexistly also referred to as positive/negative units), which overlap in a Taoist yin/yang scheme. Nature is also a reflection of God, who experiences emotions in human fashion, His/Her most essential characteristic being "heart," the impulse to love, to be united in love with the object of that love. All living things have to pass through three stages of growth, Moon teaches, during which God relates to them through His "divine principle," His universal law. Mankind, when passing through these stages, must develop his/her capacity to love. Moon's mankind has free will and needs to seek a direct relationship with God.

If Moon's basic theology seems a tossed salad of Western Christianity, so too does his discussion of Creation recapitulate various earlier ideas. According to Moon, Adam and Eve were created by God so that they could pass through the obligatory three stages and only then be united in matrimony, becoming "True Parents" of the rest of mankind. This is what he calls the "Ideal Four Position Foundation," a quadrilateral figure with God at the top, Husband and Wife in the middle, and Children at the bottom, which allows mankind to fulfill the "Three Blessings" of God: to perfect his character, to have an Ideal Family, and to assert his right of dominance over the whole of Creation. (As we shall see, this notion of dominance over Creation will be essential for the Christian Reconstructionist or Dominion Theology movement, which has become much more prominent in recent years, even to the extent of influencing mainstream premillennials such as Pat Robertson.)

Sadly, this was not to be. God had entrusted Adam's care to the Archangel Lucifer, who became jealous of the Almighty's love for the first man and developed an emotional relationship with Eve, who then persuaded Adam to have a physical relationship with her. This premature union of Adam and Eve replaced God with Lucifer, and caused original sin to be transmitted to their descendants. The cause of the Fall was the misuse of love, the most powerful of all forces. God, for His part, has tried to restore the original equilibrium and to establish His kingdom on earth. Ultimately, this will be possible only when a Messiah comes to mankind to take on the role in which Adam failed. Before this can happen, however, mankind must prepare the way for the coming of the Messiah by "indemnifying" God, canceling the bad debts of his forebears. Jesus might have been able to restore the balance, but He was not recognized as the Messiah because of the wavering faith of John the Baptist, as a result of which the Jews of the time did not accept Jesus, and He was crucified before He was able to marry and establish the Ideal Four Position Foundation. Yet through His death, Jesus was at least able to offer mankind a spiritual salvation and to restore equilibrium with God. After the crucifixion, Satan took the physical body of Jesus in order to indemnify mankind for its past sin; having lost the physical object of its faith, man must now await the future establishment of a further Foundation for another messiah, the "Lord of the Second Coming," Adam III.

Not content with rehearsing Anselm's eleventh-century doctrine of salvation, Moon goes on to repeat conventional ideas about patterns in temporal history. The sequence of years between Israel's captivity in Egypt and the birth of Jesus is precisely that of the period from Jesus to our own times, he tells us (although his charts are distinctively scrappy compared with their nineteenth-century originals, or even the sketches of Joachim of Fiore). In the last chapter of *Divine Principle*, he explains that the Messiah will not come in the clouds, but will be born as a physical being. He also gives a short curriculum vitae of the Messiah, including the important details that He will be born between 1917 and 1930, in an Eastern country, in a nation which has suffered, has within its borders a number of different religions, and in a place where the forces of democracy and satanic Communism confront each other. The Messiah, Moon reports, will almost certainly be a Korean born, say, in 1920.

An interesting feature of Moon's message is how adaptable it is. There are versions of his teaching in which all quotations from the Bible are replaced with passages from the Koran. In California, the thrust of the argument is often New Age, with frequent references to psychology and self-fulfillment. Moon's picture may be absent, and the man himself may not be introduced until much general discussion has taken place. A sociological study of Moon's Unification Church suggests that the number of full-time members in the United States has never exceeded four thousand, with no more than fifty thousand worldwide, with maybe five times that number affiliated with Moon's movement in one form or another. Moon's fanatical anti-Communism, which led him to support both the Vietnam War and President Richard Nixon even at the height of the Watergate scandal, lost him allies at one end of the political spectrum, and his marketing methods and his suspicious religious message has repelled Fundamentalists and mainstream Christians.[46]

| VI |

Marion Gordon "Pat" Robertson (b. 1930) is another important figure in the messianic world, who created an empire much more impressive than an unhappy commune in South America. The son of A. Willis Robertson, a Democratic senator from Virginia, Pat Robertson is a graduate of the Yale Law School (although he failed the bar exam) and head of the Christian Broadcasting Network (CBN), one of cable television's giants. He is also a former Marine officer and a Golden Gloves boxer.[47] His *700 Club* on CBN (named after an early telethon that hoped for seven hundred pledges) is a Christian institution; not many people remember that its first host was the notorious Jim Bakker, who with his wife, Tammy, joined CBN in 1965, learned the trade secrets, and defected to found their own corrupt PTL evangelical empire. A subsidiary of CBN, Middle East Television, beams a beguiling mixture of American pulp and missionary programs to Israel, in the hope that its population will eventually include what Robertson calls "completed Jews," those who have accepted Christ as their savior. As Robertson put it:

> TV is a national pastime in Israel. Whole families are going to watch and be blessed. News of the Messiah is going to reach families in . . . Jerusalem [and in] Tel Aviv . . . Everyone is about to hear the Gospel! . . . God's Holy Spirit is about to be poured out on the Holy Land! Miracles are about to abound. God's chosen ones are about to see more and more of the direct revelation of Jesus Christ! And when they see Him, they're going to believe.[48]

Before the introduction of cable television to Israel in 1991, Robertson's station was the only alternative to the Israel state television, whose standard fare was less than exciting.

One reason for Robertson's interest in this medium may be his notion that the return of Jesus to earth will first be witnessed on television, so that, as the Bible says, "every eye shall behold him." He has told audiences that Jesus appearing to him in a vision told him that he, Robertson, was the modern-day John the Baptist who would usher in the Second Coming on TV. Gerard Straub, who was producer of *The 700 Club* until he was dismissed over an affair with an employee, said the televising of the Second Coming began to be discussed in 1979 under the code GSP ("God's Secret Project"):

> The greatest show on earth was in our hands. I wondered where we would put the cameras. Jerusalem was the obvious place. We even discussed how Jesus' radiance might be too bright for the cameras and how we would have to make adjustments for that problem. Can you imagine telling Jesus, "Hey, Lord, please tone down your luminosity; we're having a problem with contrast. You're causing the picture to flare."[49]

Robertson's campaign for the presidency of the United States in 1988 made clear his political activism on behalf of conservative causes, as did his attempt in 1992 to acquire the bankrupt United Press International (UPI) group. His Christian Coalition was founded in October 1989 "to give Christians a voice in their government again to reverse the moral decay that threatens our nation by training Christians for effective political action and getting more Christians involved in influencing public policy." The CC now claims more than 400,000 members and supporters, with nearly nine hundred branches in all fifty states, whose goal is to teach Evangelicals how to succeed in local politics, especially by being elected to school boards.[50] Robertson also founded the American

Center for Law and Justice in 1990, which gives free legal counsel for Christians in conflict with "anti-God, anti-family groups."[51]

Robertson is also more connected than other Fundamentalist or Evangelical preachers to Pentecostalism, groups whose members believe in faith healing, speaking in tongues, exorcisms, and direct messages from God. This movement of Christian renewal is based on the scene of the first Christian Pentecost, when the Holy Spirit descended on the Apostles and transformed them into evangelists. But the real beginning of Pentecostalism took place on January 1, 1901, when a Sunday school teacher at a Bible school in Topeka, Kansas, named Agnes Ozman began to speak in an unknown language. Others began to repeat the experience, especially in the area around Azusa Street, Los Angeles, which drew hundreds of Christians from around the world.

At least 7 million members of congregations are dedicated Pentecostalists, but millions of others, known as Neo-Pentecostalists, or Charismatics, belong to more mainstream Evangelical congregations which use Pentecostalist practices.[52] Oral Roberts, Jim Bakker, and Jimmy Swaggart are all Charismatics. Jerry Falwell and the television preacher Robert Schuller of Garden Grove, California, reject the entire Pentecostalist phenomenon of "glossolalia," claiming that these New Testament gifts existed only during the days of the early Church. But Robertson embraces it, even at the expense of distancing himself from those more firmly in the Fundamentalist camp, and has been known to speak in tongues himself—his sounds like an African dialect, he writes, and his wife Dede's sounds like French—and when he preached in English to people in China, he writes, each listener heard him in his native dialect. He also claims to have repulsed Hurricane Betsy from Virginia Beach, and when Hurricane Gloria tried to slip by him in 1985, he diverted her path simply by saying, "In the name of Jesus I command you to stop." At first he suggested that the Tribulation would begin in 1982, then changed the date to 1984.[53]

Two authors used as authoritative sources by Pat Robertson in his book *The New World Order* (1991) are Nesta Webster (1876–1960) and Eustice C. Mullins (b. 1923). Neither of them is a millenarian or a messianic revolutionary, but both provide powerful ammunition to anyone wanting to justify a claim that the Jews are a dangerous anti-Christian force who must be countered at any cost. Webster, writing just after the First World War, noted in passing the exploitation of Arab workers by Jewish colonists, but she was more concerned with the Jewish part in the Bolshevik Revolution.[54] Like many right-wing conspiracy buffs, Webster was obsessed by the supposed pernicious influence of the eighteenth-century Bavarian Order of the Illuminati, founded on May 1, 1776, by Adam "Spartacus" Weishaupt (1748–1830) as a secret rationalist, anticlerical society.[55] Mullins was more direct. "Born in an atmosphere of murder and extortion," he wrote, "nurtured in clouds of poison gas and the invention of the Jewish Hell-Bomb, the State of Israel proved from its very inception that it was the embodiment of absolute evil."[56]

Mullins is important to the militias and the Aryan Nation/Christian Identity followers. According to his own biographical notices in his books, he was born in Roanoke, Virginia, in 1923, and served for more than three years in the Air Force during the Second World War. He notes his education at Washington and Lee University (where Pat Robertson studied), New York University, and the Washington Institute of Contemporary Arts, and boasts of abilities as a painter. He claims to have worked as a legislative researcher for Senator Joseph McCarthy, and for the Library of Congress and the American Petroleum Institute. Curiously, he says he was active in the attempts to free Ezra Pound from his confinement at St. Elizabeth's Hospital in Washington, D.C., where he was detained as a result of his treasonous activities during the Second World War. Mullins writes that it was Pound who commissioned him to begin his research into the history of the Federal Reserve, which culminated in one of the two books which have brought him notoriety. Since Pound could not use the Library of Congress, Mullins was sent to do four hours of research each day and to discuss his findings with Pound at the hospital. Mullins claims that he "was designated the only authorized biographer of Ezra Pound by letter from him dated July 24, 1958," and indeed he did produce a biography of the poet.[57]

Mullins's history of the Federal Reserve Bank, published in 1952, raised eyebrows, and his continuing interest in this topic shows in his history of the Jews, published in 1968.[58] Mullins claimed in the book to have discovered the great betrayal of President Woodrow Wilson in turning America's banking system over to a cabal of Jewish financiers, and Mullins contends that the law instituting the Federal Reserve Bank was the result of a Jewish plot to undo the provision of the Constitution that "Congress shall have power to coin money, and regulate the value thereof; and of foreign coin," a clause inserted into the Constitution in order to "safeguard the people from Jewish bankers." It was because of this act of foresight that from "the moment the Constitution was adopted, the Rothschilds began to spend money to abrogate this provision." According to Mullins, this effort began with Alexander Hamilton, "the bastard son of a Jewish merchant in the West Indies, named Levine, and his mulatto mistress," the first Secretary of the Treasury who advocated a national bank.[59]

When the Federal Reserve Act was passed in 1913, Jewish bankers—Paul Warburg, Jacob Schiff, Bernard Baruch, and others—finally succeeded in gaining control of the American monetary system. The only congressman to oppose it was the father of Charles Lindbergh. But the bankers were merely tools in the hands of the House of Rothschild, which had controlled the Bank of England since Napoleonic times and hoped to extend to America their system of establishing central banks which they then dominated and controlled. Indeed, the Great Crash of 1929 was engineered by the Federal Reserve for its benefit.[60]

Mullins continued his analysis of the Jewish noncontribution to civilization on a wider scale in his *New History of the Jews* (1968).

Mullins claimed that the Jews in ancient times were known only as destroyers: "They produced no art, founded no dynasties, built no great cities, and, alone of ancient peoples, had no talent for the finer things of civilized life." They were merely parasites on the civilizations of others: "In all of the vast records of peace and wars and rumors of wars, one great empire after another has had to come to grips with the same dilemma . . . the Jews.[61]

Jesus was not a Jew, Mullins insisted, but rather a flaxen-haired gentile from Galilee, where few Jews lived. The Jews themselves are the satanic descendants of Cain, and racially different from gentiles, on whom they prey parasitically.[62] This distinct nature of the Jew comes out clearly in Mullins's elaboration of the blood libel. According to Mullins, blood rites and ritual murder are forms of Stone Age tribal behavior that only the Jews and primitive groups continue to practice. In a lengthy chapter on the subject, Mullins wrote that it was part of the Jewish religion to drink the blood of young children and that all sorts of devious means were devised to obtain this essential ritual fluid. We need to be informed that Jews continue to kidnap children from hospitals in order to drain their blood for religious purposes; this was the true motive behind the kidnapping of the Lindbergh baby, whose blood was drained in revenge for his grandfather's opposition to the establishment of the Federal Reserve Bank. As Mullins explains, in "the United States, Jews have been able to practice ritual murder of gentile children with impunity, because they control the press, and because they hold so many high public offices."[63]

Mullins's creative account of the Jews in history combines excerpts from published histories with mysterious private conversations. He tells us of the existence of a secret "Manual of Discipline" discovered among the Dead Sea Scrolls, which teaches the Jews to follow orders. He tells us that it was the Jews who confined themselves in ghettos in order to hide from the gentiles, and once they swarmed out of these sanctuaries they never ceased to cause misery for the surrounding Christian populations. Indeed, "the continent of America was settled solely because of the desire of the European workers to escape further exploitation by the Jews." By that time, the Jews had managed to reduce the number of gentiles by causing the Black Death. It was Jews who started the Spanish Inquisition too, and they prevented Luther from reforming the Church and thereby caused religious warfare. Both Nazism and Communism were Jewish creations, and both world wars were Jewish plots to make money and to kill Christians, so that at the end of the day, over "one hundred million gentiles lost their lives in these two Jewish wars."[64]

It comes as no surprise to learn that the Holocaust was also a Jewish plot. According to Mullins, it is well documented that Hitler was financed by Jewish money at the beginning of his career. Germany was less anti-Semitic than other countries, so the Nazis had to carry on their attacks on Jewish businesses at night so the local people would not have a chance to interfere. The German mood changed only when the Allies began to bomb Germany, finding their targets thanks to signals sent by German Jews. Hitler was forced to intern the Jews for the duration of the war in concentration camps. No Jews were murdered there; they died from "typhoid, because of their refusal to maintain clean living conditions among themselves." Once the Jews had died of disease, the Germans had no choice but to burn the bodies and introduced ovens for this purpose. Most of the Jews actually killed during the war were Polish, murdered by Stalin in order to prevent them from betraying Russian defenses to the advancing Germans. The claim of the murdered six million was merely a Jewish scheme to extort reparations from the German people. After the war, with "the German reparations, the Jews in Israel were able to live comfortably without working, as they lounged in the homes seized from the hardworking Arabs who had built them."[65]

Generally speaking, Mullins explained, "the Jewish parasite has held to the religious belief that he can achieve absolute power over the gentile host only if he re-establishes his headquarters at the ancient crossroads of world civilization in Palestine." In 1917, the Jews got the British to promise them Palestinian land in exchange for the use of a deadly poison gas invented by Chaim Weizmann, later Israel's first president. After the end of the Second World War, the Jews used terrorist groups such as the Irgun and the Stern Gang to murder gentiles. After the King David Hotel in Jerusalem had been blown up, a "heartsick England reluctantly agreed to give them the country, and the State of Israel came into being after a series of murders which had horrified the civilized world." From its inception, the State of Israel "was the embodiment of absolute evil."[66]

But Mullins reserved his greatest invective for what Jews did in America. The big question, Mullins insisted, is:

> How did this happen? How did the freedom-loving American people become slaves of the Jews? First of all, Americans do not stick together. Second, many sincere and misguided Americans believe the blasphemy that Christ was a Jew, and that the Jews are our natural rulers because our God is a Jew. Third, the Jews spend fortunes every year to cover up their crimes, while Americans spend nothing to find out what the Jews are doing.[67]

Mullins offered a solution to the Jewish problem. "There is no need to kill the Jews," he cautioned in conciliatory fashion. The answer to the Jewish problem is simple: "Get the Jews out of banking and they cannot control the economic life of the community. Get the Jews out of education and they cannot pervert the minds of the young to their subversive doctrines. Get the Jews out of government and they cannot betray the nation." As for non-Jews, "the gentile must become serene in the Love of Jesus Christ, he must acknowledge that he has been chosen as the instrument of Christ's love which the Jews rejected . . . when the gentile begins to know himself, and to acknowledge his identity as the chosen instrument of Christ's love for all men, he will be armed against every wile, every bit of poison which the parasite seeks to inject in him."[68] The aroused gentile community will have to unite to drive out the Jews and their "shabbos goy" agents from positions of power: "Then we will be able to live in a community of kindness and love, because we will have rescued our nation from the beggars, thieves and jackals who seek to install the Antichrist as our master."[69]

Although Mullins is not a millenarian and gives no indication of accepting dispensationalist Fundamentalism, his small picture of the Federal Reserve Bank scandal, and his big picture of the Jewish conspiracy throughout history, feed only too easily into the paranoia of the Aryan Nation/Christian Identity groups and the American militias. His erudition may even look impressive to such people, for whom Mullins has made himself available as an adviser and "expert." It is more surprising that a sophisticated media man like Pat Robertson should take Mullins seriously. Indeed, although critics immediately noted his use of Nesta Webster, they paid less attention to Robertson's use of Mullins as a source.[70] But Robertson's account of the establishment of the Federal Reserve Bank closely follows Mullins, the anti-Semitism left out, with the bankers in the conspiracy just happening to be Jews. Even the title of Robertson's book mimics Mullins's work *The World Order*, published six years earlier.[71] Robertson adds the conspiracy theories of Nesta Webster about the role of the Jews and Freemasons in creating a new world order after the French Revolution. Robertson turns Mullins and Webster around by putting their theories into a Christian Zionist framework, arguing that God's work goes on as prophesied in Revelation, and that the establishment of the State of Israel is one sign that the divine plan is in motion. He therefore argues for the strengthening of Israel and support for her prosperity. As he put it to the Anti-Defamation League of B'nai B'rith in 1980:

It is my considered judgment that there is a firm Biblical mandate in both the Old and New Testament for the establishment of the Nation of Israel in the Holy Land. I believe it is the shared belief of the majority of evangelical Christians in the United States that the possession of all of Jerusalem by the Nation of Israel is of utmost significance in the fulfillment of Biblical prophecy as an evangelical Christian. I have pledged my personal effort and support to gain a just peace in the Middle East and the homeland promised Israel by Almighty God.[72]

At the same time, like Mullins, Robertson urges political action to repeal the law establishing the Federal Reserve Bank, argues for the abolition of the Internal Revenue Service, and hopes for legislation against pornography, abortion, and so on.

Professor Harvey Cox, a recent visitor to Pat Robertson's Regent University (formerly CBN University), recounts that when he raised the problem of the questionable sources used in *The New World Order*, he was told that Robertson "doesn't write all his own books, and the guys he gets to ghost them are just not that dependable." Cox reported a great debate going on within the Robertson camp about whether to adopt Dominion Theology, since Robertson's latest book looks very much like the program suggested by Rousas J. Rushdoony's Christian Reconstructionist movement over thirty years ago. As Gary DeMar, one of Rushdoony's lieutenants, wrote in 1992:

> I was a bit confused when Pat Robertson claimed that he doesn't "agree with Reconstructionism" but does believe that "Jesus is the Lord of all the world, of the government, and the church, and business, and, hopefully, one day, Lord of the press." This is the heart and soul of Reconstructionism. Robertson says he wants "the church to move into the world." Reconstructionists have been saying this and getting criticized for it for over 30 years. At the very least, Pat Robertson, as I've always suspected, is an operational Reconstructionist.[73]

Robertson's Law of Reciprocity, by which God operates according to eight immutable universal laws, and his belief that Christians can create a utopia on earth which they will hand over to Jesus when He returns, look very much like Dominion Theology. They show a marvelous predilection for flexibility by a premillennial preacher who has proclaimed, "I firmly expect to be alive when Jesus Christ comes back to earth," but who at the same time seeks to assimilate views that are different from his own.[74] This resurgence of the Christian Reconstructionist movement and its Dominion Theology, and with it the entire concept of postmillennialism, may point to the direction messianic revolution will take in the future. Instead of advocating a violent change in society and government, based on millenarian theology, the proponents argue that we are *already* in Christ's millennium, whose progress will only bring us greater and greater good until the personal reappearance of Jesus at the end of this thousand-year period. Reconstructionism is a social gospel that insists on the importance of imposing biblical law even on unbelievers, so that Jesus can return and take up the reins of his kingdom on earth. An important document for Reconstructionists is the *Christian Manifesto* (1981), by the late Swiss theologian Francis Schaeffer. Schaeffer argued that America must not fall below a minimum standard of "Judao-Christian consensus," and that Christians must defend this bottom line by all means necessary. If legal means fail, then they are allowed to resort to civil disobedience and, ultimately, force.[75]

Apart from the pioneering but lonely efforts of Thomas Brightman in the late sixteenth century, the other important expression of postmillennialism was that of Daniel Whitby's *A Treatise of the True Millennium* (1703). Whitby's new interpretation of the Second Coming gave the Jews a starring role. According to Whitby, when Paul makes reference in Romans 11:26 to the fact that "all Israel shall be saved," he was alluding to the thousand-year messianic era: "the true *Millennium* is only a Reign of Converted Jews, and of the Gentiles flowing into them." Indeed, the entire concept of resurrected dead people populating a messianic kingdom simply did not make sense: "Can a spiritual body, free from grossness and ponderosity, from needing rest, sleep, clothing, sustenance, receive advantage from that universal plenty?" When we think again, Whitby wrote, we should wonder:

> Can the Devil, when loosed, be so foolish, as to summon up his Armies to fight against, and kill them who are immortal, and can die no more? Can Gog and Magog, with all their numerous Host, hope to prevail against them, or even dare to assault such shining radiant Bodies as they then will have? In a word, can such bodies need or receive any farther Exaltation to fit them for heaven, or for their elevation into the Clouds, to be forever with the Lord? If not, why should they live a thousand Years after God had thus fitted and prepared them for their Habitation in the highest Heavens?

The very notion of believing in a supernatural millennial paradise on earth was a travesty of the "true Genius of the *Christian Faith*," which calls upon mankind to renounce the things of this world. The millennium would come, Whitby said, when the Jews would convert to Christianity and "become a most famous Church again," but it would take place before the Second Coming, and be characterized by a thousand years of peace and prosperity.[76]

The key figure in Christian Reconstructionism today is Rousas J. Rushdoony, head of the Chalcedon Foundation, who with the help of his son-in-law Gary North of Tyler, Texas (where David Koresh is buried), and David Chilton has advocated a Dominion Theology of Christian Reconstructionism that is far more aggressive than Brightman's benign seventeenth-century postmillennialism. When they speak of "Christian values," the Christian Reconstructionists are not really offering them as a possible choice. "Our goal is world dominion under Christ's lordship, a 'world takeover' if you will," explains David Chilton. "We are the shapers of world history."[77]

"The Creed of Christian Reconstruction" by the Reverend Andrew Sandlin is presented for public view on the Web site of the
Chalcedon Foundation. Short and to the point, the philosophy of
Rushdoony is easy to comprehend. "A Christian Reconstructionist
is a Calvinist," he begins, and on the way also explains that he is
a "Presuppositionalist," in that he "does not try to 'prove' that God
exists or that the Bible is true": he simply accepts these axioms on
faith. He is also, of course, a postmillennialist: "He believes Christ
will return to earth only after the Holy Spirit has empowered the
church to advance Christ's kingdom in time and history."

But it is the two other characteristics which are most worrying.
"A Christian Reconstructionist is a Theonomist," Sandlin writes:

> Theonomy means "God's law." A Christian Reconstructionist
> believes God's law is found in the Bible. It has not been abol-
> ished as a standard of righteousness. It no longer accuses the
> Christian, since Christ bore its penalty on the cross for him.
> But the law is a description of God's righteous character. It
> cannot change any more than God can change. God's law is
> used for three main purposes: First, to drive the sinner to trust
> in Christ alone, the only perfect law-keeper. Second, to pro-
> vide a standard of obedience for the Christian, by which he
> may judge his progress in sanctification. And third, to main-
> tain order in society, restraining and arresting civil evil.

No wonder, then, that many of Rushdoony's critics claim that, in
his perfect world, children would be executed for smiting their parents.

"A Christian Reconstructionist is a Dominionist," Sandlin goes
on, referring to God's command in the very first chapter of Genesis:

> And God said, Let us make man in our image, after our like-
> ness: and let them have dominion over the fish of the sea, and
> over the fowl of the air, and over the cattle, and over all the

earth, and over every creeping thing that creepeth upon the earth.

So God created man in his *own* image, in the image of God created he him; male and female created he them.

And God blessed them, and God said unto them, Be fruitful, and multiply, and replenish the earth, and subdue it: and have dominion over the fish of the sea, and over the fowl of the air, and over every living thing that moveth upon the earth.[78]

According to Sandlin, presumably with Rushdoony's blessing, a Christian Reconstructionist

takes seriously the Bible's commands to the godly to take dominion in the earth. This is the goal of the gospel and the Great Commission. The Christian Reconstructionist believes the earth and all its fullness is the Lord's: that every area dominated by sin must be "reconstructed" in terms of the Bible. This includes, first, the individual; second, the family; third, the church; and fourth, the wider society, including the state. The Christian Reconstructionist therefore believes fervently in Christian civilization. He firmly believes in the separation of church and state, but not the separation of the state or anything else from God. He is not a revolutionary; he does not believe in the militant, forced overthrow of human government. He has infinitely more powerful weapons than guns and bombs, he has the invincible Spirit of God, the infallible word of God, and the incomparable gospel of God, none of which can fail. He presses the crown rights of the Lord Jesus Christ in every sphere, expecting eventual triumph.

Ultimately, the Christian Reconstructionist hopes to establish a biblical state in God's America, even against the wishes of those who reject entirely the divine authority of Scripture. Even if this is accomplished on a small scale and by democratic means, Rushdoony's vision still would contradict any concept of minority rights.

Why would Pat Robertson, in many ways a traditional premillennialist, be attracted to such a philosophy? Premillennialists have quite naturally been somewhat skeptical of political action, believing that there was no point in improving a doomed world. Robertson in the past left no doubt that he believes the end is nigh.[79] But his presidential campaign in 1988 in a sense signaled his conversion to a new theology, which attempts to combine pre- and postmillennialism in an original amalgam, both expecting the imminent Second Coming of Christ and attempting to improve the world so as to ease His descent. Robertson's social activism, American style, joined with enthusiastic millenarianism, puts one in mind of the Fifth Monarchy Men of seventeenth-century England, whose manifestos, as we have seen, combined the abolition of the tax on imported leather with the certainty that Christ would return in their day.[80] The continued success of Pat Robertson may be a clear indication of one way in which the ideas of messianic revolution can evolve into a much more benign and socially conservative political force.

Each stage in the development of the concept of messianic revolution not only left something behind but remained connected to evolving themes that have stayed influential until our own times. Joachim of Fiore in twelfth-century Italy bequeathed the significance of looking for God's grand design, and the effective use of visual media, especially the prophetic timeline, complete with arrows and exploding trumpets. He also explored the possibility of setting definite dates for the coming of the Messiah, preferably after one's own expected demise. Millenarian strategists in the Renaissance three hundred years later knew of Joachim's work, and emphasized the importance of looking outside the Christian tradition for the eternal truths. They placed great weight on supernatural forces of every origin, and used Egyptian and Jewish wisdom, arguing that ultimately everything connects.

In the sixteenth-century European Reformation, Christian attention was focused on the biblical text itself, positing through the doctrine of *sola scriptura* that all of the answers to both divine and everyday life could be found in the pages of holy writ. It was also during this period that the prime model of a revolutionary society based on messianic principles was created, in the northern German city of Münster (1534–35). A second touchstone emerged a century later in the 1650s in England's Fifth Monarchy movement, a group of revolutionaries who fervently believed that King Jesus would not return to rule over them unless they first altered completely the existing society on earth. Among their contemporaries were the imaginary Rosicrucians, who also became a model, in this case for a highly secret society based on esoteric lore known only to a select group of initiates.

Isaac Newton at the end of the seventeenth century looked back on what had been accomplished in the millennial field, and hoped that here, combined with his scientific work, he might reduce this imposing jumble of ideas into a Unified Messianic Theory. Part of this work of unification involved an attempt to synchronize all the histories of the world, and to interpret all existing mythologies, especially the religion and culture of ancient Egypt. It was a noble undertaking, and ensured that Newton would remain a key secular prophet for later messianic thinkers.

The French Revolution was the first great historical event which seemed to indicate the working out of divine promises in this world. Many people thought that what was happening in France and America was no less than the fall of Satan and the creation of a new messianic society on both sides of the Atlantic. Richard Brothers and Joanna Southcott sought through their prophecies to prepare mankind to receive the Messiah in His imminent arrival. Emanuel Swedenborg in voluminous Latin volumes took the Renaissance axiom that "everything connects" to an even higher plane of sophistication, building on the Bible, modern science, and the possibility of direct access to the spirit world.

But much of this messianic theorizing remained in the realm of pure speculation until the nineteenth century, when dispensationalism came into vogue. A new Joachimite ground plan gained acceptance, positing a seven-year period of tribulation before the coming of the Messiah, a time of troubles which the faithful would be spared by being "raptured" into a blissful and undefined waiting mode. A number of key biblical texts provided the raw data which could be used for setting dates, and the role of the Jews came to be emphasized even more. The spectacular failure of William Miller, who looked with his followers for the Messiah in the spring and autumn of 1844, splintered messianic fellow travelers into different groups, notably the Jehovah's Witnesses and the Seventh-day Adventists. From the Adventists evolved the Branch Davidians, whose fiery finish at Waco, Texas, on April 19, 1993, not only provided yet another model for messianic revolutionaries but also demonstrated the dangerous consequences of the failure to understand the entire millenarian concept.

Another contribution of the nineteenth century was the reemphasis of the place of Jewish history in the Messiah's grand plan. The Reformation set the principle of regarding the biblical text as the ultimate authority, and the most perfect utopia as the kingdom of Christ on earth. The British Israelites sought to simplify the biblical plan by demonstrating that the Anglo-Saxon races were the literal descendants of the Israelites through the Lost Ten Tribes, and God's promises to the Children of Israel applied directly to Englishmen and Americans alone, the Germans being disowned by the First World War. In true Newtonian fashion, the British Israelites succeeded in uniting divine and secular history. But there was an inherent danger in seeing one's own ethnic group as the Chosen People, and British Israelism developed in the United States into an extreme variety of racism which was attractive to individuals who already inclined to militancy and survivalism. The bombing at Oklahoma City on the second anniversary of the fire at Waco was part of this dark world.

At the same time, both devotion to the inerrant Bible and the concept of Rapture through the dispensationalist schema of world history found expression in mainstream American Fundamentalism. In some ways, the Fundamentalists have been the heirs of the entire messianic revolutionary tradition, even down to their Joachimist penchant for setting millennial dates and illustrating the Second Coming by means of impressive charts and maps. Some religious leaders in this vein have been proclaimed as "living Gods," like Jim Jones and Sun Myung Moon. But most are still more benign, such as Hal Lindsey, Jerry Falwell, and Pat Robertson. At the same time, even they are truly messianic revolutionaries, since they envisage the End of Days as a nuclear holocaust and the destruction of millions of lives. Indeed, the Second Coming is one of the few things a Fundamentalist can long for without guilt, and the accompanying devastation may be the price we have to pay to inaugurate the Kingdom of God. When the man who has the power to launch a nuclear war has some sympathy with such a scenario, as was the case with Ronald Reagan, then the notion of messianic revolution takes on truly apocalyptic proportions. The slight shift in the direction of postmillennial Christian Reconstructionist/Dominion Theology, according to which mankind's lot must improve before the Messiah can return, may indicate that at least Fundamentalist messianism may be more biblical and less nuclear in the coming years.

━━⬧━━

The distance between Joachim of Fiore in the twelfth century and Hal Lindsey eight hundred years later can be measured in many different ways: by language, geography, nationality, religious affiliation, and indeed by almost any criterion known to sociological man. But in at least one very fundamental way, as it were, they are very similar, in that both were driven to comb the Bible in search of divine clues about the course of history and the time of its prophetic conclusion. Both Joachim and Lindsey thought Christ would return in their own lifetimes or shortly thereafter. They both even like to express themselves in diagrams, which make their millenarian vision easier to grasp.

Another tie which binds Joachim and Lindsey is that both men are primarily theoreticians of messianism, who point the way to the

End of the World without feeling the need to take any practical steps to help bring that day closer. Yet despite this caution, both Joachim and Lindsey inspired others to prepare the way for the enthronement of King Jesus. Joachim was responsible for the emergence of the Spiritual Franciscans and the heretical groups that expected Jesus to return about 1260. Hal Lindsey's followers included Randy Weaver, whose survivalism was meant to protect him from the Tribulation, but instead led to the fatal shooting of his wife and teenage son by the FBI.

We need to see men like Joachim of Fiore and Hal Lindsey on the same level plane, and to recognize the persistent existence of a tradition of messianic revolution in the West, stretching from the Middle Ages until our own time. Groups like the Christian Identity movement, or the followers of David Koresh at Waco, or the conspirators who killed so many people at Oklahoma City have a clear place on the timeline of messianic revolution, in the company of many other groups before them who transformed into practical and violent action the belief that Jesus would soon return in power and in glory. Had the federal authorities understood that Waco and Oklahoma were not police problems alone, they would have stood a better chance at preventing the loss of life. So too did the soldiers who exterminated the Kingdom of the Saints at Münster in 1535 see the Anabaptists in the same light. All indications are that the law-enforcement agencies will need a deeper knowledge of the messianic tradition in the coming years, unless, of course, Joachim of Fiore and Hal Lindsey are proved right about the imminent Apocalypse.

Notes

INTRODUCTION

1. "Waco: The Decision to Die," an ABC News Special, April 20, 1993: transcript quoted by J. D. Tabor and E. V. Gallagher, *Why Waco? Cults and the Battle for Relgious Freedom in America* (Berkeley, 1995), pp. 109–10.
2. Ibid., p. 108. For more on Waco, see pp. 161–169.
3. George Orwell, *The Road to Wigan Pier* (London, 1937), chap. 11.
4. See A. Ravitsky, *Messianism, Zionism, and Jewish Religious Radicalism* (Chicago, 1996). The Hisbollah even have a home page on the Internet.
5. G. Gallup, "Religion at Home and Abroad," *Public Opinion* (Mar.–May 1979), pp. 38–39.
6. *The Economist*, Nov. 1995. For many more statistics of this type, see B. A. Kosmin and S. P. Lachman, *One Nation Under God: Religion in Contemporary American Society* (New York, 1993).
7. On Joachim generally, see M. E. Reeves, *The Influence of Prophecy in the Later Middle Ages* (Oxford, 1969); idem, *Joachim of Fiore and the Prophetic Future* (London, 1976); idem, and B. Hirsch-Reich, *The Figurae of Joachim of Fiore* (Oxford, 1972); B. McGinn, *The Calabrian Abbot* (New York, 1985).
8. B. McGinn, *Visions of the End: Apocalyptic Traditions in the Middle Ages* (New York, 1979), p. 314, citing Reeves, *Influence of Prophecy*, pp. 6–10.
9. Will printed in McGinn, *Visions*, pp. 140–41, where he notes that as it is in

the form of a letter prefaced to Joachim's *Expositio in Apocalypsim*; some authorities have questioned its authenticity.

10. N. Cohn, *The Pursuit of the Millennium* (2nd ed., Oxford, 1970), p. 108.

11. For the role of Islam and Saladin in Joachim's thought, see E. R. Daniel, "Apocalyptic Conversion: The Joachite Alternative to the Crusades," *Traditio*, 25 (1969), 127–54; and M. Reeves, "History and Prophecy in Medieval Thought," *Mediaevalia et Humanistica*, n.s., 5 (1974), 51–75.

12. Quoted in McGinn, *Visions*, p. 316.

13. From the reference in Revelation 14:6.

14. More than twenty-five works have been wrongly or falsely attributed to Joachim of Fiore: McGinn, *Visions*, p. 320.

15. Ibid., p. 29.

1 | RENAISSANCE MESSIANISM

1. The best and most recent translation is *Hermetica*, ed. B. P. Copenhaver (Cambridge, 1992).

2. *The Nag Hammadi Library in English*, ed. J. M. Robinson (Leiden, 1988).

3. See R. H. Popkin, *The History of Scepticism from Erasmus to Spinoza* (Berkeley, 1979).

4. On Pico generally, with reference to the Cabala, see Ernst Cassirer, "Giovanni Pico della Mirandola: A Study in the History of Renaissance Ideas," *Jnl. Hist Ideas*, 3 (1942), 123–44, 319–46; B. P. Copenhaver, "Astrology and Magic," in *The Cambridge History of Renaissance Philosophy*, ed. C. B. Schmitt and Q. Skinner (Cambridge, 1988), pp. 264–300; idem, "Platonism," esp. section on "Giovanni Pico and Nicholas of Cusa" in *Renaissance Philosophy*, ed. B. P. Copenhaver and C. B. Schmitt (Oxford, 1992).

5. On Cabala generally, see Gershom Scholem, *Major Trends in Jewish Mysticism* (Jerusalem, 1941); idem, *Kabbalah* (Jerusalem, 1974). On Christian Cabala, see J. L. Blau, *The Christian Interpretation of the Cabala in the Renaissance* (New York, 1944); F. Secret, *Les Kabbalistes chrétiens de la Renaissance* (Paris, 1964); W. J. Bousma, "Postel and the Significance of Renaissance Cabalism," *Jnl. Warburg & Courtauld Inst.*, 17 (1954), 318–32; Frances A. Yates, *The Occult Philosophy in the Elizabethan Age* (London, 1979).

6. Johannes Reuchlin, *De rudimentis Hebraicis* (Pforzheim, 1506); idem, *De verbo mirifico* (Basel, 1494); idem, *De arte Cabalistica* (Haguenau, 1517). For an interesting discussion of the Egyptian tradition, see Martin Bernal, *Black Athena* (London, 1987).

7. Quoted from a manuscript source in Moshe Idel, "The Magical and Neopla-

tonic Interpretations of the Kabbalah in the Renaissance," in B. Cooperman, ed., *Jewish Thought in the Sixteenth Century* (Cambridge, 1987), pp. 186–242, esp. pp. 186–87. See also idem, "Hermeticism and Judaism," in I. Merkel and A. Debus, eds., *Hermeticism and the Renaissance* (Washington, D.C., 1988), pp. 59–76; and J. Friedman, *The Most Ancient Testimony: Sixteenth-Century Christian-Hebraica in the Age of Renaissance Nostalgia* (Athens, Ohio, 1983).

8. See generally, S. Simonsohn, "Some Well-Known Jewish Converts During the Renaissance," *Rev. Etud. Juives*, 148 (1989), 17–52, esp. 20–26.

9. Published as Flavius Mithridates, *Sermo de Passione Domini*, ed. C. Wirszubski (Jerusalem, 1963), where it is shown that much of the sermon was cribbed from the *Pugio Fidei* of Raimundus Martini. See also F. Secret, "Notes pour une histoire du *Pugio Fidei* à la Renaissance," *Sefarad*, 29 (1960); idem, *Les Kabbalistes chrétiens de la Renaissance* (Milan, 1985).

10. F. Secret, "Qui était l'orientaliste Mithridate," *Rev. Etud. Juives*, 116 (1957).

11. Idel, "Magical," p. 187; idem, "Kabbalah and Ancient Theology in R. Isaac and Judah Abrabanel" (Hebrew), in M. Dorman and Z. Levy, eds, *The Philosophy of Love of Leone Ebreo* (Haifa, 1985), pp. 73–112. Cf. idem, "Kabbalah, Platonism and Prisca Theologia: The Case of R. Menasseh ben Israel," in Y. Kaplan, M. Mechoulan, and R. H. Popkin, eds., *Menasseh ben Israel and His World* (Leiden, 1989), pp. 207–19; and David B. Ruderman, *Kabbalah, Magic, and Science: The Cultural Universe of a Sixteenth-Century Jewish Physician* (Cambridge, Mass., 1988); idem, *Jewish Thought and Scientific Discovery in Early Modern Europe* (New Haven, 1995).

12. Jacob Burckhardt, *The Civilization of the Renaissance in Italy* (London, 1960), p. 295: first pub. 1860.

13. On Savonarola generally, see D. Weinstein, *Savonarola and Florence: Prophecy and Patriotism in the Renaissance* (Princeton, 1970).

14. *Compendio di Rivelazione: testo volgare e latino e dialogus De veritate prophetica: Girolamo Savonarola*, ed. Angela Crucitti (Rome, 1974), pp. 148–49: quoted and translated by McGinn, *Visions*, pp. 281–82.

15. *Supplementum Ficinianum*, ed. P. O. Kristeller, 2 (Florence, 1937), 76–77: quoted in McGinn, *Visions*, pp. 282–83.

16. See also J. L. Phelan, *The Millennial Kingdom of the Franciscans in the New World: A Study of the Writings of Geronimo de Mendieta (1525–1604)* (Berkeley, 1956).

17. G. B. Spotorno, *Memorials of Columbus* (London, 1823), p. 224: repr. in P. M. Watts, "Prophecy and Discovery: On the Spiritual Origins of Christopher Columbus's 'Enterprise of the Indies,' " *Amer. Hist. Rev.*, 90 (1985), 73.

18. The original MS. of Columbus's letter is at the Biblioteca Colombina, Seville. It is partially printed as the *Libro de las Profécias*, ed. C. de Lollis, in *Raccolta di Documenti e Saudi*, part 1, 2 (Rome, 1894), 148, quoted in McGinn, *Visions*, p. 284. The so-called prophecy from Joachim of Fiore is actually from Arnold of Villanova (c. 1250–1312) and circulated in Aragon as part of the propaganda effort by the brothers James II of Aragon and Frederick III of Sicily: Watts, "Prophecy."

19. Christopher Columbus, *Select Letters*, ed. R. H. Major (London, 1847), pp. 196–98: repr. in McGinn, *Visions*, p. 285. The Spanish text is to be found in de Lollis, p. 202. Cf. M. Reeves, "Joachimist Influences on the Idea of a Last World Emperor," *Traditio*, 17 (1961), 323–70.

20. For what follows concerning d'Ailly, see Watts, "Prophecy." See also J. V. Fleming, "The 'Mystical Signature' of Christopher Columbus," in *Iconography at the Crossroads*, ed. B. Cassidy (Princeton, 1993), pp. 197–214.

21. M. Bloomfield and M. Reeves, "The Penetration of Joachimism into Northern Europe," *Speculum*, 29 (1954), 772–93; and Watts, "Prophecy."

22. P. J. Alexander, "Byzantium and the Migration of Literary Works and Motifs: The Legend of the Last Roman Emperor," *Medievalia et Humanistica*, n.s., 2 (1971), 47–82.

23. See, generally, Thomas Frognall Dibdin, *An Introduction to the Knowledge of Rare and Valuable Editions of the Greek and Latin Classics*, vol. 1 (4th ed., London, 1827); B. Hall, "Biblical Scholarship: Editions and Commentaries," in *The Cambridge History of the Bible*, 3, ed. S. L. Greenslade (Cambridge, 1963), 38–93.

24. He was made a cardinal in 1507, and in an expedition to Africa two years later captured Oran. He was regent of Castile for Charles V (1516–17) and died within hours of being sacked by the emperor.

25. Others included Corpus Christi College at Oxford, the Collège de France, and the University of Wittenberg, which was endowed by Frederick of Saxony with chairs in each of the three languages.

26. According to J. Le Long, *Bibliotheca sacra* (Leipzig, 1709).

27. Another reason to pinpoint 1522 as the date of circulation is that Erasmus's third edition of his Greek New Testament (1522) shows no clear influence of the Complutensian Polyglot, whereas his fourth edition does.

28. He also made Henry VIII "Defender of the Faith" (Oct. 11, 1521). Leo X died of malaria and was replaced by Adrian VI (1522–23), a Dutchman, who was the last non-Italian pope until John Paul II.

29. Gomecius, *De Rebus gestis a Francisco Ximenio Cisnerio Archiepiscopo Tole-*

tano (Alcalá, 1569). See also the histories of Baudier (trans. Vaughan), Fléchier, and Marsolier. Cf. Butler, *Horae Biblicae*, pp. 123–27: Dibdin.

30. A photograph of a typical page is printed as plate 12, *Cambridge History*, vol. 3.

31. Cited in *Cambridge History*, vol. 3, p. 51.

32. Ibid.

33. This curious Jewish codex was not the only manuscript which was lost, to the intense frustration of modern scholars; only four of the Hebrew codices used can still be traced. It seems that in about 1750 they were sold by the librarian at Alcalá to a manufacturer of fireworks. There must have been quite a quantity of material, as the money was paid by the rocket man, a certain Toyro, in two installments. A contemporary scholar, hearing of this tragic transaction, immediately intervened, but arrived in time only to save a few scattered pages. J. D. Michaelis, the great nineteenth-century German biblical scholar, summed up the incident exclaiming, "Oh, that I had it in my power to immortalize both librarian and rocket-maker! The author of this inexcusable act was the greatest barbarian of the present century, and happy only in being unknown": T. F. Dibdin, *An Introduction to the Knowledge of Rare and Valuable Editions of the Greek and Latin Classics* (4th ed., London, 1827), vol. 1, pp. 6–7.

34. Tarscio Herrero del Collado, "El proceso inquisitorial por delito de hereija contra Hernando de Talavera," *Anuario de Historia del Derecho Español. Instituto Nacional de Estudios Jurídicos* (Madrid, 1959), pp. 671–706; R. H. Popkin, "Jewish Christians and Christian Jews in Spain, 1492 and After," *Judaism*, 41 (1992), 248–67.

35. Printed as *El Manuscrito Apologético de Alfonso de Zamora* (Madrid, 1950).

36. See esp. Francis Losa, *La Vie de Grégoire Lopez dans la nouvelle Espagne* (Paris, 1644), trans. from the Spanish; and the English translation, *The Holy Life of Gregory Lopez: A Spanish Hermite in the West-Indies* (2nd ed., n.p., 1675). John Wesley was a great admirer of López, and wrote a biography of him which appeared in *The Christian Library* (London, 1826): E. Duffy, "Wesley and the Counter-Reformation," in *Revival and Religion Since 1700* [John Walsh Festschrift], ed. J. Garnett and C. Matthew (London, 1993), esp. pp. 12–19. See also F. C. Doyle, *The Life of Gregory Lopez* (London, 1876).

37. On Paracelsus generally, begin with H. Trevor-Roper, "The Paracelsian Movement," in his *Renaissance Essays* (London, 1985), chap. 9. See also W. Pagel, *Paracelsus: An Introduction to Philosophical Medicine in the Era of the Renaissance* (New York, 1985); A. G. Debus, *The Chemical Philosophy: Paracelsian Science and Medicine in the Sixteenth and Seventeenth Centuries* (New York, 1977).

2 | THE MESSIANIC IDEA DURING THE REFORMATION

1. Thomas Müntzer, *Politische Schriften*, ed. C. Hinrichs (Tübingen, 1950), pp. 5–28: trans. in *Renaissance and Reformation 1300–1648*, ed. G. R. Elton (3rd ed., New York, 1976), pp. 190–93.
2. Friedrich Engels, *The Peasant War in Germany* (New York, 1926).
3. Martin Luther, *Against the Robbing and Murdering Hordes of Peasants* (May 1525): trans. *Culture and Belief in Europe, 1450–1600* (Oxford, 1990), pp. 191–95.

3 | THE MESSIAH DURING THE SEVENTEENTH-CENTURY WORLD WAR

1. See, generally, C. Webster, *From Paracelsus to Newton: Magic and the Making of Modern Science* (Cambridge, 1982), pp. 29–30, 41.
2. See esp. F. A. Yates, *The Rosicrucian Enlightenment* (London, 1972), and the very stern criticism of it by B. Vickers, "Frances Yates and the Writing of History," *Jnl. Mod. Hist.*, 51 (1979), 287–316. Also: J. W. Montgomery, *Cross and Crucible: Johann Valentin Andreae (1586–1654)* (The Hague, 1973); C. McIntosh, *The Rose Cross and the Age of Reason: Eighteenth-Century Rosicrucianism in Central Europe and Its Relationship to the Enlightenment* (Leiden, 1992); P. Arnold, *Histoire des Rose-Croix et les origines de la Franc-Maçonnerie* (Paris, 1955): (2nd ed., Paris, 1990) with preface by U. Eco. Older works include A. E. Waite, *Real History of the Rosicrucians* (London, 1887); idem, *The Brotherhood of the Rosy Cross* (London, 1924); T. De Quincey, "Historico-Critical Inquiry into the Origin of the Rosicrucians and the Freemasons," *Collected Writings*, ed. D. Masson, 13 (Edinburgh, 1890), 384–448.
3. This was Gassendi's view: see M. L. Kuntz, *Guillaume Postel: Prophet of the Restitution of All Things: His Life and Thought* (The Hague, 1981), p. 174.
4. There seem to have been two stars, which appeared in the constellations Serpentarius and Cygnus: they were discussed by Kepler in two books published in Prague in 1606. See also Kuntz, *Postel*, p. 175, and now S. Åkerman, *Rose Cross over the Baltic: The Spread of Rosicrucianism in Northern Europe* (Leiden, 1998).
5. H. R. Trevor-Roper, "The Paracelsian Movement," in his *Renaissance Essays* (London, 1985), p. 183n.
6. Ibid., p. 182.
7. Yates, *Rosicrucian*, p. 69.

8. See, generally, W. R. Shea, "Descartes and the Rosicrucian Enlightenment," in *Metaphysics and Philosophy of Science in the Seventeenth and Eighteenth Centuries* (Gerd Buchdahl Festschrift), ed. R. S. Woolhouse (Dordrecht, 1988), pp. 73–99.

9. See, generally, R. G. Clouse, "The Rebirth of Millenarianism," in *Puritans, the Millennium and the Future of Israel*, ed. P. Toon (Cambridge and London, 1970), pp. 42–65.

10. B. S. Capp, *The Fifth Monarchy Men* (London, 1972), p. 38.

11. D. S. Katz, "English Redemption and Jewish Readmission in 1656," *Journal of Jewish Studies*, 34 (1983), 73–91.

12. See A. Woolrych, *Commonwealth to Protectorate* (Oxford, 1982), pp. 271–72.

13. [John Cotton], *An Abstract of the Lawes of New England* (London, 1641). The 1655 edition included a preface by Fifth Monarchist William Aspinwall. Others who advocated adopting the Mosaic law included John Brayne, *The New Earth* (London, 1653), and John Spittlehouse, *The first Addresses* (London, 1653)

14. Woolrych, *Commonwealth*, p. 272.

15. Taken from William Medley, *A Standard Set Up* (London, 1657), pp. 12–22.

16. Thomas Gataker, *Of the Nature and Use of Lots* (2nd ed., London, 1627).

17. Quoted in R. H. Tawney, *Religion and the Rise of Capitalism* (London, 1926), contents.

18. B. Hilton, *The Age of Atonement: The Influence of Evangelism on Social and Economic Thought, 1785–1865* (1989).

19. J. Bossy, *Christianity in the West* (Oxford, 1985).

20. [Henry Jessey], *1654. The Scripture-Kalendar* (London, 1654), title page, last page; idem, *1661. The Scripture-Kalendar* (London, 1661), sig. B^{r-v} and passim: the almanacs for 1656–59 and 1662 are now missing. Jessey's Scripture Kalendar was revived later by "J. S." in 1668. See generally B. S. Capp, *Astrology and the Popular Press* (London, 1979), pp. 365, 377.

21. H[enry] J[essey], *The Lords Loud Call to England* (London, 1660), title page, p. 4.

22. All anonymous, without notation of publisher or place: *Mirabilis Annus, Or The year of Prodigies and Wonders* (1st imp., 1661); *Mirabilis Annus Secundus: Or The Second Year of Prodigies* (1662); *Mirabilis Annus Secundus Or, The Second Part Of the Second Years Prodigies* (1662).

23. The computation of prodigies was made by Ball, *Great Expectations*, pp. 111–15. On these works, see also K. Thomas, *Religion and the Decline of Magic* (Penguin ed., Harmondsworth, 1973), p. 111; and C. E. Whiting, *Studies in*

English Puritanism (London; 1931), pp. 547–51. See also P. C. Cohen, *A Calculating People: The Spread of Numeracy in Early America* (Chicago, 1982), chap. 3.

24. *Mirabilis Annus*, sig. A4ᵛ (preface).

25. *Mirabilis Annus Secundus* (first part), sig. A3ᵛ (preface).

26. E[dward] W[histon], *The Life and Death of Mr. Henry Jessey* (n.p., 1671), pp. 84, 94; White Kennett, *A Register and Chronicle*, 1 (London, 1728), 833.

27. *The Journal of Christopher Columbus*, ed. C. Jane and L. A. Vigneras (London, 1960), pp. 51, 206. Cf. A. B. Gould y Quincy, "Nueva Lista Documentada de los Tripulantes de Colón en 1492," *Bol. de la Real Acad. de la Hist.*, 75 (1924), pp. 34–49.

28. II Kings 17:6, 23.

29. II Esdras 13:41–42, 46–47.

30. See Richard H. Popkin, *Isaac La Peyrère (1596–1676): His Life, Work and Influence* (Leiden, 1987).

31. See, generally, D. S. Katz, *Philo-Semitism and the Readmission of the Jews to England, 1603–1655* (Oxford, 1982), chap. 4, and passim for much of what follows. See also D. S. Katz, *The Jews in the History of England, 1485–1850* (Oxford, 1994), chap. 3.

32. See, generally, *Menasseh ben Israel and His World*, ed. Y. Kaplan, H. Méchoulan, and R. H. Popkin (Leiden, 1989). See also Cecil Roth, *A Life of Menasseh ben Israel: Rabbi, Printer, and Diplomat* (Philadelphia, 1934).

33. D. S. Katz, "Menasseh ben Israel's Mission to Queen Christina of Sweden," *Jewish Soc. Stud.*, 45 (1983–4), 57–72.

34. "The Relation of Master Antonie Monterinos," in *Ievves in America*, ed. T. Thorowgood (London, 1650). Cf. Menasseh ben Israel, *The Hope of Israel*, ed. Henry Méchoulan and Gerard Nahon (Oxford, 1987), pp. 105–11.

35. Edward Winslow, *The Glorious Progress* (London, 1649), repr. *Coll. Mass. Hist. Soc.*, 3rd ser., 4 (1834), 73.

36. John Dury, "An Epistolicall Discourse," in Thorowgood, *Ievves*, sigs D-E2, dated January 27, 1649–50. Dury promises to send Thorowgood a copy of Menasseh's book as soon as it is published.

37. For the publishing history of *The Hope of Israel*, see the edition of Méchoulan and Nahon, pp. ix–xi. We now know that it was John Dury who decided that the English versions be dedicated to Parliament: Ernestine van der Wall, "Three Letters by Menasseh ben Israel to John Durie: Philo-Judaism and the 'Spes Israelis,' " *Nederlands Archief voor Kerkgeschiedenis*, 65 (1985), pp. 46–63.

38. Isaiah 11:12; Deuteronomy 28:64; Cecil Roth, "New Light on the Resettlement," *Trans. Jew. Hist. Soc. Eng.*, 11 (1928), 113–14.

39. Most of this narrative comes from the first book of Nephi, in *The Book of Mormon* (Palmyra, N.Y., 1830), and the introductory material therein, which is part of the canon. See also Whitney R. Cross, *The Burned-Over District* (Ithaca, N.Y., 1950); Fawn M. Brodie, *No Man Knows My History: The Life of Joseph Smith, the Mormon Prophet* (New York, 1946); Leonard J. Arrington and Davis Bitton, *The Mormon Experience: A History of the Latter-day Saints* (London, 1979). For analogous evidence, see David Philipson, "Are There Traces of the Ten Lost Tribes in Ohio?" *Pubs. Amer. Jew. Hist. Soc.*, 13 (1905), pp. 37–46; Lee M. Friedman, "The Phylacteries Found at Pittsfield, Mass.," *Pubs. Amer. Jew. Hist. Soc.*, 25 (1917), pp. 81–85.

40. The Articles of Faith are signed by Joseph Smith, and are often printed in *The Book of Mormon*.

41. *The Book of Mormon*, III Nephi 21:23–26.

42. Ibid., 20:29–33.

43. Quoted in Arrington and Bitton, *Mormon Experience*, p. 30.

44. Joseph Smith's new translation is published by the Reorganized Church of Jesus Christ of Latter-day Saints, Independence, MO. See R. J. Matthews, *"A Plainer Translation": Joseph Smith's Translation of the Bible* (Provo, Utah, 1975).

4 | MEASURING THE APOCALYPSE: ISAAC NEWTON AND THE MESSIAH

1. See, generally, J. E. Force and R. H. Popkin, *Essays on the Context, Nature, and Influence of Isaac Newton's Theology* (Dordrecht, 1990); and M. Goldish, *Judaism in the Theology of Sir Isaac Newton* (Dordrecht, 1998).

2. Isaac Newton, *Observations upon the Prophecies of Daniel, and the Apocalypse of St. John* (London, 1733).

3. F. E. Manuel, *Isaac Newton Historian* (Cambridge, 1963), p. 35, blames William Whiston for the book's publication. According to his view, Whiston was still angry with his former patron and wanted to see the book in print so he could publicly refute it. According to Richard S. Westfall, *Never at Rest: A Biography of Isaac Newton* (Cambridge, 1980), however, Newton's heirs were anxious to capitalize on his reputation, and sold the manuscript to a bookseller at once. Conduitt was married to Newton's niece Catherine Barton in 1717, and became very involved with Newton during the last years of his life.

4. Westfall, *Never at Rest*, p. 815.
5. Ussher to Selden, Nov. 12, 1627: James Ussher, *The Whole Works*, ed. C. R. Elrington, 15 (Dublin, 1847–64), 383–84. On chronology generally, see A. T. Grafton, "Joseph Scaliger and Historical Chronology: The Rise and Fall of a Discipline," *History & Theory*, 14 (1975), 156–85; idem, "Scaliger's Chronology," *Jnl. Warburg & Courtauld Inst.*, 48 (1985), 100–43; J. Barr, "Why the World was Created in 4004 B.C.: Archbishop Ussher and Biblical Chronology," *Bull. John Rylands Lib.*, 67 (1984–85), 575–608; idem, "Luther and Biblical Chronology," *Bull. John Rylands Lib.*, 72 (1990), 51–67; H. Trevor-Roper, "James Ussher, Archbishop of Armagh," in his *Catholics, Anglicans and Puritans* (London, 1987), chap. 3; F. E. Manuel, *Isaac Newton, Historian* (Cambridge, Mass., 1963).
6. Edward Gibbon, *Memoirs of My Life* (Penguin ed., Harmondsworth, 1984), pp. 72–73.
7. Trevor-Roper, "Ussher," p. 159.
8. P. Hazard, *The European Mind, 1680–1715* (Penguin ed., Harmondsworth, 1973), p. 60 [French ed., 1935].
9. Isaac Newton, *The Chronology of Ancient Kingdoms Amended. To which is Prefix'd, A Short Chronicle* (London, 1728), p. 43: ded. to the queen by John Conduitt.
10. Ibid., pp. 79–95. See also J. E. Force, *William Whiston: Honest Newtonian* (Cambridge, 1985).
11. Ibid., pp. 51–57.
12. The manuscript is far more disorganized than some recent commentary would suggest. Most of it is in the Jewish National and University Library, Jerusalem, MS. Yahuda 16.2. Some of it is in Latin, some in English; some in Newton's hand, and some in the hand of his assistant (but no relation) Humphrey Newton. Further details regarding the MS. can be found in Westfall, *Never at Rest*, pp. 351–52n. See also idem, "Isaac Newton's *Theologiae Gentilis Origines Philosophicae*" in *The Secular Mind*, ed. W. Wager (New York, 1982), pp. 15–34; and R. H. Popkin, "The Crisis of Polytheism and the Answers of Vossius, Cudworth, and Newton," in Force and Popkin, *Newton's Theology*, pp. 9–26.
13. Newton, *Chronology*, pp. 332–46 and following three plates.
14. Isaac Newton, "A Dissertation upon the *Sacred Cubit* of the *Jews* and the *Cubits* of the several Nations; in which, from the Dimensions of the greatest *Egyptian* Pyramid, as taken by Mr. *John Greaves*, the antient Cubit of *Memphis* is determined," in John Greaves, *Miscellaneous Works*, ed. Thomas Birch, 2 (London, 1737), 405–33. John Greaves (1602–52) was professor of astronomy at Oxford. Between 1638 and 1640 he traveled in the Middle East and climbed

the Great Pyramid twice. His work was summarized in his *Pyramidographia: or a description of the Pyramids in Aegypt* (London, 1646), including a very accurate cross section of the Great Pyramid. For the ultimate pyramid book, see P. Lemesurier, *The Great Pyramid Decoded* (London, 1977).

15. Jewish National and University Library, Jerusalem, MS. Yahuda 17.3, fols. 8–11: repr. Westfall, *Never at Rest*, p. 354.

16. Isaac Newton, *Correspondence*, ed. H. W. Turnbull, 3 (Cambridge, 1961). See letter #384 for proof that Newton did not know that the letters had been sent on.

17. *Two Letters of Sir Isaac Newton to Mr. Le Clerc, Late Divinity Professor of the Remonstrants in Holland. The Former Containing a Dissertation upon the Reading of the Greek Text, I John, v. 7. The Latter Upon That of I Timothy, iii. 16. Published from authentick MSS in the Library of the Remonstrants in Holland* (London, 1754).

18. "An Historical Account of Two Notable Corruptions of Scripture, in a Letter to a Friend. Now first published entire from a MS. in the Author's hand-writing in the possession of the Rev. Dr. Ekens, Dean of Carlisle," in Horsley, 5 (1785), 493–550. The original letter is the one which bears study, being among the New College manuscripts deposited at the Bodleian Library at Oxford: Bodl. Lib., MS. New College 361/4, fols. 2–41: repr. Newton, *Correspondence*, vol. 3, pp. 83–129 (#358): Newton to a Friend, Nov. 14, 1690. It is in fact two letters, the first dealing with the passage from John and the second from Timothy, written carefully in Newton's hand. Ibid., pp. 129–44 (#359): Newton to a Friend [?John Locke], [?Nov. 1690], is headed by Newton "The Third Letter," and is a sequel to the previous text. It exists in two manuscripts: Bodl. Lib., MS. New College 361/4, fols. 49v–68; and fols. 70–83.

19. Actually, the manuscript turned up in Dublin in the mid-eighteenth century, but Newton was correct that it was "new"—that is, late medieval—and therefore without authority.

20. King's College MS. 5, fol. 55: repr. S. Mandelbrote, " 'A duty of the greatest moment': Isaac Newton and the Writing of Biblical Criticism," *Brit. Jnl. Hist. Sci.*, 26 (1993), 296. See, generally, R. H. Popkin, "Newton as a Bible Scholar," in Force and Popkin, *Newton's Theology*, pp. 103–18.

21. See, generally, R. H. Popkin, "Newton and the Origins of Fundamentalism," in *The Scientific Enterprise*, ed. E. Ullmann-Margalit (Dordrecht, 1992), 241–59; and idem, "Newton and Fundamentalism, II," in Force and Popkin, *Newton's Theology*, pp. 165–80.

5 | **THE RADICAL ENLIGHTENMENT**

1. E. Cassirer, *The Philosophy of the Enlightenment* (Princeton, 1951), p. 134: first pub. 1932.

2. A major dissenter to this view was the conservative Edmund Burke, who wrote his classic *Reflections on the Revolution in France* the following year, arguing that the Glorious Revolution was an aberration, and not indicative of English constitutional history.

3. See N. O. Hatch, *The Sacred Cause of Liberty: Republican Thought and the Millennium in Revolutionary New England* (New Haven and London, 1977); E. L. Tuveson, *Millennium and Utopia* (2nd ed., New York, 1964).

4. His chief work is David Hartley, *Observations on Man, his Frame, his Duty, and his Expectations* (London, 1749). For more on Hartley, see Richard Haven, "Coleridge, Hartley, and the Mystics," *Jnl. Hist. Ideas*, 20 (1959), 477–94; Robert Marsh, "The Second Part of Hartley's System," *Jnl. Hist. Ideas*, 20 (1959), 264–73; Hoxie N. Fairchild, "Hartley, Pistorius, and Coleridge," *Proc. Mod. Lang. Assoc.*, 62 (1947), 1010–21; R. H. Popkin, "Divine Causality: Newton, the Newtonians and Hume," in *Greene Centennial Studies*, ed. P. J. Korshin and R. R. Allen (Charlottesville, 1984), pp. 40–56.

5. See his works, *The Three Woe Trumpets* (2nd ed., London, 1793); *Lectures on the Prophecies that Remain to be Fulfilled* (London, 1789–90), in four volumes. Edward Martin Stone, *Biography of Elchanan Winchester* (Boston, 1836); E. W. preface to G. P. Siegvolk (pseud.), *The Everlasting Gospel* (London, 1792). See also Geoffrey Rowell, "The Origins and History of Universalist Societies in Britain, 1750–1850," *Jnl. Eccl. Hist.*, 22 (1971), 35–56.

6. On Richard Brothers, see J. F. C. Harrison, *The Second Coming: Popular Millenarianism 1780–1850* (London, 1979), chap. 4.

7. These works were numbered and indexed by a follower named Philip Pullen in 1815. Another follower, Daniel Jones, did a fuller index in 1852. Her works were reprinted between 1912 and 1924, and there is a modern catalogue of the Southcott Collection at the University of Texas at Austin. Southcott's "communications" are now fourteen sets of bound manuscripts, originally kept in the families of believers. The British Library has the largest collection; there are others at Texas, and still more at the Blockley Antiquarian Society, which rescued the MSS. when Rock Cottage burned down in 1971. Wonderfully, there is also a "Great Box" weighing 156 pounds containing further MSS., still sealed, its location known to only a few chosen believers.

8. M. C. Jacob, *Living the Enlightenment: Freemasonry and Politics in Eighteenth-Century Europe* (New York, 1991), p. 224.

9. J. M. Roberts, *The Mythology of the Secret Societies* (London, 1972), pp. 17–31. Unlike Jacob, who stresses the role of loyal Whig Freemasons, Roberts notes that French Freemasonry was popularized by Jacobite exiles from Scotland and Ireland, who wanted to bring down the entire *ancien régime*: pp. 28–29.

10. See, generally, the important new work by M. K. Schuchard, esp. "Swedenborg, Jacobitism, and Freemasonry," in *Swedenborg and His Influence*, ed. E. J. Brock et al. (Penn. and London, 1988), pp. 359–79; and "Yeats and the 'Unknown Superiors': Swedenborg, Falk, and Cagliostro," in *Secret Texts*, ed. M. Roberts and H. Ormsby-Lennon (New York, in press).

11. See, generally, P. J. Lineham, "The English Swedenborgians 1770–1840: A Study in the Social Dimensions of Religious Sectarianism" (PhD thesis, Univ. of Sussex, 1978), p. 11. Cf. idem, "The Origins of the New Jerusalem Church in the 1780s," *Bull. John Rylands Lib.*, 70 (1988), 109–22.

12. Emanuel Swedenborg, *The True Christian Religion* (Everyman ed., London, 1933), pp. 270, 280 (#191, 201). See also the very useful book *A Compendium of the Theological Writings of Emanuel Swedenborg*, ed. S. M. Warren (London, 1896).

13. Swedenborg, *True Christian Religion*, pp. 280–81, 332 (#202, 275).

14. Ibid., pp. 282–84, 335 (#204–5, 279). Swedenborg also notes that scriptural truths might be found in China: cf. D. S. Katz, "The Chinese Jews and the Problem of Biblical Authority in Eighteenth- and Nineteenth-Century England," *Eng. Hist. Rev.*, 105 (1990), 893–919.

15. *True Christian Religions*, pp. 285–86 (#209).

16. Ibid., pp. 334–35 (#278).

17. Ibid., p. 340 (#281). See also M. Idel, "The World of Angels in Human Form," in *Studies in Jewish Mysticism, Philosophy, and Ethical Literature* (Isaiah Tishby Festschrift), ed. J. Dan and J. Hacker (Jerusalem, 1986), pp. 1–66, esp. pp. 64–66, where Idel argues that Swedenborg's idea of a *homo maximus* was closer to cabalistic ideas than to the Cosmic Man of Jaina.

18. On Boehme and Law, see Edward Taylor, *Jacob Boehme's Philosophy Unfolded* (London, 1641); D. Hirst, *Hidden Riches: Traditional Symbolism from the Renaissance to Blake* (London, 1964), esp. chaps. 3 and 7.

19. John Wesley, *Journal*, ed. N. Curnock, 5 (London, 1938), 354, 440, quoted in W. R. Ward, "Swedenborgianism: Heresy, Schism or Religious Protest?" in *Stud. Ch. Hist.*, 9 (1972), 303–9, esp. p. 304. Cf. Wesley's fullest discussion of Swedenborg's works in *Arminian Magazine*, 6 (London, 1783), 437–680.

20. See esp. Lineham, "Origins," pp. 112–13. On Cagliostro, see W. R. H. Trow-

bridge, *Cagliostro, Splendour and Misery of a Master of Magic* (London, 1910); M. Harrison, *Count Cagliostro* (London, 1942); F. Funck-Brentano, *Cagliostro and Company* (London, 1910); and H. R. Evans, *Cagliostro and his Egyptian Rite of Freemasonry* (New York, 1930).

21. Lineham, *English Swedenborgians*, chap. 3; Ward, "Swedenborgianism." The standard history of the sect is R. Hindmarsh, *Rise and Progress of the New Jerusalem Church in England, America and other Parts*, ed. E. Madeley (London, 1861).

22. William Blake, "The Marriage of Heaven and Hell," (c. 1790–93), in *Complete Writings*, ed. G. Keynes (London, 1957), pp. 148–60, esp. pp. 157–58. The title itself, of course, is a reference to Swedenborg's book *Heaven and Hell*.

23. Generally, see S. Schwarzfuchs, *Napoleon, the Jews, and the Sanhedrin* (London, 1979); *Le Grand Sanhedrin de Napoléon*, ed. B. Blumenkranz and A. Soboul (Toulouse, 1979); *Les Juifs et la Revolution française*, ed. B. Blumenkranz and A. Soboul (Toulouse, 1979).

24. Some of Grégoire's notes about the deliberations are in his papers in the Bibliothèque de Port-Royal: R. H. Popkin, "La Peyrère, the Abbé Grégoire, and the Jewish Question in the Eighteenth Century," *Stud. 18th Cent. Culture*, 4 (1975), 209–22.

25. Norman Cohn, *Warrant for Genocide* (London, 1966).

26. L. Hyman, *The Jews of Ireland from Earliest Times to the Year 1910* (London, 1972).

27. For more on this, see R. H. Popkin, "Mordecai Noah, the abbé Grégoire and the Paris Sanhedrin," *Mod. Jew. Rev.*, 2 (1982), 131–48.

28. See, generally, G. Scholem, *Sabbatai Sevi* (London, 1973).

29. S. E. Bloemgarten, "De Amsterdame Joden gedurende deerste Jaren van de Bataafse Republiek, 1795–98," *Stud. Rosenthaliana*, 2 (1968), 42–65.

30. Generally, see D. W. Bebbington, *Evangelicalism in Modern Britain* (London, 1989).

31. Among the important works in this regard are George Stanley Faber, *A Dissertation on the Prophecies, That Have Been Fulfilled, Are Now Fulfilling; or Will Hereafter be Fulfilled, Relative to the Great Period of 1260 Years* (5th ed., London, 1814): first pub. 1805; James Hatley Frere, *A Combined View of the Prophecies of Daniel, Esdras and St. John* (London, 1815), who predicted before Waterloo the downfall of Napoleon, but went wrong in positing the Second Coming in 1822–23.

32. "J. J. Ben-Ezra" (Emanuel Lacunza), *The Coming of Messiah in Glory and Majesty*, trans. Edward Irving (London, 1827). The British Library has a copy

of this work with copious notes by S. T. Coleridge. See A. L. Drummond, *Edward Irving and his Circle* (London, 1938).

33. The conferences are described in detail in Ernest R. Sandeen, *The Roots of Fundamentalism: British and American Millenarianism 1800–1930* (Chicago, 1970).

6 | RAPTURE, GREAT DISAPPOINTMENT, AND WACO

1. For more on these Powerscount Conferences, see Ernest R. Sandeen, *The Roots of Fundamentalism: British and American Millenarianism 1800–1930* (Chicago, 1970), pp. 35–37.

2. See Paul S. Boyer, *When Time Shall Be No More: Prophecy Belief in Modern American Culture* (Cambridge, Mass., 1992), p. 185.

3. See esp. John N. Darby, *The Hopes of the Church of God in Connexion with the Destiny of the Jews and the Nations as Revealed by Prophecy* (2nd ed., London, 1842); idem, *Lectures on the Second Coming* (London, 1909).

4. George M. Marsden, *Fundamentalism and American Culture: The Shaping of Twentieth-Century Evangelicalism 1870–1925* (New York, 1980), p. 52.

5. On this see the *Narrative of Mission of Inquiry of the Jews from the Church of Scotland in 1839* (Philadelphia, 1839), pp. 142–43.

6. Sandeen, *Fundamentalism*, pp. 70–80. For the earlier period see R. Bloch, *Visionary Republic: Millennial Themes in American Thought, 1756–1800* (Cambridge, 1985); idem, "The Social and Political Base of Millennial Literature in Late Eighteenth-Century America," *Amer. Qly*, 40 (1988), 378–96; J. B. Moorhead, "Between Progress and Apocalypse: A Reassessment of Millennialism in American Religious Thought, 1800–1880," *Jnl. Amer. Hist.*, 71 (1984), 524–42.

7. On the Niagara Conferences, see Sandeen, *Fundamentalism*, chap. 6.

8. David A. Rausch, *Zionism Within Early American Fundamentalism, 1878–1918* (New York, 1979), pp. 220–21.

9. Marsden, *Fundamentalism*, p. 51.

10. James H. Brookes, "How to Reach the Jews," *The Truth*, 19 (1893), 135.

11. Arno C. Gaebelein, *The History of the Scofield Reference Bible* (New York, 1943), p. 11; Rausch, *Zionism*, pp. 77–78; Boyer, *Time*, p. 97.

12. Oxford University Press claims that they sold perhaps as many as ten million copies by 1967, when they put out a revised version: ibid., p. 98.

13. Rausch, *Zionism*, p. 286.

14. Ibid., p. 285.

15. See David A. Rausch, "Arno C. Gaebelein (1861–1945): Fundamentalist Protestant Zionist," *Amer. Jew. Hist.* (Sept. 1978), 43–55; idem, *Messianic Judaism: Its History, Theology, and Polity* (New York, 1982), pp. 62–63; Y. Ariel, *On Behalf of Israel: American Fundamentalist Attitudes Toward Jews, Judaism, and Zionism, 1865–1945* (Brooklyn, 1991), chap. 5.

16. S. Maxwell Coder, *Israel's Destiny* (Chicago, 1978), p. 55. Coder described the petition to President McKinley, and then digressed to report on some Jews who went to Palestine at the time and converted to Christianity: pp. 55–56.

17. On Hechler, see Richard H. Popkin, "The Christian Roots of Zionism," *Contentions*, 2 (1993), 99–125.

18. Isaac M. Haldeman, *The Signs of the Times* (3rd ed., New York, 1912); Marsden, *Fundamentalism*, p. 125.

19. A. E. Thompson, "The Capture of Jerusalem," in *Light on Prophecy*, ed. W. L. Pettingill et al. (New York, 1918), pp. 144–75; Marsden, *Fundamentalism*, p. 151; Sandeen, *Fundamentalism*, pp. 233–34.

20. Arno C. Gaebelein, "The Capture of Jerusalem and the Great Future of That City," in his *Christ and Glory* (New York, 1919), pp. 145–60.

21. David L. Cooper, *The Eternal God Revealing Himself to Suffering Israel and to Lost Humanity* (Los Angeles, 1928), esp. p. 331.

22. Ibid., 1953 ed., p. 1.

23. Boyer, *Time*, pp. 192, 209, 216, 404–5 (where Boyer notes the Fundamentalist authors who have given similar "positive" interpretations of the Holocaust).

24. See, for example, Jack van Impe and Roger F. Campbell, *Israel's Final Holocaust* (Nashville, 1979); Arthur Bloomfield, *Before the Last Battle: Armageddon* (Minneapolis, 1971); and Charles L. Feinberg, *Israel at the Center of History and Revelation* (Portland, Oreg., 1980), who cites Gaebelein, pp. 136–39. For rabbinical interpretations, see Aviezer Ravitsky, *Messianism, Zionism, and Jewish Religious Radicalism* (Chicago, 1996).

25. On Miller's life and intellectual development, see Leroy B. Froom, *The Prophetic Faith of Our Fathers*, 4 (Washington, D.C., 1954), 455–62. More academic studies of the Millerites include: D. L. Rowe, *Thunder and Trumpets: Millerites and Dissenting Religion in Upstate New York, 1800–1850* (Chicago, 1985); M. Barkun, *Crucible of the Millennium: The Burned-Over District of New York in the 1840s* (Syracuse, 1986); R. A. Doan, *The Miller Heresy, Millennialism, and American Culture* (Philadelphia, 1987); *The Disappointed: Millerism and Millenarianism in the Nineteenth Century*, ed. R. L. Numbers and J. M. Butler (Bloomington, 1987).

26. William Miller, *Wm. Miller's Apology and Defence* (Boston, 1845), pp. 9, 11–12.

27. Generally, see Froom, *Prophetic Faith*, pp. 445–55.

28. For Miller and the Jews, see Sandeen, *Fundamentalism*, p. 52.

29. Generally, see G. Scharnhorst, "Images of the Millerites in American Literature," *Amer. Qly.*, 32 (1980), 19–36.

30. Nathaniel Hawthorne, *Centenary Edition of the Works*, 10 (Columbus, Ohio, 1974), 181–82, 247, 262, 381, 403.

31. Moncure Conway, *Emerson at Home and Abroad* (Boston, 1882), p. 232: quoted in Scharnhorst, "Images," pp. 23–24. Cf. Ralph Waldo Emerson, *Journals and Notebooks*, ed. R. H. Orth and A. R. Ferguson, 9 (Cambridge, Mass., 1971), 30.

32. "The World's End" first appeared in 1844, and in England four years later under the title "Father Miller": John Greenleaf Whittier, *Writings*, 5 (Boston, 1889), 419–27.

33. James Fenimore Cooper, *Wyandotté* (New York, 1892), p. 117.

34. Henry Wadsworth Longfellow, *Kavanagh: A Tale*, ed. J. Downey (New Haven, 1965), pp. 8, 102.

35. Oliver Wendell Holmes, *Works*, 1 (Boston, 1892), 24–25.

36. Robert Coover, *The Origin of the Brunists* (New York, 1966).

37. See, generally, M. J. Penton, *Apocalypse Delayed: The Story of Jehovah's Witnesses* (Toronto, 1985).

38. Cited in Malcolm Bull and Keith Lockhart, *Seeking a Sanctuary: Seventh-day Adventism and the American Dream* (San Francisco, 1989), p. 35. For more on the background of the Saturday Sabbath, see D. S. Katz, *Sabbath and Sectarianism in Seventeenth-Century England* (Leiden, 1988).

39. Generally, see William L. Pitts, Jr., "Davidians and Branch Davidians, 1929–1987," in *Armageddon in Waco*, ed. Stuart A. Wright (Chicago, 1995), pp. 21–26; idem, "The Davidian Tradition," in *From the Ashes: Making Sense of Waco*, ed. J. R. Lewis (Lanham, Md., 1994), pp. 33–39; idem, "The Mount Carmel Davidians: Adventist Reformers, 1935–1959," *Syzygy*, 2 (1993), 39–54.

40. See, generally, David G. Bromley and Edward G. Silver, "The Davidian Tradition from Patronal Clan to Prophetic Movement," in *Armageddon in Waco*, ed. Wright; R. Lawson, "Seventh-day Adventist Responses to Branch Davidian Notoriety," *Jnl. Sci. Stud. Rel.*, 34 (1995), 323–41.

41. See, generally, the very hostile picture of Koresh given in Clifford L. Linedecker, *Massacre at Waco, Texas: The Shocking Story of Cult Leader David Koresh and the Branch Davidians* (New York, 1993), esp. pp. 87–89.

42. Books on Waco include J. D. Tabor and E. V. Gallagher, *Why Waco? Cults and the Battle for Religious Freedom in America* (Berkeley, 1995); D. J. Reavis, *The Ashes of Waco* (New York, 1995); Linedecker, *Massacre at Waco*; D. Leppard, *Fire and Blood: The True Story of David Koresh and the Waco Siege* (London, 1993). One group which alleges a government conspiracy is the American Justice Foundation of Linda and Al Thompson, who are actively involved in the militia movement and have produced videos detailing their charges: A. Heard, "The Road to Oklahoma City," *New Republic*, 212 (May 15, 1995), 15–20; M. Vollers, "The White Woman from Hell," *Esquire*, 124 (July 1995), 50–51.

43. Curiously, when Koresh was buried by his mother in Tyler, Texas, she had his coffin draped in an Israeli flag that she had obtained from the local Conservative rabbi: Tabor and Gallagher, *Why Waco?* p. 215.

44. *Report of the Department of the Treasury on the BATF Investigation of Vernon Wayne Howell also known as David Koresh* (Washington, D.C., 1993); *United States Department of Justice Report to the Deputy Attorney General on the Events at Waco, Texas, February 28 to April 19, 1993, Redacted Version* (Washington, D.C., 1993); S. Labaton, "Report on Initial Raid on Cult Officials Erred and Lied," *NY Times*, Oct. 1, 1993, A1, A20; idem, "Report on Assault on Waco Cult Contradicts Reno's Explanations," *NY Times*, Oct. 9, 1993, 1, 11; R. Pear, "G.O.P. Report Faults Reno in Texas Siege," *NY Times*, July 12, 1996, A14.

45. S. Verhovek, "No Martyrs in Waco," *NY Times*, July 9, 1995, 6.33; idem, "On Anniversary, Sect's Members Commemorate Fatal Fire," *NY Times*, Apr. 20, 1996, 1.7.

46. R. D. McFadden, "Terror in Oklahoma: The Far Right," *NY Times*, Apr. 22, 1995, 1.1; S. H. Verhovek, "Tight Security Gets Tighter as a Sad Anniversary Nears," *NY Times*, Apr. 15, 1996, A1.

7 | FROM BRITISH ISRAEL TO CHRISTIAN IDENTITY AND ARYAN NATION

1. [John Sadler], *Rights of the Kingdom* (London, 1649), pp. 38–40. Generally, see D. S. Katz, *Philo-Semitism and the Readmission of the Jews to England, 1603–1655* (Oxford, 1982), chap. 4: "The Debate over the Lost Ten Tribes of Israel"; and a partisan view in A. H. Godbey, *The Lost Tribes a Myth* (Durham, 1930). See also S. Say, *Israel and England Compared* (London, 1741).

2. *Banner of Israel*, Apr. 5, 1899, quoted in John Wilson, "British Israelism: The

Ideological Restraints on Sect Organisation," in *Patterns of Sectarianism*, ed. Bryan R. Wilson (London, 1967), pp. 345–76, esp. p. 352.

3. Ralph Wedgwood, *Book of Remembrance* (London, 1814), which was supposed to be only the first volume of a series, although no more were published. He also produced cards on which were printed the multiplication table: *The Multiplication Table* (London [1843?]); *The Additional Table* (London [1843?]).

4. *The Time of the End and Prophetic Witness* (1844) and *The Watchmen of Ephraim* (1866–68).

5. John Wilson, *Lectures on Ancient Israel, and the Israelitish Origin of the Modern Nations of Europe* (Cheltenham, 1840); idem, *Lectures on Our Israelitish Origin* (5th ed., London, 1876): the preface from the first edition is dated Liverpool, Aug. 1840. The fifth edition included a biographical sketch of Wilson, "The Re-Discovery of Our Israelitish Origin," pp. 411–42, in which it is claimed that "Mr Wedgwood's 'Book of Remembrance,' also, did not come into his hands till long after the publication of the second edition of 'Our Israelitish Origin' " (pp. 411–12). Cf. idem, *Sixty Anglo-Israel Difficulties Answered. Chiefly from the correspondence of the Late John Wilson, compiled by his daughter* (London [1878?]); idem, *The Book of Inheritance: and Witness of the Prophets, respecting Ephraim, and the Raising up of Israel* (London, 1846).

6. Other contemporaries who emphasized Britain as the sole heir include R. Govett, *English Derived from Hebrew: with glances at Greek and Latin* (London, 1869); F. R. A. Glover, *England, the Remnant of Judah and the Israel of Ephraim* (London, 1861): the author describes himself as sometime chaplain to the British consulate at Cologne, and he would later be active in the British-Israel movement as well.

7. Wilson, *Lectures*, pp. v–vi (preface from 1st ed. of 1840), vii.

8. Ibid., pp. 192–93, 197, 229–31, 293, 302–99, and chap. 2 generally: "Relation of Abraham's Posterity to the Three Grand Races of Mankind."

9. Ibid., pp. 391, 397.

10. Ibid., pp. 397–98. Cf. John Wilson's *The Millennium, or, World to Come; and its relations to preceding dispensations* (Cheltenham, 1842), with a chart of the Dispensations (p. 76); idem, *The Mission of Elijah to Restore All, previous to our Lord's Second Advent* (London [1861]); idem, *England's Duty in Relation to the Christians of Turkey* (London [1876?]); idem, *A Vindication of Christ's character as the Prophet* (London, 1878).

11. See Edward Hine, *Memoirs, and a Selection of Letters* (London, 1909).

12. Edward Hine, *The English Nation Identified with the Lost Ten Tribes of Israel, a Lecture* (Warrington, 1872). Cf. idem, *Seventeen Positive Identifications of*

the English Nation with the Lost House of Israel (London, 1870); idem, *Twenty-seven Identifications of the English Nation with the Lost House of Israel* (7th ed., London, 1870); idem, *Forty-seven Identifications of the British Nation with the Lost Ten Tribes of Israel* (London, 1874).

13. John Lowthian, *A Narrative of a Recent Visit to Jerusalem and Several Parts of Palestine in 1843–4* (Carlisle, 1847).

14. Hine, *The English Nation Identified with the Lost Ten Tribes*, p. 32.

15. This was also the case with the Christadelphians, who also lacked any formal organization: see Wilson, "British Israelism," p. 363n.

16. The weekly was called *Leading the Nation to Glory*, and later *The Nation's Glory Leader* (1875–80); and the monthly *Life From the Dead* (1873–79).

17. Wilson, "British Israelism," p. 364.

18. "Philo-Israel" [E. W. Bird], *Are the English People the Lost Ten Tribes of Israel?* (London, 1875), with two editions the same year.

19. *Life From the Dead*, Jan. 1877; Nov. 1879; JW, 369.

20. J. Wilson, "British Israelism," *Sociological Rev.*, 16 (1968), 41–57; idem, "The History and Organization of British Israelism: Some Aspects of the Religious and Political Correlates of Changing Social Status" (Oxford Univ. D.Phil. thesis, 1966).

21. These views are nicely expressed by Thomas R. Howlett, *Anglo-Israel and the Jewish Problem* (Philadelphia, 1892): quoted by C. G. Howie, "British-Israelism and Pyramidology," *Interpretation*, 11 (1957), 307–23, esp. 309.

22. E. P. Ingersoll, *Lost Israel Found* (Topeka, 1886). Cf. Ezekiel 17:22.

23. See the voluminous writings of Adam Rutherford of the "Institute of Pyramidology" at Stanmore, London, in the 1930s, especially his monumental *Anglo-Saxon Israel or Israel-Britain* (4th ed., Stanmore, 1939) (1st ed., 193); subtitled "A Call to all the Anglo-Saxon, Celtic, Dutch and Scandinavian nations with A Special Call to Iceland." Iceland, indeed, was one of his favorite subjects, on which he published many books on everything from that country as the key to biblical prophecy to its transportation system. The predictions cited above are on pp. 556, 569, 579–89, 613, 615, 620, 630, 655, 656, 676.

24. See, generally, the ultimate pyramid book, P. Lemesurier, *The Great Pyramid Decoded* (London, 1977), esp. p. 181.

25. Rutherford, *Anglo-Saxon Israel*, p. 329.

26. Joseph Wild, *The Lost Tribes and 1882* (New York, 1879), preface: pp. [6–7]; Michael Barkun, *Religion and the Racist Right* (Chapel Hill, 1994), pp. 17–18.

27. See, for example, his "A Late Discovery in the Great Pyramid, and the Mode of it," in *The Great Pyramid of Egypt. A Digest of Great Pyramid Teaching,*

ed. "Philo-Israel" (London [1881?]), pp. 20–24, dated from Edinburgh, Dec. 5, 1876.

28. Charles A. L. Totten, *The Romance of History, Lost Israel Found; or Jeshurun's Pilgrimage* (1888), preface: pp. xv–xvi, xix.

29. Generally, see Barkun, *Religion and the Racist Right*, pp. 20–21.

30. J. H. Allen, *Judah's Sceptre and Joseph's Birthright* (Boston, 1902). The seventh edition was published at Boston in 1930.

31. F. Odum, *God's Covenant Man. British-Israel. Great and Greater Britain* (London, 1916), pp. v–vi.

32. Ibid., pp. 13, 30, 73, 76.

33. Barkun, *Racist Right*, pp. 22–23.

34. N. Cohen, *Warrant for Genocide: The Myth of the Jewish World Conspiracy and the Protocols of the Elders of Zion* (London, 1966); L. P. Ribuffo, "Henry Ford and *The International Jew,*" *Amer. Jew. Hist.*, 69 (1980), 437–77.

35. Generally, see G. Jeansonne, *Gerald L. K. Smith: Minister of Hate* (New Haven, 1988).

36. Barkun, *Racist Right*, pp. 54–67, and, generally, chap. 4, "Creating Christian Identity, 1937–1975."

37. Ibid., pp. 51–52.

38. Cf. Wesley A. Swift, *Was Jesus Christ a Jew?* (n.p., n.d.). The Web site of the Aryan Nation distributes this and other texts like it.

39. Herbert W. Armstrong, *Mystery of the Ages* (Pasadena, 1985), pp. 11–25.

40. Ibid., p. 11.

41. Cf. *The New York Times*, Nov. 26, 1995.

42. Generally, see the Anti-Defamation League [B'nai B'rith] Fact Finding Report, *Armed and Dangerous: Militias Take Aim at the Federal Government* (New York, 1994); and M. Dees, *Gathering Storm: America's Militia Threat* (New York, 1996). See also J. Smolowe, "Enemies of the State," *Time*, May 8, 1995, pp. 58–69; J. Thomas, "Kansas City Journal; Militias Hold a Congress, and Not a Gun Is Seen," *NY Times*, Nov. 1, 1996, A20; A. W. Bock, "Weekend Warriors," *National Review*, 47 (May 29, 1995), 39–42; C. J. Farley, "Patriot Games," *Time*, Dec. 19, 1994, pp. 48–49; G. Wills, "The New Revolutionaries," *NY Rev. Books*, 42 (Aug. 10, 1995), 50–52; P. Doskoch, "The Mind of the Militias," *Psych. Today*, 28 (July–Aug. 1995), 12–14; M. Barkun, "Militias, Christian Identity and the Radical Right," *Christian Century*, 112 (Aug. 2–9, 1995), 738–40; idem, "Millenarian Aspects of 'White Supremacist' Movements," *Terrorism & Political Violence*, 1 (1989), 409–34; J. Kaplan, "A Guide to the Radical Right," *Christian Century*, 112 (Aug. 2–9, 1995), 741–44; M. Janofsky, "Groups Gain New Members Since Attack," *NY Times*, June

18, 1995, 1.19; P. Applebome, "Radical Right's Fury Boiling Over," *NY Times*, Apr. 23, 1995, 1.33.

43. See, e.g., the Militia of Montana (MOM)—"we are everywhere"—especially their Internet site. Generally, see M. Cooper, "Montana's Mother of All Militias," *Nation*, 260 (May 22, 1995), 714ff.; M. Kelly, "The Road to Paranoia," *New Yorker*, 71 (June 19, 1995), 60–64; D. Voll, "At Home with M.O.M.," *Esquire*, 124 (July 1995), 46–49. Cf. an account of the visit of their leader John Trochmann to Yale University in October 1995: Y. Cheong, "Militia Chief Assails Federal Stewardship," *Yale Daily News*, Oct. 27, 1995. Trochmann was a featured speaker at the Aryan Nation congress in 1990; and has been to the compound at Hayden Lake four or five times by his own admission: D. Junas, "The Rise of the Militias," *Covert Action Qly* [n.d.: Internet repr.]. For information on the Michigan Militia Corps, see T. S. Purdum, "Clinton Assails the Preachings of the 'Militias,'" *NY Times*, May 6, 1995, 1.1; M. Janofsky, "'Militia' Man Tells of Plot to Attack Military Base," *NY Times*, June 25, 1995, 1.14. For E Pluribus Unum, another patriot group, see M. Janofsky, "Demons and Conspiracies Haunt a 'Patriot' World," *NY Times*, May 31, 1995, A18. Generally, see M. Navarro, "At Fair for Survivalists, Fallout from Oklahoma," *NY Times*, June 12, 1995, A10.

44. The full text is given in *Extremism in America: A Reader*, ed. L. T. Sargent (New York, 1995).

45. Ibid., p. 334. See also R. Sanders, *Lost Tribes and Promised Lands: The Origins of American Racism* (New York, 1978).

46. For more on Pelley, see E. V. Toy, "Silver Shirts in the Northwest: Politics, Prophecies, and Personalities in the 1930s," *Pacific Northwest Qly*, 80 (1989), 139–46.

47. Barkun, *Religion,* pp. 217ff. Many of these Posse Comitatus groups have Web sites, such as "The Watchman: The Voice of the Christian Posse Comitatus in Pennsylvania." Mark Thomas, its editor, proclaims that "I am a Two-Seedline Identity minister and was ordained by Pastor Butler at Aryan Nation in 1990."

48. A full statement of their political, economic, and legal views, taken from a pamphlet issued in Oregon in the 1980s, appears in Sargent, *Extremism*, pp. 343–50. Cf. T. Heath, "A Law of Their Own," *Newsweek*, Sept. 25, 1995, p. 27. See also the Web site of "The Fully Informed Jury Association" (FIJA), which proclaims as its object "to re-establish the trial jury not only as the decider of justice in the case before it, but as a commentator on the law itself, so that lawmakers enjoy ongoing access to the will of the people, expressed through the verdicts of citizen juries." The concept of "leaderless resistance"

is one developed recently by Louis R. Beam, a former Texas Ku Klux Klan member who also lives in Idaho: K. Schneider, "Bomb Echoes Extremists' Tactics," *NY Times*, Apr. 26, 1995, A22; T. Reiss, "Home on the Range," *NY Times*, May 26, 1995; G. Niebuhr, "Sandpoint Journal: Spreading a Message of Love Where Hate Has Found a Home," *NY Times*, Oct. 29, 1995, 1.24; and generally on Beam, Dees, *Gathering Storm*.

49. Generally, see Richard H. Popkin, *Isaac La Peyrère (1596–1676): His Life, Work and Influence* (Leiden, 1987).
50. See, for example, Morgan Godwyn, *Negro's and Indian Advocate* (London, 1680).
51. See, generally, Richard H. Popkin, "Pre-Adamism in Nineteenth-Century American Thought: 'Speculative Biology' and Racism," *Philosophia*, 8 (1978), 205–39.
52. Alexander Winchell, *Preadamites or a Demonstration of the Existence of Men before Adam, together with a Study of their Condition, Antiquity, Racial Affinities, and Progressive Dispersion Over the Earth, with Charts and Illustrations* (Chicago, 1880).
53. Charles Carroll, *"The Negro a Beast" or "In the Image of God." The reasoner of the Age. The Revelator of the Century. The Bible as it is. The Negro and his Relation to the Human Family. The Negro a Beast but Created with Articulate Speech and Hands, that he may be of Service to his Master, the White Man. The Negro and the Son of Ham* (St. Louis, 1900). For more on Carroll, see Barkun, *Racist Right*, pp. 158–60.
54. David Davidson and H. Aldersmith, *The Great Pyramid. Its Divine Message* (11th ed., London, 1948): 1st pub. 1924.
55. See Barkun, *Racist Right*, chap. 7.
56. See esp. Paul Wexler, *The Ashkenazic Jews: A Slavo-Turkic People in Search of a Jewish Identity* (Columbus, Ohio, 1993).
57. Richard Kelly Hoskins, *Our Nordic Race* (6th ed., Los Angeles, 1966), esp. pp. 24–27. See also Barkun, *Racist Right*, pp. 126–42.
58. More than three hundred people came to the conference there in July 1995: M. Janofsky, "True Believers Gather to Honor White Race," *NY Times*, July 23, 1995, 1.14; G. Niebuhr, "Sandpoint Journal," *NY Times*, Oct. 29, 1995, 1.24.
59. See, generally, K. S. Stern, *A Force Upon the Plain: The American Militia Movement and the Politics of Hate* (New York, 1995), written by the American Jewish Committee's expert on hate groups, who calls the militia movement "the fastest-growing grass-roots mass movement" in memory: *NY Times* review, Jan. 28, 1996, 7.13.

60. The Christian Defense League (Arabi, La.) sells a video entitled "Death & Taxes: The Story of Gordon Kahl," and writes endlessly about Kahl in *The CDL Report*.

61. See K. Flynn and G. Gerhardt, *The Silent Brotherhood* (New York, 1989); J. Coates, *Armed and Dangerous: The Rise of the Survivalist Right* (New York, 1987); J. W. Gibson, *Warrior Dreams* (New York, 1994). Ironically, Judge Richard P. Matsch, the man who presided over the trial of the four Order members, was also the judge appointed to try Timothy McVeigh and Terry Nichols in the Oklahoma bombing case: J. Thomas, "U.S. Judge in Colorado to Hear Bombing Case," *NY Times*, Dec. 5, 1995, A16.

62. J. Thomas, "Oklahoma City Building Was Target of Plot as Early as '83, Official Says," *NY Times*, May 20, 1995; G. Niebuhr, "A Vision of an Apocalypse: The Religion of the Far Right," *NY Times*, May 22, 1995, p. A6; S. H. Verhovek, "Leader of Apocalyptic Sect Denies Knowing McVeigh," *NY Times*, May 25, 1995, A26; J. L. Graff, "The White City on a Hill," *Time*, Feb. 24, 1997, pp. 29–30; J. Thomas, "Oklahoma Grandparents Turn Grief into a Quest," *NY Times*, Mar. 5, 1996, p. A12.

63. See Paul J. Hill, "Should We Defend Born and Unborn Children with Force?" (July 1993), an expansion of the views he expounded on the Phil Donahue television show five days after the murder of Dr. David Gunn on March 10, 1993 (Internet version). We know that Hill attended one of the Christian Reconstructionist seminaries in Alabama, and had read some of the works of Rousas J. Rushdoony, although he and his followers have denied any connection with violent action.

64. Associated Press, "Extremist Group Suspected in Spokane Bombings," *NY Times*, Apr. 3, 1996, D21; J. Brooke, "Arrests Add to Idaho's Reputation as a Magnet for Supremacists," *NY Times*, Oct. 27, 1996, 1.34.

65. For more on *The John Franklin Letters*, see D. Bell, "The Dispossessed," in his *The Radical Right* (Garden City, 1964), and Coates, *Armed*, p. 48. According to J. Sutherland, "Higher Man," *London Review of Books*, May 22, 1997, 3–6, both novels are based on Jack London's *The Iron Heel*. Sutherland also supplies the additional biographical information about Pierce that he took his BA from Rice University (1955), spent 1955–56 at Caltech, and finished his PhD in physics at Colorado (1962), teaching at Oregon State University from 1962 to 1965, after which time he went to work for Rockwell, editing the American Nazi Party's magazine, *National Socialist World*.

66. The work was first published privately in 1978 under the pseudonym of "Andrew Macdonald" and circulated underground. It was reprinted by Barricade Books in New York in 1996, ironically by a Jewish publisher, Lyle Stuart,

who in a (rather unconvincing) introduction explained why he thought it important to make the book available to the general public. Pierce's publishing group, National Vanguard Books, claimed they sold 198,000 copies by February 1995. Many more must have been sold since the events in Oklahoma. See also D. Carvajal, "Group Tries to Halt Selling of Racist Novel," *NY Times*, Apr. 20, 1996, 1.8.

67. McVeigh would hawk the book at gun shows as well: J. Kifner, "Oklahoma Blast: A Tale in 2 Books?" *NY Times*, Aug. 21, 1995, A12; P. Applebome, "A Bombing Foretold, in Extreme-Right 'Bible,' " *NY Times*, Apr. 26, 1995, A22. The other book which McVeigh had was Coates, *Armed and Dangerous*, which his co-conspirator Terry Nichols had in his living room when arrested (ibid.). Cf. J. Kifner, "The Gun Network: McVeigh's World," *NY Times*, July 5, 1995, A1; idem, "McVeigh's Mind," *NY Times*, Dec. 31, 1995, 1.1. Another text, *Report from Iron Mountain*, a spoof written by freelance writer Leonard Lewin in 1967, has had a similar success among right-wing groups; V. S. Navasky, "Anatomy of a Hoax," *Nation*, 260 (June 12, 1995), 815–17.

68. A summary can be found in "The Gun Network: Excerpts from One Right-Wing Author's Script for the Future," *NY Times*, July 5, 1995, A18.

69. W. L. Pierce, "Disney and the Jews: Eisner and His Kind Must Stop Harming Our Children," *Free Speech*, vol. 1, no. 9 (1996): National Alliance Internet site.

70. On Pierce generally, see C. Mollins, "At Home with a Racist Guru," *Maclean's*, 108 (May 8, 1995), 42–43; M. Janofsky, "One Man's Journey from Academia to Extremism," *NY Times*, July 5, 1995, A18; R. Smothers, "Supremacist Told to Pay Black Family," *NY Times*, May 20, 1996, A13.

71. S. Labaton, "F.B.I. Studies Note for Clues on Derailment," *NY Times*, Oct. 11, 1995, A1; idem, "Officials Release Note Found Near Derailed Train," *NY Times*, Oct. 14, 1995, 1.7. Another extremist group in Arizona is the "Viper Militia": J. Brooke, "As Trial Nears for Militia, Some Charges Are Dropped," *NY Times*, Oct. 9, 1996, A15.

72. For more on Ruby Ridge, see J. Walter, *Every Knee Shall Bow: The Truth and Tragedy of Ruby Ridge and the Randy Weaver Family* (New York, 1995), which was the basis of a CBS miniseries, "Ruby Ridge: An American Tragedy" (1996), starring Randy Quaid and Laura Dern as the Weaver couple. See also A. W. Bock, "Ambush at Ruby Ridge," *Reason*, 25 (Oct. 1993), 22–28; T. Morgenthau, "The Siege That Won't Go Away," *Newsweek*, Aug. 28, 1995, 40–42; "What Really Happened at Ruby Ridge?" *Midwest Today*, Dec. 1995 (Internet version). The Justice Department issued a 542-page report on the events at Ruby Ridge in 1994, which concluded that the FBI overreacted.

Twelve agents and employees were disciplined, including Larry Potts, then head of the FBI criminal division, who was nevertheless promoted to deputy director in May 1995, a post which he held for only two months before FBI director Louis Freeh demoted him, when information about the suppression of key evidence was revealed. On August 15, 1995, the U.S government settled with the Weaver family for $3.1 million. A federal deputy marshal was also killed in the initial confrontation at Ruby Ridge.

73. C. Goldberg, "Freemen in Court, But Not Without a Struggle," *NY Times*, June 15, 1996, 1.10; idem, "The Freemen Sought Refuge in an Ideology That Kept the Law, and Reality, at Bay," *NY Times*, June 16, 1996, 1.14; Associated Press, "Standoff Cost $7.5 Million," *NY Times*, Nov. 22, 1996, A22.

8 | THE END OF THE WORLD AND THE NUCLEAR MESSIAH

1. The term "Evangelicalism" is sometimes merely a code word for "Fundamentalism," adopted after the Second World War by those adherents who wished to distance themselves from the ridicule that had been attached to the movement since the Scopes "monkey" trial of 1925. George M. Marsden ("Defining American Fundamentalism," in *The Fundamentalist Phenomenon* [Grand Rapids, 1990], ed. N. J. Cohen, pp. 22, 34) postulates that a Fundamentalist is "an evangelical who agrees with Billy Graham." On Fundamentalism generally, see G. M. Marsden, *Fundamentalism and American Culture* (Oxford, 1980); E. R. Sandeen, *The Roots of Fundamentalism: British and American Millenarianism, 1800–1930* (Chicago, 1970); S. G. Cole, *The History of Fundamentalism* (New York, 1931); L. Gasper, *The Fundamentalist Movement* (The Hague, 1963); James Barr, *Fundamentalism* (London, 1977). For earlier connections, see David S. Katz, *Sabbath and Sectarianism in Seventeenth-Century England* (Leiden, 1988), "Epilogue."

2. Hal Lindsey, *The Late Great Planet Earth* (Grand Rapids, 1970), pp. 45–47.

3. Ibid., pp. 48–55, 60, 69.

4. Ibid., chaps. 7–10.

5. Ibid., pp. 135–42.

6. Ibid., pp. 144 (where the map is printed), 148. Lindsey thanks Colonel R. B. Thieme, Jr, for helping him with the military aspects of the final war. Colonel Thieme is the leader of a small Fundamentalist group that is preparing for the end of the world by combining religious and military observances. Marilyn Quayle, the wife of the former U.S. Vice President, belongs to Colonel Thieme's group. Lindsey's later work *The Road to Holocaust* (New York, 1989) is dedicated to "Colonel Robert B. Thieme, Jr., whose systematic teaching of

God's word and personal encouragement changed the entire direction of my life."

7. Lindsey, *Late Great*, pp. 150, 156. See also J. Nederveen Pieterse, "The History of a Metaphor: Christian Zionism and the Politics of Apocalypse," *Archives de Sciences Sociales des Religions*, 36 (1991), 75–103; D. A. Rausch, "The Evangelicals as Zionists," *Midstream*, 31 (1985), 13–17.

8. Lindsey, *Late Great*, pp. 165–74. Lindsey's book *Satan Is Alive and Well on Planet Earth* (Grand Rapids, 1972) describes in detail the spiritual ills that have beset the United States, and blames this state of affairs on the effects of skepticism and relativism brought about by the study of Kant, Hegel, Kierkegaard, and Marx.

9. Hal Lindsey, *The Final Battle* (Palos Verdes, Calif., 1995), esp. pp. 143ff.

10. Lindsey, *Holocaust*, chap. 1. See also his *Israel and the Last Days* (Eugene, Ore., 1983).

11. See A. J. Magida, *Prophet of Rage: A Life of Louis Farrakhan and His Nation* (New York, 1996); M. Gardell, *Countdown to Armageddon: Louis Farrakhan and the Nation of Islam* (London, 1997), and the bizarre *The Secret Relationship between Blacks and Jews* (Chicago, 1991).

12. Meanwhile, see *Time* and *Newsweek* for Apr. 7, 1997.

13. T. Daniels, "The Life and Death of the Order of the Solar Temple," *Millennial Prophecy Report*, vol. 3 (1994).

14. Gore Vidal, "Armageddon," in his *At Home: Essays 1982–1988* (New York, 1988), pp. 98–104, orig. pub. in the London *Observer*, Nov. 15, 1987. Cf. L. Jones, "Reagan's Religion," *Jnl. Amer. Culture*, 8 (1985), 59–70; R. D. Linder and R. V. Pierard, "Ronald Reagan, Civil Religion and the New Religious Right in America," *Fides et Historia*, 23 (1991), 57–73.

15. *Christian Life*, May 1968, quoted in G. Halsell, *Prophecy and Politics: Militant Evangelists on the Road to Nuclear War* (Westport, Conn., 1986), p. 42. The second edition of Halsell is subtitled *The Secret Alliance between Israel and the U.S. Christian Right* (Westport, Conn., 1989).

16. Ibid., p. 43.

17. Ibid., p. 47.

18. James Mills, in the *San Diego Magazine*, Aug. 1985, pp. 140–41.

19. Halsell, *Prophecy*, pp. 46–47. See also R. V. Pierard, "Religion and the 1984 Election Campaign," *Rev. Relig. Res.*, 27 (1985), 98–114; R. R. Stockton, "Christian Zionism: Prophecy and Public Opinion," *Middle East Jnl.*, 41 (1987), 234–53, esp. 240–41; R. Dugger, "Reagan's Apocalypse Now," *Manchester Guardian Weekly*, May 6, 1984, p. 17 (orig. pub. *Washington Post*).

20. R. N. Ostling, "Armageddon and the End Times," *Time*, Nov. 5, 1984, p. 73.

Cf. *New York Times*, Oct. 22, 1984, A24; Stockton, "Christian Zionism," p. 242.

21. Cf. Billy Graham, *Till Armageddon* (Waco, Tex. [!], 1981).

22. See Falwell's autobiography, *Strength for the Journey* (New York, 1987). Cf. R. N. Ostling, "Jerry Falwell's Crusade," *Time*, Sept. 2, 1985, pp. 30–37; F. Lipsius, "Evangelicals and Jews," *Survey of Jewish Affairs*, 1988, pp. 154–67.

23. The alternative to Darwinism is still "Creation Science," very popular among Evangelicals, even though teaching it as science was ruled unconstitutional by the U.S. Supreme Court in 1987: see R. L. Numbers, *The Creationists* (Berkeley, 1992) and *Creationism, Science, and the Law: The Arkansas Case*, ed. M. C. La Follette (Cambridge, Mass., 1983).

24. R. B. Flowers, "President Jimmy Carter, Evangelicalism, Church-State Relations, and Civil Religion," *Jnl. Church & State*, 25 (1983), 113–32.

25. See, generally, Halsell, *Prophecy*; W. H. Capps, *The New Religious Right* (Columbia, S.C., 1995); Clyde Wilcox, *God's Warriors: The Christian Right in Twentieth-Century America* (Baltimore, 1992); Gabriel Fackre, *The Religious Right and Christian Faith* (Grand Rapids, 1982); G. Wills, *Under God: Religion and American Politics* (New York, 1990); E. Jorstad, *The Politics of Doomsday: Fundamentalists of the Far Right* (Nashville, 1970); idem, *Holding Fast/Pressing On: Religion in America in the 1980s* (New York, 1990).

26. On Falwell's financial affairs, see J. W. Kennedy, "Jerry Falwell's Uncertain Legacy," *Christianity Today*, Dec. 9, 1996, pp. 62–67; and M. Ruthven, "Rapture and the American Right," *Times Lit. Supp.*, Jan. 29–Feb. 4, 1988, pp. 110, 120. For more on Oral Roberts, see D. E. Harrell, *Oral Roberts: An American Life* (Bloomington, Ind., 1985), and his own books, published by the Oral Roberts Evangelistic Association, especially his *Miracles of Seed-Faith*, explaining his famous self-help doctrine of that name. His son Richard Roberts is trying to continue his father's ministry, not helped by his ex-wife, Patti Roberts Thompson, who published her own views as *Ashes to Gold* (Waco, Tex., 1983). Tammy Bakker has also come forward with her two books, *I Gotta Be Me* (Charlotte, N.C., 1978) and *Run to the Roar* (Harrison, Ark., 1980). Jim Bakker was convicted of federal fraud charges and spent nearly five years in prison, being released in 1994. Tammy Bakker divorced him during that period and married his best friend from PTL days. Jimmy Swaggart Ministries maintains a Web site from their headquarters at Baton Rouge, La.

27. C. J. Church, "The Clinton Hater's Video Library," *Time*, Aug. 1, 1994, p. 21; "Scandalous Charges in a Falwell Video," *Christian Century*, June 1–8, 1994, pp. 566–67.

28. M. Simon, *Jerry Falwell and the Jews* (Middle Village, N.Y., 1984), where Falwell answers a series of questions about his views on Jews, including forty-five pages about his ideas concerning Israel.

29. Robert Scheer, *Los Angeles Times*, Mar. 1981.

30. Jerry Falwell, *Nuclear War and the Second Coming of Jesus Christ* (Lynchburg, 1983).

31. Distributed by the *Old Time Gospel Hour*, Lynchburg, Va.

32. Some of the sermon is quoted by Halsell, *Prophecy*, pp. 30–32.

33. G. Greenberg, "Fundamentalists, Israel and Theological Openness," *Christian Jewish Relations*, 19 (1986), 27–33.

34. Simon, *Falwell*, p. 62.

35. The program Falwell offers for doing this is basically the same as that of the Christian Reconstructionists.

36. Generally on Jim Jones and Jonestown see D. Chidester, *Salvation and Suicide: An Interpretation of Jim Jones, the People's Temple, and Jonestown* (Bloomington and Indianapolis, 1988); J. Reston, Jr., *Our Father Who Art in Hell* (New York, 1981); J. M. Weghtman, *Making Sense of the Jonestown Suicides* (New York, 1983); G. Klineman, S. Butler, and D. Conn, *The Cult That Died: The Tragedy of Jim Jones and the People's Temple* (New York, 1980); C. A. Krause, *Guyana Massacre* (New York, 1978); P. Axthelm et al., "The Cult of Death," *Newsweek*, Dec. 4, 1978, pp. 12–44; "Cult of Death," *Time*, Dec. 4, 1978, pp. 6–14; "The Horror Lives On," *Time*, Dec. 11, 1978, pp. 28–38.

37. On Father Divine, see J. Watts, *God, Harlem USA: The Father Divine Story* (Berkeley, 1992); R. Weisbrot, *Father Divine and the Struggle for Racial Equality* (Urbana, 1983); K. E. Burnham, *God Comes to America: Father Divine and the Peace Mission Movement* (Boston, 1979); Mrs. M. J. Divine, *The Peace Mission Movement* (Philadelphia, 1982); B. Satter, "Marcus Garvey, Father Divine and the Gender Politics of Race Difference and Race Neutrality," *Amer. Qly*, 48 (1996), 43–76. The Peace Mission movement still maintains a Web site.

38. See E. D. Andrews, *The People Called Shakers* (New York, 1953).

39. Klineman et al., *Tragedy*, pp. 52–55.

40. M. J. Divine, *Peace Mission*, p. 139, quoted in Watts, *God*, p. 174.

41. Watts, *God*, pp. 106–8.

42. Father Divine may have had a similar idea in his establishment of a racially mixed community in 1933 on a tiny island off the coast of Washington State: see C. P. LeWarne, "Vendovi Island: Father Divine's 'Peaceful Paradise of the Pacific,' " *Pacific Northwest Qly*, 75 (1984), 2–12.

43. See his sermon of 1973, quoted in Chidester, *Salvation*, pp. 55–56.

44. Generally, see esp. E. Barker, *The Making of a Moonie: Choice or Brainwashing?* (Oxford, 1984); J. Lofland, *Doomsday Cult: A Study of Conversion, Proselytization, and Maintenance of Faith* (rev. ed., New York, 1977); and P. Maass, "Moon at Twilight," *New Yorker*, Sept. 14, 1998, pp. 41–50.

45. One of these mediums was Arthur Ford. See Arthur Ford, *Unknown But Known: My Adventure into the Meditative Dimension* (New York, 1968), chap. 10: "The Sun Myung Moon Sittings."

46. It would be enlightening to compare Moon's Unification Church with the Children of God/Family of Love, founded in 1968 and led by David Berg (b. 1919). Berg and his companion, Karen "Maria" Zerby, have been bombarded with accusations ranging from kidnapping and assault to tax evasion, and fled the United States for Tenerife in 1974. The group claims a membership of 3,000 adults and 6,000 children throughout the world.

47. See his autobiography, *Shout It from the Housetops* (Plainfield, N.J., 1972). Cf. Robert Boston, *The Most Dangerous Man in America? Pat Robertson and the Rise of the Christian Coalition* (Amherst, N.Y., 1996); J. Taylor, "Pat Robertson's God, Inc.," *Esquire*, Nov. 1994, pp. 76–83. See also "The Expanding CBN Empire," *Christian Century*, 111 (July 27–Aug. 3, 1994), 712–13; M. Isikoff and M. Hosenball, "With God There's No Cap," *Newsweek*, Oct. 3, 1994, pp. 42–44; and G. Cohen, "On God's Green Earth," *U.S. News & World Report*, Apr. 24, 1995, pp. 31–32, regarding Robertson's investments. Robertson also had nonreligious development investments in Zaire, presumably with the blessing of Mobutu Sese Seko: A. Purvis, "Jewels for Jesus," *Time*, Feb. 27, 1995, p. 30.

48. Quoted in L. J. Epstein, *Zion's Call* (Lanham, Md., 1984), p. 134.

49. Gerard Thomas Straub, *Salvation for Sale: An Insider's View of Pat Robertson's Ministry* (Buffalo, N.Y., 1988): quoted in M. Gardner, "Giving God a Hand," *NY Rev. Books*, Aug. 13, 1987, p. 22. This is also a common claim of New Age writers.

50. For more on the CC, see "Christian Coalition Goes Interfaith," *Christian Century*, 111 (1994), 891–92; J. M. Swomley, "Pat Robertson's Contract on America," *Humanist*, 55 (July–Aug. 1995), 35–36.

51. For more on the ACLJ, see E. Gleick, "Onward Christian Lawyers," *Time*, Mar. 13, 1995, pp. 57–59.

52. The largest Pentecostalist denominations in the United States are concentrated around Arkansas and in the South, in part because of the large percentage of African-Americans in the movement. The largest groups are the Assemblies of God, the Church of God, the Pentecostal Holiness Church, and the Inter-

national Church of the Four Square Gospel (of Aimee Semple McPherson). In England, the key groups are the Elim Alliance and the House Churches. There are 14 to 15 million Pentecostalists in Latin America alone, and perhaps 22 million Pentecostalists altogether, making this the fifth-largest Protestant group in the world.

53. See Robertson's book *Beyond Reason: How Miracles Can Change Your Life* (New York, 1985); and Gardner, "God," pp. 17–23.

54. Nesta H[elen] Webster, *Secret Societies and Subversive Movements* (London, 1924), repr. in at least seven editions. Cf. her book *World Revolution: The Plot Against Civilization* (London, 1921), also in editions at least until 1971; and esp. her *Surrender of an Empire* (3rd ed., London, 1931), chap. 19: "The Surrender to Zionism." See esp. N. H. Webster, *Spacious Days: An Autobiography* (London, 1950), which carries the story up to 1920. The second part, never published, recounts her life as an active Fascist and English supporter of Hitler, but it was allegedly stolen from a publisher in 1972 by an unknown American: see the little book by R. M. Gilman, *Behind World Revolution: The Strange Career of Nesta H. Webster* (Ann Arbor, 1982); R. Griffiths, *Fellow Travellers of the Right: British Enthusiasts for Nazi Germany* (London, 1980); J. R. Carlson, *Undercover* (New York, 1943); T. P. Weber, "Finding Someone to Blame: Fundamentalism and Anti-Semitic Conspiracy Theories in the 1930s," *Fides et Historia*, 24 (1992), 40–55. Some of Webster's MSS. are in the Bodleian Library, Oxford.

55. See esp. Nesta H. Webster, *The French Revolution* (London, 1921), pp. 491–97. Pat Robertson adopts Webster's view of the Illuminati in chapters 4 and 8 of his book, blandly citing the "British author Nesta Webster" and the "English historian Nesta Webster." For more on the Illuminati, see the original work on the conspiracy theory, John Robison, *Proofs of a Conspiracy Against all the Religions and Governments of Europe. Carried on in the Secret Meetings of Free Masons, Illuminati, and Reading Societies* (London, 1797). See also *The Fear of Conspiracy: Images of Un-American Subversion from the Revolution to the Present*, ed. D. B. Davis (Ithaca, N.Y., 1971).

56. Eustace Mullins, *The New History of the Jews* (Staunton, Va., 1968), pub. by the "International Institute of Jewish Studies," p. 147.

57. Eustace Mullins, *This Difficult Individual, Ezra Pound* (Hollywood, 1979): first pub. 1961. Cf. his short work *My Life in Christ* (Staunton, Va., 1968).

58. Eustace Clarence Mullins, *A Study of the Federal Reserve* (New York, 1952), with further editions at least in 1954, 1971, and 1983: a number of unauthorized editions appeared, one of which, under the title *Secrets of the Federal Reserve* (1983), being the edition that Pat Robertson used in his controversial

book *The New World Order* (1991); idem, *New History*. Other works by him in this vein include: *Murder by Injection: The Story of the Medical Conspiracy Against America* (Staunton, Va., 1988); *The Rape of Justice: America's Tribunals Exposed* (Staunton, Va., 1989), and *A Writ for Martyrs* (Staunton, Va., 1985).

59. Mullins, *New History*, pp. 127–28.

60. Mullins, *Federal Reserve*, pp. 128–33. Cf. some interesting parallels in *The Fear of Conspiracy: Images of Un-American Subversion from the Revolution to the Present*, ed. D. B. Davis (Ithaca, N.Y., 1971).

61. Mullins, *New History*, pp. 5, 22.

62. Mullins developed the racial aspect of his ideology in another work published at the same time, *The Biological Jew* (Staunton, Va., 1968), also produced by the "International Institute of Jewish Studies" and containing a foreword dated Sept. 25, 1967.

63. Mullins, *New History*, chap. 6: "The Jews and Ritual Murder," pp. 49–66, esp. p. 58.

64. Ibid., chap. 7: "Jews in Europe," esp. pp. 69, 91.

65. Ibid., pp. 116–17.

66. Ibid., pp. 146–47.

67. Ibid., pp. 119, 124.

68. Ibid., p. 18.

69. Mullins, *Biological Jew*, p. 85.

70. In his bibliography, Robertson cites both Mullins, *Secrets of the Federal Reserve* (Staunton, Va., 1983), and Webster, *Secret Societies* (New York, 1924), reprinted by the Christian Book Club of America. In Boston, *Dangerous Man*, pp. 126–30, four pages are devoted to Nesta Webster, but Mullins is mentioned only once. See also G. Niebuhr, "Pat Robertson Says He Intended No Anti-Semitism," *NY Times*, Mar. 4, 1995, 10; M. Lind, "Rev. Robertson's Grand International Conspiracy Theory," *NY Rev. Books*, 42 Feb. 2, 1995), 21–25; idem, "On Pat Robertson," *NY Rev. Books*, 42 (Apr. 20, 1995), 67–71; A. Lewis, "The Crackpot Factor," *NY Times*, Apr. 14, 1995, A15; C. Hitchens, "Minority Report," *Nation*, Apr. 10, 1995, p. 479; J. L. Sheler, "Mending Fences Between the Christian Right and Jews," *U.S. News & World Report*, Apr. 24, 1995, p. 32; "Coalition Tries to Mend Jewish Relations," *Christian Century*, 112 (Apr. 26, 1995), 448–49; F. Rich, "Bait and Switch," *NY Times*, Mar. 25, 1995, A23; idem, "Bait and Switch II," *NY Times*, Apr. 6, 1995, A31 (last three articles regarding the efforts of Ralph E. Reed, Jr., of the CC before the Anti-Defamation League of B'nai

B'rith to repair the damage caused by Robertson, the head of the CC); M. Kinsley, "Long Sentence," *New Republic*, May 8, 1995, pp. 10–11; P. Steinfels, "Getting It Right about the Religious Right," *NY Times*, July 23, 1994, p. 26; D. Levitas, "A. D. L. and the Christian Right," *Nation*, June 19, 1995, p. 882 (last two articles discussing the change in public policy by the Anti-Defamation League: in their report "The Religious Right" (June 1994) they had condemned Robertson, and now were courting his support once again); N. Podhoretz, "In the Matter of Pat Robertson," *Commentary*, Aug. 1995; pp. 27–32; E. Radner, "New World Order, Old World Anti-Semitism," *Christian Century*, 112 (Sept. 13–20, 1995), 844–49. Robertson's historical views, especially regarding the creation of the Federal Reserve Bank, have also been compared to those of Louis Farrakhan, who may also be using Mullins and Webster: F. Rich, "The Jew World Order," *NY Times*, Mar. 9, 1995, A25.

71. Eustace Mullins, *The World Order: A Study in the Hegemony of Parasitism* (Staunton, Va., 1985).

72. Quoted by Epstein, *Zion's Call*, p. 133. See also R. Mouly and Roland Robertson, "Zionism in American Premillenarian Fundamentalism," *Amer. Jnl. Theo. & Phil.*, 4 (1983), 97–109; I. Kristol, "The Political Dilemma of American Jews," *Commentary*, 78 (July 1984), 23–29.

73. *Christianity Today*, Aug. 17, 1992: repr. in the Web site of "Biblical Discernment Ministries."

74. Harvey Cox, "The Warring Visions of the Religious Right," *Atlantic Monthly*, Nov. 1995, pp. 59–69. Cf. Pat Robertson, *The Secret Kingdom* (Nashville, Tenn., 1982); idem, *Answers to 200 of Life's Most Probing Questions* (Nashville, Tenn., 1984).

75. On Christian Reconstructionism generally, see Bruce Barron, *Heaven on Earth: The Social and Political Agendas of Dominion Theology* (Grand Rapids, 1992); D. A. Rausch and D. E. Chismar, "The New Puritans and Their Theonomic Paradise," *Christian Century*, 100 (Aug. 3–10, 1983), 712–15; A. Shupe, "The Reconstructionist Movement on the New Christian Right," *Christian Century*, 106 (Oct. 14, 1989), 880–82; R. J. Neuhaus, "Why Wait for the Kingdom? The Theonomist Temptation," *First Things*, 3 (1990), 13–21; D. A. Oss, "The Influence of Hermeneutical Frameworks in the Theonomy Debate," *Westminster Theological Jnl.*, 51 (1989), 227–58.

76. Daniel Whitby, *A Paraphrase and Commentary of the New Testament* (London, 1727), pp. 9, 10, 11–15, 25, 27–28, where the *Treatise* is reprinted. Cf. J. W. Davidson, *The Logic of Millennial Thought* (New Haven and London, 1977), pp. 141–145.

77. Quoted in Paul S. Boyer, *When Time Shall Be No More: Prophecy Belief in Modern American Culture* (Cambridge, Mass., 1992), p. 303.

78. Gen. 1:26–28. Cf. J. Cohen, *"Be Fertile and Increase, Fill the Earth and Master It": The Ancient and Medieval Career of a Biblical Text* (Ithaca, N.Y., 1989).

79. See Robertson, *Secret Kingdom*.

80. This combination is also apparent in the evolving theology of Billy Graham, who more than anyone could be called America's Protestant pope. His preaching in Oklahoma at the memorial service for the victims of the bombing, standing beside the President of the United States, provides a striking image of his position. His message there was also a "smooth blend" of Calvinism, pre- and postmillennialism.

INDEX

Anglo-Ephraim Association, 175–77
Anglo-Israel Research Society, 187
Anglo-Saxon Christian World
    Movement, 188
Apocrypha, 81
Apostles, 56, 236
Applewhite, Marshall Herff, 211
Armstrong, Herbert W., 189–91
Arnold of Villanova, 258n18
Aryan Nation, xii, xv, 80, 189, 192,
    193, 237, 242, 276n43
Aspinwall, William, 261n13
Athanasius, St., 98
Augsburg, Peace of, 41
Augustine, St., 44, 210

B

Babylonian Codex, 24–25
Bacon, Roger, 20
Bakker, Jim, 214, 218, 234, 236,
    282n26
Bakker, Tammy, 234, 282n26
Balfour Declaration, 151–52, 206
Balzac, Honoré de, 134
Baptists, 78, 153; Southern, 216,
    219
Barruel, Abbé, 132
Barth, Karl, 42
Baruch, Bernard, 238
Batavian Confederation, 138
Baudelaire, Charles, 134
Baxter, Richard, 47
Beach, Henry "Mike," 193
Begin, Menachem, 222

Behmen, Jacob, 134
Benedict, St., xxiii
Benzelius, Eric, 120–21
Berg, Alan, 198
Berg, David, 284n46
Bernini, Gian Lorenzo, 53
Beukels, Jan, 40
Bible, xiv–xvi, 12, 34, 35, 41, 55,
    76–78, 96, 103–4, 115, 149, 158,
    182, 185, 189, 194, 204, 211,
    215, 223, 233, 235, 247, 250,
    252; Hebrew, 7, 21; inerrancy of,
    85, 251; Latin Vulgate, 22, 23;
    Mormon attitude toward, 87–88;
    New Testament, 18, 102, 242;
    Old Testament, 18, 242; Polyglot,
    21–26, 102, 258n27; Scofield
    Reference, 147–48; Seventh-day
    Adventists' study of, 159, 162;
    Swedenborg's interpretation of,
    119, 127, 134; *see also specific
    books*
Bible Society, 177
Bicheno, James, 109
Bird, Edward Wheler, 177–79, 181
Black Death, 240
Blackstone, William, 150–51
Blake, William, 49, 133–34
Blakey, Deborah Layton, 227–28
Blavatsky, Madame, 119
B'nai B'rith, Anti-Defamation
    League of, 242
Boehme, Jacob, 129, 130
Bokelson, Jan, 40
Bolingbroke, Lord, 121
Book, Mary, 118